Y0-BCG-326

Труд П

ABU

Taijiquan

The Art of Nurturing,
The Science of Power

Taijiquan

The Art of Nurturing,
The Science of Power

YANG YANG

with Scott A. Grubisich

ZHENWU PUBLICATIONS · CHAMPAIGN, ILLINOIS USA

Editor: Kathryn Enders
Design: Evelyn C. Shapiro
Production assistance: Randee Bowlin
Calligraphy: Xie Feng
Photography: Benjamin Lapid

© 2005 Yang Yang. All rights reserved.
ISBN 0-9740990-0-7

Cataloging-in-Publication Data

Yang, Yang, 1961–
    Taijiquan : the art of nurturing, the science of power / Yang Yang
with Scott A. Grubisich.
        p.   cm.
    Includes bibliographical references and index.
    ISBN 0-9740990-0-7 (cloth : alk. paper)
    1. Tai chi. I. Title. II. Grubisich, Scott A.
GV504.Y38   2005
613.7148—dc22   2004096572

This book is printed on acid-free paper
Manufactured in the United States of America

ZHENWU PUBLICATIONS is the publication group of the Center for Taiji Studies™ in
Champaign, Illinois. To order more copies of *Taijiquan: The Art of Nurturing, The Science of Power*,
please contact us at zhenwu@chentaiji.com. Other instructional materials are available through
our website at **www.chentaiji.com**.

ZHENWU PUBLICATIONS · P.O. Box 11386 · Champaign, Illinois 61826 · USA

Contents

Yang Yang with Grandmaster Feng Zhiqiang in Shanghai, 1982.

foreword
Grandmaster Feng Zhiqiang

WHEN YANG APPROACHED ME with an invitation to introduce this book, it gave me cause to reflect on his years as a student with me. Knowing that Yang has completed multiple degrees in China and America and is now a Ph.D. candidate, it brought a smile to remember the day when, as a youngster in the early 1980s, Yang announced his intention to quit college and devote his energy to learning and teaching Taiji. With gentle persuasion (I told him that if he quit college I wouldn't teach him), I was able to convince him to stay in school. At that time, of course, my primary intention was to convey the importance of an education. Who knew that, some twenty years later, Yang would ultimately marry his love of Taiji with an academic career and be in a unique position to both study the art from a Western scientific perspective and share it with the Western world?

Anyone wishing to learn Taiji must research and ponder the theory and meaning of the art, and practice seriously. This book makes clear the fundamental exercises that must be practiced, and explains the theories and principles of the art from both Eastern and Western perspectives. It is a valuable work bridging East and West. I am pleased that Yang has endeavored to uphold the oath of a disciple: to study and practice diligently, achieve both virtue and the art, and devote his life to the promotion of Taijiquan, a treasure of the Chinese culture.

Feng Zhiqiang
President, Beijing Chen Style Taiji Research Association
President, Beijing Hunyuan Taiji Association
Beijing, 2004

foreword
Robert Schlagal

I HAVE HAD THE PRIVILEGE of reading *Taijiquan: The Art of Nurturing, The Science of Power* at several stages during its creation. This book embodies a remarkable blend of rich experience, deep reflection, and fresh, directly stated insight. Each time I read it I come away with further understanding of the art, science, and spirit of Taijiquan and a quickened sense of purpose in my training. This volume has the potential to revolutionize one's thinking and practice.

Master Yang is a top disciple and close personal friend of Grandmaster Feng Zhiqiang, who is widely acknowledged as one of the most accomplished Taiji experts in the modern era. Grandmaster Feng, in turn, was a top student of the great Chen Fake. The training that Yang received, therefore, comes directly from the heart of Taiji tradition at its best.

As is invariably the case with mastery, Yang worked closely under a great teacher and long and hard on his own to perfect the art he was given. He stands at the center of a rich and practical vein of Taiji lineage. From this vantage alone, he has an exemplary knowledge of the art. But Yang has also worked to understand the power and mechanics of Taijiquan by reaching beyond traditional explanatory frameworks. Thus, in order to better demonstrate and promote the benefits of Taiji practice in the West, he is currently conducting doctoral research in kinesiology at the University of Illinois. His research focuses directly on Taiji. Yang's detailed study of Taiji from these commanding points of view—as a master practitioner and as a scientific researcher—enable him to clarify and/or de-mystify what are often obscure points of theory and practice.

Despite Yang's detailed and multifaceted knowledge of Taiji, this book is highly readable. It should be of compelling interest to beginners—or even curious non-practitioners—as well as to initiates. Throughout, Yang offers thoughtful advice to beginners and to veterans. I valued his advice to beginners every bit as much as his advice to veterans. Yang possesses a unique ability to go clearly and directly to the heart of things. *Taijiquan: The Art of Nurturing, The Science of Power* is an exposition on Taijiquan in its essential expressions, apart from questions of style; and it is a discussion of the means for efficiently maximizing growth within those expressions. Yang's candid discussions of the central role of energy cultivation, of the requirements of Taiji movement, and his careful guidelines and advice for push-hands training are unique and of lasting value.

Taijiquan: The Art of Nurturing, The Science of Power represents the thinking, experience, and straightforward confidences of an acknowledged master of Taijiquan. This is a book replete with life-wisdom. For Master Yang, Taiji is a spiritual practice as well as martial discipline. The cornerstone of Taiji development lies in effectively training in ways that promote health, relaxed strength, balance, integrity, and spiritual well-being as the necessary foundations for and accompaniments of real martial advancement. To build upon this foundation and take these gains to their highest level, Yang explains, requires in students the presence and continued development of solid moral character, what some have called martial virtue. This book should be the central volume in any Taijiquan practitioner's library.

Robert Schlagal, Ph.D.
Appalachian State University
Boone, North Carolina, 2004

Acknowledgments

THIS WORK HAS BEEN A GROUP EFFORT, and I am indebted to many friends, students, and advisors. I would like to thank Bob Schlagal for his elegant foreword and helpful editing, Wendy Heller for her edits and contribution to the description of the human nervous system, Lillian Hoddeson for her contribution discussing the relation between memory and history, and Brian Ragan and Sharon DeCelle for their review and contribution to the discussion of biomechanics. Thanks also to my academic advisor, Karl Rosengren, and to Stephen Kaufman, Elizabeth Hsiao-Wecksler, Sunshine VanBael, Ron Burr, Bob Parker, Dan Ferber, Barbara Poss, and Weng Cho Chew, for their editorial suggestions and review of the book, to Jessica Beverly for her assistance with references, and to Master Chun Man Sit for his review of Taiji principles and translations of Chinese.

Thanks also to the editor, Kathryn Enders, for her patience and transformation of my writing into comprehensible prose, Evelyn Shapiro for her cover artwork, book design, and valuable guidance on the processes of publishing, Randee Bowlin for her production assistance, Benny Lapid for his photography, Xie Feng for her calligraphy, and Stephen Smith for his assistance with the cataloging-in-publication data.

Finally, I would like to especially recognize and thank my student and co-author, Scott Grubisich, and my sister Yang Ying for her encouragement and inspiration. It was Ying who first suggested that we write this book.

Note on the Transliteration of Chinese

THE ART OF TAIJIQUAN was traditionally a guarded secret, handed only to select and trusted students. Through the centuries, a strong oral tradition evolved as a tool for teachers to pass the art to successive generations. Since many of the traditional teachings of Taijiquan, and the internal martial arts in general, are preserved in the sayings or aphorisms of this oral tradition, it is necessary to share many of these throughout the book, both because of the obvious utility in explaining the art and because of the need to document these sayings and guard against inevitable misunderstandings due to differences in dialect or poor translations.

Many of the Chinese words will be unfamiliar to the average reader, so in convention with standard writing styles, they are represented in *italics* in the text. Exceptions to this are the words "Taiji" and "Taijiquan," which, as the subject of the book, should be familiar to the reader, and the words "yin" and "yang," which are used commonly enough in American English to be considered vernacular.

Except where directly quoting works that relied on the older Wade-Giles system, I use *pinyin* to transliterate Chinese characters. Developed in the mid-20th century by the Chinese government, the *pinyin* system is now the world standard for transliterating Chinese text. According to the Library of Congress website, the *pinyin* system "has already been the standard for the United States Government for more than two decades; it is also the standard used by the United Nations and most of the world's media."

The *pinyin* representation, however, is still not sufficient to fully document the Chinese word. In standard Mandarin dialect, four possible intonations for each word determine different meanings. Further, the same intonation can have multiple meanings. To fully document the Chinese words, I have included Chinese characters within the text at the first occurrence of each word or saying. An index of Chinese sayings is also provided at the end of the book. This index summarizes the sayings by chapter, and for those inclined to learn correct pronunciations, includes diacritical marks for intonation cues with the *pinyin* spelling.

I realize that the name of the art may be more widely recognized in the older Wade-Giles spelling as "T'ai Chi Chuan," or simply "T'ai Chi." However, for reasons stated above, the *pinyin* spelling as "Taijiquan" or simply "Taiji" is used throughout.

Yuan
Origin

Chapter One

Introduction

THE ART OF TAIJIQUAN IS ONE OF THE GREATEST GIFTS that China has to share with the world. I feel strongly about this, and about my commitment to share the art with others, because I literally owe my life to the practice of Taijiquan. At the time I was born, precious little food was available in China. Many pregnant mothers did not have enough food for themselves, let alone enough to support healthy pregnancies, and so in my hometown many children my age had problems resulting from poor prenatal nutrition. In my case, I was born with a congenital heart defect, and I was especially weak as a young boy. The doctors warned my parents that I might not live much longer and recommended that I travel to Shanghai for an operation. Such drastic measures, however, were entirely beyond the resources of my family.

For a time it seemed there was no hope that I would ever be healthy. When I was twelve, however, a visiting uncle suggested, "You live so close to the Chen family village, why not try Taiji?" All modern styles of Taiji trace their lineage to the Chen Village in Henan Province, only miles from my home.[1] With just this passing comment, my life took a new direction. I began practicing with Wu Xiubao, a government official in my hometown of Jiaozuo and a well-respected teacher of Taiji who was himself a student of Chen Zhaopei and Chen Zhaokui, the two preeminent representatives of the Chen family at that time. I can picture the day my mother took me as a small boy to meet Wu Xiubao to ask him to take me as a student—I had to wear my best clothes and be on my very best behavior.

With my father's loving but not-so-subtle encouragement—every morning he would wake me at 5:30, saying, "Get up! You have to go to the park to practice Taiji or you will die!"—I persevered through the beginning stages of practice and began to learn the art. Although the doctors had previously forbidden any strenuous activity, I soon found that I was not only able to play sports, I could wrestle with and hold my own against older and stronger boys. My health and strength had improved tremendously, and even at this early age I began to develop a profound appreciation for the art as well as a desire to pursue higher levels of skill and understanding. By the age of sixteen, I was easily able to pass the physical examination necessary for entrance into college, without which students were not admitted and therefore had little hope of improving their living condition.

And so, even if I had not died from the heart defect, without Taijiquan I certainly would never have been able to attend college and likely would never have left my hometown. Attending college in Shanghai and Beijing, working as an engineer and lawyer, and later traveling to America to pursue my doctorate in kinesiology and to teach Taiji have all been made possible by the curative effects of Taiji practice. Beyond the health benefits, the experience and knowledge I garnered from Taiji practice have been a continuing source of inspiration and guidance in my daily life. Because the influence of Taiji on my life has been so profound, and because the benefits of practicing Taiji are real and available to anyone ready and willing to follow the path of this holistic art, I have dedicated myself to promoting and sharing this treasure of Chinese culture.

What is Taijiquan?

The word *taiji* (太极) is an ancient Daoist philosophical term symbolizing the interaction of yin and yang, which are opposite manifestations of the same forces in nature. The dynamic interaction of yin and yang, underlying the relation and changing nature of all things, is epitomized in the famous "Taiji Diagram."[2] *Taiji* is often translated as "grand extreme" (as opposed to *wuji*, 无极, which means "no extreme"), and *quan* (拳) means "fist" or "boxing." Thus, "grand extreme boxing," or *Taijiquan*, is a pugilistic art rooted in the Daoist concepts of the interplay and necessary balance of yin and yang.[3]

It is helpful to think of yin and yang as complementary opposites—each necessarily relies upon, and gives birth to, the other. For example, a fundamental theory of Taijiquan is that hardness comes from softness and quickness comes from slowness. In Taiji practice, emphasis is placed on relaxing the body and calming and focusing the mind. Taiji form movement is performed

The Taiji Diagram

slowly, accentuating the intention, mechanics, accuracy, and precision of the motion. By practicing in accordance with Taiji principles of softness and slowness, the practitioner will paradoxically begin to experience a quality of hardness and strength and efficiency of movement that is significantly different from that of ordinary natural ability. Throughout this book, I suggest possible explanations from the perspective of Western neural science and kinesiology for how improvements in power, quickness, and agility are made possible by the seemingly contradictory Taiji training principles of softness and slowness.

The martial arts of China are typically categorized as either "internal" or "external." Taijiquan downplays brute strength and natural ability and emphasizes learned motor skills, nurturing, and the accumulation of hardness through softness, and thus it is considered an internal martial art. Other popular internal martial arts include *Xinyiquan, Baguazhang,* and *Yiquan.* Classification of a particular art as internal or external is useful in describing beginning training practices to novices, but it is ultimately an oversimplification of the martial arts. In their complete form many, if not most, external or "hard" styles also eventually seek to develop and incorporate an internal or "soft" aspect in their practice. Similarly, all practices of the internal martial arts are intended to develop *gong* (功), the physical aspect of which includes improvements in strength and power. In the classical literature, Taijiquan is referred to as the "science of power." And so it can be seen that the practices of internal and external martial arts eventually merge toward common ground (if not unification).

While Taijiquan was originally created as a martial art, it is also, importantly, a holistic art that develops and informs one's life. Physical, mental, and spiritual components are all integral to its practice. This must be thoroughly understood to grasp the complexity of Taijiquan, to achieve high levels of skill, and to obtain the full benefits of practice. The balance of yin and yang, which is a central theory of the art, explains the linking of spiritual (yin and internal) and martial (yang and external) aspects. The classical literature and poetry of Taijiquan emphasize the importance of this dual cultivation of the martial and spiritual. For example, Chapter 19 of *The Yang Family Forty Chapters* explains,

> Without self-cultivation, there would be no means of realizing the *Tao*… The spiritual is cultivated internally and the martial externally… Those whose practice is successful both internally and externally reach the highest level of attainment. Those who master the martial arts through the spiritual aspect of internal cultivation, or those who master the spiritual aspect through the martial arts attain the middle level. However, those who know only internal cultivation but not the martial arts, or those who know only the martial arts without internal cultivation represent the lowest level of attainment.[4]

The holistic nature of Taiji is perhaps best summarized in the classical *Song of Real Meaning*, where its highest goal and purpose are distilled into a single sentence:

> With your whole being, develop your life.[5]

Unfortunately, this important aspect of Taijiquan is often underemphasized in current books and teaching.

I would also characterize Taiji as a living and growing art. It is not static or restricted to traditions and understandings of past generations, but continues to be enriched by thoughtful insights of each successive generation. Further, as with all art forms, Taiji is ultimately a deeply personal experience and expression of one's feelings, outlook, and understanding of life. One's inner spirit is not only nurtured and molded *by* Taiji practice, but also is inherently reflected *in* practice. The practitioner's spirit and competence is mirrored first in the mechanical movements of the form and later, as one assimilates the lessons from practice, in one's entire relation and interaction with the world.

The fact that Taiji is a personal, living, and growing art is apparent in the different "styles" that have developed over the years. Chen, Yang, Sun, Wu, and Wu (Hao) family styles are currently accepted as standard, orthodox forms, and there are several variations within these styles, as well. Turn to Appendix I, "A Brief History of Taijiquan and the Modern Chen Style," for more information on the evolution of various styles and for further explanation why I believe that Taiji is a living art that cannot possibly be limited to the understandings of previous generations.

Common Misunderstandings

A tradition of secrecy is embedded in many aspects of Chinese culture. Chinese martial arts in general are steeped in enigma and mystery, and Taijiquan is no exception. The martial arts in China were often held as closely guarded secrets that were passed on only to select members of successive generations. Often, an art was held within a single family, as was the case with the original Chen style of Taiji. Largely, I believe, because of the mystery surrounding the art, there are three common misunderstandings about Taiji:

1. That there is a difference between practicing for health and practicing for martial arts;

2. That "slow form movement" is all there is to Taiji practice; and

3. That Taiji is a mysterious oriental practice that cannot be understood without decades of practice.

These misconceptions are prevalent in China as well as the West, and need to be refuted before we go further.

Health versus Martial Arts

I mentioned above that the training exercises of Taiji, like those from all the internal martial arts traditions of China, are designed to build *gong*. What does it mean to build *gong*? Physically, the accumulation of *gong* refers to constant improvements in balance, coordination, agility, flexibility, sensitivity, and strength or power. Mentally and spiritually, the accumulation of *gong* refers to improved awareness and confidence, and constant advancements toward realizing tranquility of heart and mind. These physical, mental, and spiritual improvements are the benefits and purpose of practice. The priority of accumulating *gong* (as opposed to martial technique or trickery) is repeatedly emphasized in many of the most famous sayings from the oral tradition of the Chinese internal martial arts.

You may have noticed that the benefits described above, as well as being essential to self-defense and fighting skill, are also fundamentally valuable for improved health. The two are inseparable. Whether your interest in Taijiquan was sparked by a desire for martial arts skill or for improving health, the benefits will simultaneously be in both, because the *gong* that is accumulated through correct practice is the source of improvement in both martial arts skill and health. The concept of *gong* is further developed and explained in Chapter 2.

The Importance of a Complete Curriculum

To study the complete art of Taijiquan, it should be recognized that, notwithstanding outward differences in styles, there are fundamental types of exercises that must be practiced and universal principles that apply to these exercises. There is often misunderstanding of these principles, just as there are incomplete curricula and incorrect ways to practice.

While the slow movement that is most commonly recognized as Taiji is certainly a cornerstone of Taijiquan training, it is only one aspect of the art. Paradoxically, one purpose of the slow movement is to increase both speed and accuracy. Chinese philosophy states that yin and yang are mutually dependent and evolve into one another. If you want one, you should start with its opposite—extreme hardness is born from extreme softness, extreme quickness comes from slowness. Of course, slow movement by itself is not so complete that it can yield all the *gong* of the internal martial arts. Three essential pillars of Taiji practice have evolved to form a complete curriculum:

- ✦ **Qigong**: Principally *wuji* sitting and standing meditation
- ✦ **Taiji form**: Mainly slow movement practice
- ✦ **Push-hands**: Two-person balance, strength, and reaction training

These form the subjects of Chapters 4, 5, and 6, respectively, and receive more explanation there.

Perhaps the least understood of these exercises are the *qigong* sitting and standing meditations. Even up to modern times, it was quite common for the meditation exercises to be withheld from all but the closest disciples. As solo Taiji form practice gained popularity and publicity, more and more practitioners were led to equate form practice with Taiji, and a smaller and smaller percentage of Taiji practitioners were aware of the other core practices of the art. The *qigong* meditation exercises are now an "open secret," but little information has been disseminated as to *why* they are important. This book outlines the purposes, methods, and interdependency of the meditation, form, and push-hands exercises, and therefore the importance of practicing a complete curriculum.

The Difference Between Subtle and Mysterious

It's true that Taijiquan is a deep and subtle art. The words of the Indian *Yoga Sutra*, "performed in all states and stages, on all planes of mind," may aptly be applied to Taijiquan as well. Precisely because Taijiquan is a deep art, there are differences in levels of understanding and points of emphasis. At the lowest level, these differences inevitably degenerate into bickering amongst proponents of (seemingly) different systems. The old adage of the blind men and the elephant helps illustrate the problem of defining Taiji at this level. Several blind men were allowed to touch one part of an elephant, and then asked to describe what an "elephant" is. Of course, the one who happened to touch a leg was absolutely convinced that his description of an elephant was correct and that the accounts of others who touched the tail, trunk, ear, or tusk were completely erroneous. We are all blind in the sense that we cannot possibly see Taijiquan in its entirety at the beginning of our practice. Those who close their minds to the possibilities of the complete art will not progress to higher levels of skill and understanding.

Although I call Taiji a subtle art, there is a difference between subtle and mysterious. The mysterious is unknown and unknowable to the intellect. God is a mystery. The *Dao* is a mystery. Whether it be Laozi telling us in the *Dao De Jing* that "The *Dao* that can be spoken of is not the true *Dao*," or Saint Thomas Aquinas introducing the *Summa Theologica*, "Since we cannot know what God is, but only what God is not, we cannot consider how God is, but only how he is not," we know that we can never intellectually understand or communicate in words the truly mysterious. Taijiquan is subtle, but it is not mysterious. Our current understanding of the art is grounded in generations of practical observation and trial and error. In this case, it *is* possible to see the whole elephant, given time, dedication, and an open mind and heart.

When Can the Benefits of Practice Be Realized?

Since coming to America, I have frequently heard that it takes "twenty years or more" to develop practical martial skills in the art of Taijiquan. Even a little contemplation would dispel this myth. Taijiquan was developed first and foremost as a fighting art, at a time and place in China when practical fighting skills were essential. Any art that would require twenty years of practice to achieve martial skill would certainly have been of no practical use and would not have survived for generations. That said, Taijiquan is an *art* and is not learned in a day. A wide variety of external fighting systems have been developed for the sole purpose of acquiring pugilistic skills as quickly as one's physical capabilities allow. If that is your desire, I would steer you toward the "external" martial arts. Indeed, for reasons explained later, if your sole motivation is to be a great fighter, the higher levels of Taijiquan will remain beyond your grasp. My point is simply that, once you have gained the trust of a competent teacher and have practiced correctly and efficiently, physical and mental health benefits and martial skill can be quickly realized.

Over the past ten years, the health benefits of Taiji practice have received increasing attention within the Western scientific community. Although the rudimentary research conducted to date has largely been limited to studies lasting six months or less, these studies have documented significant improvements in strength, balance, cardiovascular function, and self-efficacy. Many other health benefits of correct practice have also been observed, such as improved quality of sleep, improved digestive and cognitive functions, stress reduction, and the prevention or treatment of arthritis or osteoporosis, among others. If students are practicing correctly, they will notice improvements within the first few months of regular practice. With daily practice, it is possible to acquire a solid foundation of *gong* in three to five years. At this point the physical and mental improvements, and therefore the self-defense potential, should be obvious to the practitioner. If, after three to five years of practice, a student is left wondering about the self-defense benefits of the art, his or her practice is not as efficient as it could be.

Of course, it is helpful to walk a straight path in practice, avoiding unnecessary detours and mistaken directions, to quickly grasp the subtleties of the art and realize the full benefits of Taiji exercise. Perhaps the highest compliment that a knowledgeable teacher can give is to say that someone is practicing in the correct way. If true, that student will ultimately reach the highest level that his or her intellect/spirit/ability and fate will allow. What more could be expected?

Walking the Straight Path

A famous Chinese saying, *"shi ban gong bei"* (事半功倍), means that if you study something—anything—in an efficient way, you can learn it in a fraction of the time. (Literally, this saying is translated as "half the work, double the result.") Conversely, if you walk a crooked path, greater investments of time and energy are required. Most of us have, for one reason or another, walked a crooked path at some point in our Taiji study. The crooked path in Taiji practice can be costly in terms of time and energy, for as anyone who has practiced knows, it often takes longer to unlearn bad habits than it does to learn them correctly in the first place. The more bad habits that develop and the longer one practices them, the deeper the hole one digs. The good news is, and I assure you of this, that if practiced efficiently and correctly, Taijiquan can be learned and the health and martial benefits of practice can be realized with reasonable investments of time. The key word is *efficiency*. With the responsibilities of work and family, few of us have the luxury of being able to practice four hours or more every day. Thus, the time we do have must be spent as constructively as possible if we hope to realize the full benefits of practice.

One unifying principle is essential for efficient and correct practice, and it is *nurturing*. In all exercises, internal and external, we are nurturing our *qi* (气), our vital energy. Taiji history is littered with those who did not fully comprehend this principle, and either never made any real progress in the art or narrow-mindedly traded the treasure of the art for relatively short-term fighting skills and reputation. The principle of nurturing is explained in Chapter 2, and addressed in each of the respective chapters on *wuji* meditation, Taiji form, and push-hands practice.

The Purpose of this Book

Those drawn to Taiji characteristically have open minds and a willingness and ability to learn new things. The Taiji community is replete with intelligent and interesting characters. Because of this, and Taiji's rapid increase in popularity in the West over the past twenty years or so, the body of technical literature is already quite prolific. So what can I add to the already crowded field of Taiji literature? Again, because Taiji is a deep art, it is not uncommon for practitioners to get lost in the minutia. They lose sight of the forest because of the trees. My primary intention in composing this book is to provide a resource documenting a complete training system. Beyond this, I shall attempt to explain why certain exercises must be practiced and how the different aspects of the art form an integral whole. People approach Taijiquan from different perspectives and with different expectations, but everyone should recognize that the full benefits can be realized only if the complete training system is embraced.

Much of the available literature on Taijiquan can be described as either technical works illustrating form movements or martial applications, or esoteric writings similar in style and substance to the original Wu/Li and Yang family "classics," or to Chen Xin's writings from the Chen Village. Neither of these approaches is fully satisfactory.

On the one hand, technical works that seek to teach form or applications run the risk of grossly oversimplifying the art, as it is impossible to convey the foundation of Taiji in drawings or pictures. The essence of form is not communicated by illustrations with arrows or foot diagrams depicting posture and direction of external movement. Similarly, the application of the art and the true reason an application works cannot be conveyed in a picture. As will be discussed in detail, movement in Taiji is meaningless without intention. Yet it is difficult to learn this intention without some deeper explanation of the art than usually occurs in "how-to" books. You will never understand an application until you understand the foundation that gives birth to and supports it.

On the other hand, the "classics" of Taiji literature have obtained nearly sacred status within the Taiji community, and it is safe and easy for teachers to emulate their tone and content. The classical genre of Taiji literature, however, is notoriously esoteric. For centuries, the art was zealously guarded and was passed only to a few trusted students. Because their meaning was (and remains) intelligible only to the initiated, the classics well preserved this secretive nature of the art. Further, it is extraordinarily difficult, if not impossible, to describe certain aspects of this subtle, internal art in words. The authors of the classics were limited by the common language and scientific knowledge of their times. In hindsight, one may argue that the poetic verse and enigmatic aura of the classics did much to preserve Taijiquan by elevating a "lowly" martial art to a more respectable intellectual and even spiritual status within the Chinese culture. Nevertheless, the downside of this esoteric style is that it can encourage the misperception of Taijiquan as a mysterious, unknowable art, making it all too susceptible to creative or fanciful interpretation. It is not uncommon to see students, convinced that they are learning to "overcome hardness with softness," playing push-hands with bodies completely devoid of internal power. That is folly, but easily understandable considering the perils of an untutored interpretation of the classics. Throughout this book I refer to sayings from the classical literature of Taijiquan and the oral tradition of the martial arts, but always with the intention to clarify the meaning of the sayings.

Besides providing a clear, yet comprehensive guide for those interested in practicing Taiji, this work is also intended to aid the academic community that has begun to research the art of Taiji. It is encouraging that this once secret art is now becoming an "open book," subject to the systematic rigors of the Western scientific process. While I remain committed to the view that many valuable aspects of the art are not quantifiable, and that understanding the philosophical, cultural, spiritual, and creative components of the art of Taiji are equally important to good practice, I recognize the potential contribution of Western science to understanding the physical and psychological benefits of Taiji. We should now be able to qualitatively identify themes experienced by practitioners, quantitatively measure some of the physical and mental health benefits, and begin to explore the mechanisms that contribute to these benefits. While the perception of Taiji as a mysterious oriental exercise will always yield a baseline of interest, only when the benefits and mechanisms of Taiji practice are thoroughly examined and documented in Western scientific terms will Taiji be acceptable to the medical community and therefore mainstream Western culture.

For this reason I believe that we are at a critical juncture in the history of Taiji. The degree to which the art is disseminated to the mainstream culture is ultimately dependent upon the results of future scientific studies. Alarmingly, however, the common misunderstanding of Taiji as simply a "slow movement exercise" is prevalent in scientific studies completed to date. For example, of the approximately one hundred studies published since 1980, not a single article has included, or even mentioned, the *qigong* meditation exercises that are a crucial component of the foundation of the art. Indeed, the meditation exercises are exactly what were omitted from public teaching when the intent was to withhold the complete art from the public. It would be a grave disservice to both the art and the world community if future scientific research perpetuated a similar misunderstanding of the art.

Organization of Contents

Following this Introduction, Chapter Two provides an overview of the foundation of Taiji practice, defines its key principles and terms, and discusses the dual cultivation of the martial and spiritual aspects of Taiji practice. To demonstrate that it is not restricted to Eastern practitioners, the spiritual tradition of Taiji is placed within the context of the world's prominent spiritual and philosophical traditions.

Chapters Three through Six present the general order of a student's progression in Taiji practice. The first task for a serious student is to find a qualified teacher, and so Chapter Three advises readers about what to seek, and what to avoid, in a teacher. Chapters Four through Six address the core sequence of Taiji practice: Wuji meditation, Taiji form, and Push-hands, respectively. Finally, Chapter Seven summarizes the book's main points and reviews the benefits of practicing Taiji.

My hope is that this book is both clear and encouraging to the average practitioner. Wherever possible, I interweave explanations from Eastern and Western perspectives. Although some of the Western explanations are simple hypotheses, they may serve to de-mystify the art, as well as help to explain why certain exercises are practiced. I am also optimistic that some of the hypotheses presented may result in research projects that will further our understanding of the art of Taijiquan.

Gong
foundation

Chapter Two

The foundation— Mental, Physical, and Spiritual Aspects of the Art

BEFORE TURNING TO THE SPECIFICS of Taiji practice, it is helpful to look at the bigger picture and try to understand the objectives of Taiji in a broader context. On several levels, the practice of Taijiquan is a process. First, in the vernacular used within the Chinese internal martial arts community, it is *the process of practicing and accumulating gong.* So what is *gong*?

Gong Practice

Gong is the foundation of Taijiquan. Physically, the accumulation of *gong* refers to constant improvements in balance, coordination, agility, and power through the accretion and replenishment of *qi*, which can be described as "vital energy," or "life force."[1] Mentally and spiritually, the accumulation of *gong* refers to constant advancement toward realizing inner tranquility. *Gong* practice means practice of essential exercises necessary to understand the art of Taiji and build a solid foundation of skill. It is indispensable. My teacher compared *gong* to the flour in noodles; that is, it is the main ingredient.[2] (Or, for my New Orleans friends, *gong* is the roux of the gumbo.)

Gong is not technique—it is the root from which the flower of technique can grow. Without *gong*, technique is empty and unreliable. The value of *gong* compared to technique is emphasized in three famous sayings:

练拳不练功, 到老一场空。

Lian quan bu lian gong, dao lao yi chang kong.

Even if you practice your whole life,
if you do not practice *gong*, your art will be empty.

力不敌法, 法不敌功。

Li bu di fa, fa bu di gong.

Brute force cannot defeat technique, and technique cannot defeat *gong*.

一功, 二胆, 三技巧。

Yi gong, er dan, san ji qiao.

First *gong*, second confidence, third technique.

Gong practice has long been considered the secret of the art. "I will teach you *quan* (external movements or technique) but not *gong*" is another well-known saying within the Chinese martial arts community. To build *gong* is to build internal power and realize the physical and mental benefits of bountiful *qi*. Internal power, in turn, is the foundation of all internal martial arts.

It is not surprising then find the word *gong* used as the foundation for other key concepts of Taiji. *Gong* is often used synonymously with *qigong*. Every Taiji exercise, if performed correctly, is a *qigong* or energy gathering/transforming exercise. Whether practicing static *qigong* (e.g., sitting or standing meditations) or dynamic *qigong* (e.g., repetitive motions, Taiji form, push-hands, or any physical activity), you should always feel the accumulation of energy afterwards. If you don't, something is not right.

The root meaning of the word *gong* as "essential foundation" is also conveyed in the compound word *gongfu* (功夫). *Gongfu* is commonly pronounced as "Kung Fu" in American English. The meaning of the term is not limited to martial arts, as is popularly understood, but rather refers to true skill in an art in general. If a person's skill is high, the Chinese may say *gongfu tebie shen* (功夫特别深), which literally means that his or her skill is very "deep." The implication is that he or she has "the real stuff." The opposite is expressed in the phrase *kong jiazi, mei you gongfu* (空架子, 没有功夫), meaning that he or she has an "empty frame and no *gongfu*," that is, form with no *gong* or internal power. The form may look impressive to the untrained eye, but it is superficial and unsupported by *gong*.

So when I tell you that Taiji is the process of practicing and accumulating *gong*, I mean that you should start with the internal aspects of the art and first begin to acquire *gong*. Each subsequent step relies upon the *gong* accumulated and is itself a means for the further accumulation of *gong*. If you do not start with *gong*, then what is the foundation of what you are doing? Some have practiced Taiji form movements for many years and have never truly gotten beyond the beginning stage; they never really began accumulating *gong*.

Nurture, Nurture, Nurture

How is *gong* accumulated? The *method*, of course, is through meditation, form, and push-hands practice. All of these exercises are essential and interrelated. The *gong* derived from standing and sitting meditation is used in form and push-hands practice; the *gong* derived from form practice is used in push-hands; and the *gong* developed in push-hands is used in fighting applications. (I will further describe the form and substance of *gong* accumulated from each of these practices in their respective chapters. If I am at all successful, the interdependency of these exercises and therefore the importance of practicing a complete curriculum will ultimately be obvious.)

Although these exercises provide the means for accumulating *gong*, they may be more or less successful, depending on how they are carried out. The key principle that affords accumulation of *gong* in all exercises is *nurturing*. My teacher would often say "*duo zhuyi yangsheng*," (多注意养生) or, "pay attention to nurturing." Every Taiji exercise should be done with this intention.

How do we nurture *gong*? Acquiring *gong* is just like saving money. We can either choose to save our money, continually and consciously adding to our principle and accumulating interest, or we can spend it whenever we get it. And so it is with *gong*. In the way that we practice, we choose to either nurture ourselves or spend our energy. If we spend it, we will not accumulate it. It's that simple. Our attitude should be to nurture, nurture, nurture, slowly and patiently, step-by-step, accumulating *gong*. Only by nurturing can we use softness to accumulate hardness. Note, however, that accumulating doesn't mean being selfish—when we practice push-hands, for example, we should nurture our partner's as well as our own energy. We should also heed the principle of moderation—not too much, and not too little. The extreme of a good thing is the birth of a bad thing. A wrong-minded focus on accumulating can lead to avariciousness. The principle of nurturing and the foundation of *gong* practice are so central to the art of Taiji that I will refer to them repeatedly when explaining how to practice.

Going one step further, the principle of constant nurturing applies to everything we do—not just Taijiquan practice. We should always nurture/replenish/balance our energy. If we are constantly harried in everyday life, if our emotions frequently swing beyond control, how can we expect to nurture *qi?* Don't expect to "save" *qi* with a couple hours of Taiji practice every day if you turn around and "spend" it in your daily life. You don't have to retreat to a secluded mountain to practice *gong*, but you do have to pay attention to moderation and nurturing in all aspects of your life. Actually, once you get started in the right direction, it's easy to keep going. The sense of improved health, peacefulness, and growing internal power will be quite obvious, and you will develop an inner repulsion for any activity that wastes your energy. (The list of wasteful activities is seemingly infinite—arguments, anger, worry, excesses of any kind.) So here we have one bridge connecting our Taiji practice with our daily lives and demonstrating that everything is interrelated and interdependent. The principles of Taiji practice extend and apply to daily activities and the attitude with which we live our daily lives directly affects our foundation of skill in Taijiquan. This leads us to a second description of the processes of Taijiquan.

Improving Ourselves Physically, Mentally, and Spiritually

Taiji is secondly a process of improving ourselves physically, mentally, and spiritually, where these three are interrelated and interdependent. Everyone knows that Taiji is beneficial to health, but many think of that simply as improvement in physical health. Yet, Western medicine now agrees that physical and mental health are inextricably related. Furthermore, Western scientific studies are increasingly showing the role of spirituality in health.[3] The importance of spirituality in the Eastern view of health is emphasized in a Chinese saying:

药补不如食补, 食补不如气补, 气补不如神补。

Yao bu bu ru shi bu, shi bu bu ru qi bu, shi bu bu ru shen bu.

To improve your health, medicine is not as good as food/nutrition;
food/nutrition is not as good as *qi(gong)*;
qi(gong) is not as good as spiritual nourishment.

This interrelationship of the physical, mental, and spiritual is clearly apparent in Taiji. Those of you who teach or have practiced Taiji for a while may have noticed something interesting: a person's form is often reflective of his or her character. A clear example of this is tension—it is astounding how much tension some beginning students carry with them, which is manifested in their inability to relax when doing the form. Or, a student may habitually do the form with very small, reserved motions, even after instructed to make the movements large. That person's form may reflect a reserved, perhaps fearful personality. If we pay close attention, Taiji practice will reveal areas that need improvement, not only in our physical selves, but also in our character. Since our Taiji form is an external manifestation of our inner spirit, and since Taiji seeks to achieve the *balanced* interactions of yin and yang, to improve our form we must work to balance yin and yang in ourselves. How can we reach a high level of skill in Taijiquan if our inner nature has an imbalance—too much yin or too much yang? This, I believe, is exactly the meaning of the following excerpt from Chapter 40, "Treatise on Zhang Sanfeng Realizing the Dao Through Martial Arts" of *The Yang Family Forty Chapters*:

> Thus the external becomes concentrated in the internal, and the internal expresses itself externally. In this way we develop within and without, the fine and gross, and with penetrating understanding we realize the work of wise men and sages.[4]

The dual cultivation of the external and internal, the martial and spiritual, is thus a common theme in all of the Chinese martial arts and is mentioned throughout the classical Taijiquan literature. A famous Chinese saying states that one's martial skill can only be as good as one's virtue:

拳以德立，无德无拳。

Quan yi de li, wu de wu quan.

Virtue is the foundation of boxing skill,
without virtue there is no (high level of) boxing skill.

Chen Xin (1849–1929), a 16th-generation practitioner from the Chen Village, further wrote that from the little dao (martial arts), we can glimpse the big Dao (spiritual truth).[5] Chapter 14 of *The Yang Family Forty Chapters*, in particular, addresses the tradition of the dual cultivation of martial and spiritual in Taijiquan:

The spiritual is the essence, the martial is the application. Spiritual development in the realm of the martial arts is applied through the *jing, qi,* and *shen*—the practice of internal cultivation. When the martial is matched with the spiritual and it is experienced in the body and mind, this then is the practice of martial arts. With the spiritual and the martial we must first speak of the proper timing, for their development unfolds according to the proper sequence. This is the root of internal cultivation. As the spiritual and the martial are applied to sparring, we must consider the appropriate use of storing and issuing. This is the root of the martial arts. Therefore, the practice of the martial arts in a spiritual way is soft-style exercise, the sinew power of *jing, qi,* and *shen*. When the martial arts are practiced in an exclusively martial way, this is hard-style, or simply brute force. The spiritual without martial training is essence without application, and the martial without spiritual is application without essence. A lone pole cannot stand; a single palm cannot clap. This is not only true of internal cultivation and martial arts, but all things are subject to this principle. The spiritual is internal principle, the martial is external skill. External skill without internal principle is simply physical ferocity. This is a far cry from the original nature of the art, and by bullying an opponent one eventually invites disaster. To understand the internal principles without the external skill is simply an armchair art. Without knowing the applications, one will be lost in an actual confrontation. When applying this art, one cannot afford to ignore the significance of the two words: spiritual and martial.[6]

Spirituality in the Art of Taijiquan

Many seek the martial aspects and health benefits of Taiji, but how is *spirituality* practiced in Taiji, and how is that an indispensable aspect of our art?

Of the twelve principles of practice emphasized by Grandmaster Feng Zhiqiang,[7] the first principle is that the mind and spirit should always be *xujing* (虚静), that is, empty and tranquil. Grandmaster Feng teaches that *xujing* is the essence of Taiji, as well as its ultimate goal. Maintaining *xujing* is essential for the practitioner to truly relax in *qigong* and form practice. In push-hands practice, one must realize *xujing* to learn the skills of how to "abandon oneself and follow others" and also how to "begin late but arrive early." "Taiji is the *gongfu* of *xujing*," teaches Grandmaster Feng, "This is the most important principle of all."

Grandmaster Feng Zhiqiang's
12 Principles of Taijiquan Practice

1. Heart and spirit empty and tranquil from beginning to end.

2. Central equilibrium.

3. Use the mind to move *qi*. The heart is the commander.

4. Start with sinking and dropping.

5. Search for soft and smooth.

6. Inside/outside and upper/lower should work together.

7. The transition of yin/yang will help you find hard/soft.

8. The silk-reeling force should be present throughout
    the body.

9. Search for open/close by folding the chest and stomach.

10. Concentrate on *dantian* to improve *neigong* (internal skill).

11. Keep your heart calm, mind quiet, and practice slowly
    (stillness in movement). The form is a moving standing
    pole (*huo zhuang*).

12. You will be successful if you know both how to practice
    and how to nurture yourself (*yang sheng*).

So how does Taijiquan lead one to achieve tranquility of mind and spirit? In learning Taiji, practitioners follow the spiritual principles of moderation, cessation of ego, and inward looking in all aspects of practice. Tranquility of mind and spirit, and the heightened awareness that arises from this tranquility, are ultimately the greatest possible benefits of our Taiji practice. Tranquility is also, in the end, a purely spiritual function.

To more clearly explain these spiritual principles and their relation to Taiji practice, it is better now to step back and look at the big picture rather than quickly get muddled in the esoteric language of Daoist spiritual practices. To do so, I have selected comparative sayings from across the world's major spiritual traditions. In using comparative quotes from a wide range of sources, my purpose is twofold:

1. To illustrate the spiritual aspect of Taiji in familiar terms to readers from various cultures and spiritual traditions, and

2. To demonstrate the commonality of the spiritual principles of moderation, cessation of ego, and inward looking, and therefore the universality of the spiritual aspects of Taiji practice.

Before beginning the discussion of spirituality in Taijiquan, though, I would first make clear a distinction between spirituality and religion. Religion is an institutionalized system of attitudes, beliefs, and practices that requires a commitment or devotion to a shared faith. *Taijiquan is not in any way a religion.* It does not require, nor espouse, any particular system of religious beliefs or practices. As exemplified below, however, core spiritual and philosophic principles common to the world's spiritual traditions are an essential aspect of the complete art of Taijiquan.

Duality and the Moderation Principle

Throughout the world's spiritual and philosophic traditions, duality lies at the core of divine creative expression. Complementary opposites are an essential (perhaps the essential) part of the dynamic action of the world. Individuals may be as attracted to one pole as they are opposed to its opposite, but both must ultimately be understood to connect more fully with reality. This idea recurs throughout texts of spirituality:

> I form the light and create darkness. I make peace and create evil. I am the Lord that doeth all these things.   —Judeo-Christian *Bible*, Isaiah 45:7

> Male and female created he them.   —Judeo-Christian *Bible*, Genesis 1:27

> And it is He who spread out the earth, and set thereon mountains standing firm and (flowing) rivers: and fruit of every kind He made in pairs, two and two.   —Islamic *Quran* 013.003[8]

> That it is He Who granted Laughter and Tears. That it is He Who granted Death and Life. That He did create in pairs—male and female.
> —Islamic *Quran* 053.043–045[9]

> And thus he created everything that exists in pairs.—Hindu *Upanishads*[10]

> Nature governs the world with her law of balance. She puts things ever in pairs, and leaves nothing in isolation. Positives stand in opposition to negatives, actives to passives, males to females.   —Zen Buddhism[11]

Whatever we may call them, the strong and the weak, or the rigid and the tender, or the male and the female, or heaven and earth, or Yang and Yin, or Chien and Kun, there are, according to the Yi Ching, two independent principles, and their interplay, governed by certain fixed laws, constitutes the universe.　　—D.T. Suzuki discussing the Chinese *Book of Changes*[12]

God is day and night, winter and summer, war and peace, surfeit and hunger...　　　　　　　　　　—Greek philosopher Heraclitus[13]

These quotes underscore that the world's spiritual and philosophical traditions widely recognize an intrinsic duality of nature. Yin and yang, of course, are the well-known Chinese terms describing this duality, and as noted in the introduction and explained in detail in Chapter 5, the recognition of the essential interrelatedness of duality is central to the core theory of the art of Taiji.

Rather than being buffeted by this world of opposites, the world's spiritual guides suggest we find wisdom and balance by avoiding excess and instead following a middle course. The avoidance of extremes is a common admonition in the world's spiritual traditions:

Nature doth ever swing between extremes, holding the balance, stands midway, her God.　　　　　　　　—Hindu *Bhava-Prakasha*[14]

Be not righteous over much, neither make thyself over wise...Be not over much wicked, neither be thou foolish.
　　　　　　—Judeo-Christian *Bible*, Ecclesiastes 7:16–17

Give me neither poverty nor riches.
　　　　　　　　—Judeo-Christian *Bible*, Proverbs 30:8

But such disciplined effort (*yoga*) is not for one who eats or sleeps too much or too little. For one whose enjoyment of food is disciplined, whose engagements in actions [are] disciplined, whose sleeping and waking are disciplined, the disciplined effort of meditation (*yoga*) becomes a remover of sorrow.　　　　　　　　—Hindu *Bhagavad Gita*[15]

Make not unlawful the good things which Allah hath made lawful for you, but commit no excess.　　　　—Islamic *Quran*[16]

If in the satisfaction of his desires man oversteps the limits of moderation, he pollutes his body and mind.　　—Shinto tenet as explained by
　　　　　　　　　Japanese author Inazo Nitobe[17]

Nothing in excess.　　　　　　　　　　—Greek maxim[18]

Of course, the entire teachings of Buddha are referred to as the "Middle Path." This avoidance of extremes is what my teacher refers to as the "moderation principle," essential to Taiji practice. We should not allow our practice to become forced dreary work, nor should we expect to realize the full benefits of practice if we lackadaisically approach it as play or hobby. We should not overemphasize one aspect of our practice to the detriment, or exclusion, of another. We should balance yin and yang, hard and soft, movement and stillness, physical and spiritual. Not too much and not too little—this is the balance we seek in all facets of Taiji practice (as well as daily life). The balanced interaction of yin and yang *is* Taiji.

Beyond calling for moderation in action, understanding the inherent duality of the world process leads, ultimately, to *transcendence* of that process. In perceiving that happiness doesn't exist without sadness, good without bad, the spiritual practitioner is increasingly unaffected by either. As the Sufis say: "The wise saw good and evil both from God, therefore from both they drew their heart aside." Recognizing God as the center and source of the intrinsic duality of the world, Jesus says in the *Gospel of Thomas* (22:4–7): "When you make the two into one, and when you make the inner like the outer and the outer like the inner, and the upper like the lower, and when you make male and female into a single one. . . then you will enter the (Father's) domain."[19] Noting that the inherent duality of the world is also mirrored within man, the *Upanishads* say: "Like two birds of golden plumage, inseparable companions, the individual self and the Immortal self are perched on branches of the self-same tree. The former tastes the sweet and bitter fruits of the trees, the latter, tasting neither, calmly observes."[20] And so in understanding that joy and woe are inextricably intertwined ("all joy wants eternity," as Nietzsche famously said), the warrior realizes that the only true battle is within—that of overcoming the ego that ensnares by attachment to pleasure and aversion to pain.

Overcoming Ego

The quintessential practice of the world's spiritual traditions is that of overcoming ego, of surpassing the petty attractions and aversions of the small self in search of union with the greater Self. Overcoming the egoistic and sensual desires of the physical body is the very definition of spirituality, inasmuch as the word "spiritual" directly contrasts with the worldly or material. Egoism or selfish desire is insatiable, and is considered the root of evil and the source of suffering and pain. Lust, hate, greed, aggression, pride of martial glory, political and religious bigotry—all spring from egoistic desire.[21] Buddha's teachings begin with the assertion that desire is the source of suffering, and that true peace can only be realized by overcoming selfish desire. Similarly, in the Christian tradition, the surrender of one's self to the greater Universal Self is succinctly stated in the Lord's prayer—"Father, *Thy* will be done." Self surrender is also the lesson in the Beatitudes, "Blessed are the poor in spirit, theirs is the kingdom of heaven...Blessed are the meek, for they shall inherit the earth" (Matthew 5:3,5), and particularly in the verse from the Gospel of Mark, "If any want to become my followers, let them deny themselves and take up their cross and follow me. For those who want to save their life will lose it, and those who lose their life will preserve it" (Mark 8:34–35). The very word "Islam" has the profound meaning of "peaceful acceptance of God," the surrender of the small self with calm resignation to the will of God.

In the Chinese tradition, the *Dao De Jing* repeatedly emphasizes the need to surpass egoistic desire:

> Is it not because he wants nothing, that he is able to achieve everything?
> The lesser man acts from his ego, and what he wants is gratification.
> Simplicity comes from letting go of what you want.[22]

The teachings of Confucius and Mencius further emphasize the role of unselfishness:

> There are only two moral principles, fellow feeling or Altruism, and its opposite, Egoism. *Ren* (仁) is the fundamental virtue. It is sympathy, fellow feeling. This fellow feeling is the reason of the Golden Rule. It is the Dao; it is the road which must be traveled by every human being. The Dao is the feeling of fellowship, and the feeling of fellowship is the Dao. Without it, one will not be kept from doing to others what one would not have done by others to him. All virtues spring from *Ren*: loyalty, filial piety, courage, wisdom, propriety, faithfulness, righteousness, long-suffering, humaneness, benevolence. *Ren* is the reason of love. Prosperity, kindheartedness, charity, sincere sympathy, and unselfishness are different shades of Ren. When a man behaves as his heart desires, yet never transgresses the mean, he has reached perfect adjustment between natural impulses and moral discipline. He is now *Ren* itself. He is *Sheng Ren* (圣人), a holy man. He behaves as freely and innocently as a child fresh from the bosom of nature, and all that he does never deviates from the Middle Way, *Zhong Dao*.[23]

The concept of surpassing egoistic desire is central to the world's understanding of spirituality. It is also central to and directly practiced in the art of Taijiquan. Surrender of the ego is exactly the requirement of the famous text from the Taijiquan classic, "*Give up yourself* and follow your opponent" (*she ji cong ren*, 舍己从人). There is deep and profound meaning in these simple words. Almost every student, when beginning push-hands practice, will respond to a push with a push. This is nothing more than the quite natural response of a threatened ego controlling the body, the end result of which is simply external fighting. The self-defense skill to which Taijiquan practitioners aspire, however, is based upon "sticking" to the opponent, following his or her attack, and leading the attack to emptiness. This can only be done if central equilibrium (*zhong ding*, 中定) is maintained. Central equilibrium, in turn, is primarily a mental/spiritual function. The physical manifestation of *zhong ding* is a perfectly balanced body. A perfectly balanced body, with the *qi* sunk to the *dantian* (i.e., relaxed), is achieved only by a calm and peaceful mind.[24] Peace and quiet of the mind, and therefore *zhong ding*, will be lost every time that the ego seeks to assert itself, and in direct proportion to the magnitude of the desire. The next time that you practice push-hands, be aware of your thoughts and intention and observe what happens to your *qi* and balance when you mistakenly "forget your partner and follow yourself." You will feel your *qi* rise and go outward, and your body and balance will follow—every time, without exception. The well-known Zen teaching that the archer will miss the target if his or her mind is intent upon winning the trophy is the same lesson: ego/desire is the downfall. Effortless action can occur only when the ego is in check. It is no easy task to give up yourself and follow your opponent, but it is necessary to advance to higher levels of skill and understanding in Taijiquan.

Another, perhaps even more obvious, exercise in which the submission of ego is directly practiced in Taijiquan is standing and sitting meditation. We have already noted that standing and sitting meditation are the foundation of *gong* practice; the *gong* from meditation is central to form, push-hands, and self-defense applications. In both sitting and standing meditation, one strives for a state of perfect quietude. Many techniques have been developed to lead the practitioner to a state of quiet awareness. A common thread in all of these is that they are intended to distract the mind from its primary, unbridled focus: selfish desire. Everybody who practices meditation is hindered by an active mind. The root source of "noisy" thoughts is desire. To find the source of a distracting thought, simply ask yourself what you "want" (and then be brutally honest with yourself). Surrender of ego is a requisite to enter stillness and begin the accumulation of *gong*. The more you can truly surrender the ego, the deeper you will go into quiet contemplation and the more *gong* you will acquire.[25] From the very beginning of Taiji practice, one is practicing the quintessential spiritual exercise, although it is not often recognized as such until much later in one's development.

At this point, we can better understand the saying that one's martial art can only be as good as one's morality, or my earlier statement that those who seek martial glory can never possibly reach the higher levels of Taijiquan skill. Surrender of ego, unselfishness, is a fundamental virtue. It is also a requisite for meditation practice from which the fundamental *gong* is extracted, and for the achievement of one of the basic principles of Taijiquan self-defense technique—forgetting oneself and following the opponent. The physical and spiritual are inexorably linked. It's paradoxical. The art of Taijiquan is a deep and profound martial art, but those with the ego-driven desire of becoming invincible fighters will never achieve higher skill in the art—their very desire to be great fighters will limit their progress in learning.

Another famous, yet elliptical, saying within the Chinese internal martial arts community suggests the necessity of surpassing ego to achieve higher levels of skill: "Quan wu quan. Yi wu yi. Wu quan wu yi qiu zhen yi" (拳无拳, 意无意, 无拳无意求真意) or "Form without form. Intention without intention. Go beyond form and intention to search for the true meaning." This saying refers to the highest level of Taijiquan, or any martial art for that matter, and few understand its meaning. I believe that the Zen Master Takuan Soho repeatedly addresses the essence of this saying in *The Unfettered Mind, Writings of a Zen Master to the Sword Master*. Takuan writes:

> If you do not think of striking your opponent and no thoughts or judgments remain, if the instant you see the swinging sword your mind is not the least bit detained, the sword that was going to cut you down will become your own … The function of the intellect disappears, and one ends in a state of No-Mind-No-Thought. If one reaches the deepest point, arms, legs, and body remember what to do, but the mind does not enter into this at all … When the mind is biased in one place and lacking in another, it is called a *one-sided mind*. One-sidedness is despicable. To be arrested by any-

thing, no matter what, is falling into one-sidedness and is despised by those traveling the Way. Not stopping the mind is object and essence. Put nowhere, it will be everywhere. Even in moving the mind outside the body, if it is sent in one direction, it will be lacking in nine others. If the mind is not restricted to just one direction, it will be in all ten.[26]

It is exactly the grasping ego that arrests and "stops" the mind. In martial arts, desiring victory, desiring to "attack," or even desiring to save oneself, are all manifestations of the ego. Only when ego is dissolved can one reach the level of "beyond form and intention," of detachment even in the face of death. It is only then that one can respond freely, spontaneously, and flawlessly, without the mind stopping in concern for any aspect of attack or defense. Dissolution of ego is a high achievement in spiritual practice and martial arts. Few indeed reach it.

It is certainly true that at times those of dubious moral character have succeeded in becoming renowned "martial artists." After all, any person may study pugilistic techniques and train the body to improve strength and endurance. The accomplishments of such persons, however, are short-lived. If practiced only on an external level with the egoistic desire to attain glory, or to harm, or to impose one's will on others, the practitioner need only await his or her inevitable downfall. Taijiquan is balance—yin and yang, movement and stillness, physical and spiritual. Through sheer will, intellect, and effort, it is possible for anyone to discover the biomechanical principles of Taijiquan movement (especially now that Taijiquan is taught commercially and "how to practice" books are readily available). For example, one may discover how to issue "short power" through the storing and releasing of the "elastic" force. Since every movement in the Taiji form is practice in storing and releasing energy, those who understand this principle can easily impress uninformed observers with their powerful *fajin* 发劲 (explosive release of energy). It is true that the power generated by physical Taijiquan movement alone can be quite impressive. However, the primary substance of true *fajin* is internal *gong*— mechanical movement is simply its expression.[27] Issuance of "short force" by mechanical movement without the foundation of *gong* is simple technique or external skill (albeit done using different muscle and tendon groups than those usually used to generate movement) and is ultimately no greater accomplishment than a carnival sideshow trick. Individuals seeking to learn Taijiquan for the single-minded, egoistic purpose of becoming great fighters may acquire a small piece of the Taiji pie, but they will never realize the full benefits of the art. Movement is a yang aspect of the art. Without the spiritual, without stillness, the yin aspect, no person can approach the complete art of Taijiquan.

Looking Within

A third important commonality between the world's spiritual traditions and Taijiquan lies in the assertion that the individual is a microcosm of the infinite, and therefore the infinite is realized by looking within. The spiritual traditions agree, disciplined self-examination leads to self-transcendence:

So God created man in his own image, in the image of God created he him.　　　　　　　　　—Judeo-Christian *Bible*, Genesis 1:27

I have said, ye are gods, and all of you are children of the most High.
　　　　　　　　　　　—Judeo-Christian *Bible*, Psalms 82:6

Jesus answered them, "Is it not written in your law, 'I said, ye are gods'?"
　　　　　　　　　　　—Christian *New Testament*, John 10:34

The kingdom of heaven is within you.
　　　　　　　　　　　—Christian *New Testament*, Luke 17:21[28]

When you know yourselves, then you will be known, and you will understand that you are children of the living Father. But if you do not know yourselves, then you live in poverty, and you are the poverty.
　　　　　　　　　　　—Jesus saying in *The Gospel of Thomas*, 3:1–5[29]

The truth is that you are always united with the Lord. But you must know this. Nothing further is there to know.　　　—Hindu *Upanishads*[30]

Now if a man worship Brahman, thinking Brahman is one and he another, he has not the true knowledge.　　　　　—Hindu *Upanishads*[31]

The Self-Existent made the senses turn outward. Accordingly, man looks toward what is without, and sees not what is within. Rare is he who, longing for immortality, shuts his eyes to what is without and beholds the Self.
　　　　　　　　　　　—Hindu *Upanishads*[32]

Shut of thy eyes, ears, lips, and senses all from outward things, surely thou wilt see God.　　　　　　　　　　—Sufi writings[33]

Although the great glad news of thee is writ plainly upon the Quran's holy page: "Nearer am I to thee than thy throat vein," my eyes blinded with selfishness, saw not. —Sufi song [34]

Know ye not that ye are the temple of God, and that the Spirit of God dwelleth in you? —Christian *New Testament*, I Corinthians 3:16

Remember what St. Augustine tells us...how he sought God in many places and at last found the Almighty within himself... We are not forced to take wings to find him, but only to seek solitude and look within ourselves. —St. Theresa of Avila [35]

He who attempts to act and do things for others or for the world without deepening his own self-understanding, freedom, integrity, and capacity to love, will not have anything to give others. He will communicate to them nothing but the contagion of his own obsessions, his aggressiveness, his ego-centered ambitions, his delusions about ends and means, his doctrinaire prejudices and ideas. —Christian monk, Thomas Merton [36]

Your real self lies hid beneath your outward self, for "I am the servant of him who looks into himself." —Sufi Prophet Rumi [37]

What the superior man seeks is in himself. —Confucius [38]

The concept that the individual is a microcosm of the Infinite is also a well-known Daoist principle. Taijiquan, as we have said, is a continual process of looking within, of continually identifying one's shortcomings with the intention of improving oneself mentally, physically and spiritually. The inward-looking process is of course the essence of meditation and is integral to form and push-hands practice. Indeed, form practice is often referred to as the practice of "knowing yourself." With concentrated awareness, "look within" during all aspects of Taiji practice. A final Chinese proverb reminds us that it is not only our physical selves that need sustenance:

吾日三省吾身。

Wu ri san xing wu shen.

One should look within three times a day.

"From the Little Dao, One Can Glimpse the Big Dao"

Some are attracted to martial arts or Eastern philosophies because of the belief that they are inherently mysterious and very different from other paths. Others refrain from or even rally against them for the same reason. Both groups are but two sides of the same coin—the product of nothing more than a lack of understanding. This is easily understandable, considering the obscure language of many Eastern spiritual disciplines. The language and culture *is* quite different from that of the West. Unfortunately, there are also those who, taking advantage of the attraction that some feel to the mysterious, poetic, and even exotic language of some Eastern spiritual traditions, seek to profit by promoting the misconception that the spiritual lessons of the East are fundamentally unique.[39]

Truth is not a unique possession of any one culture. Truth has been expressed to all people by the sages of all spiritual traditions. In the wisdom literature of all cultures there is the insistence that, with reference to ultimate reality, truth is singular and unchanging. It is ever present to be discovered by any person at any time. It is unvaried from age to age, despite the many labels we may give it and despite its different contemporary trappings. As the author of Ecclesiastes wrote, "Is there anything whereof it may be said, 'See this is new'? It hath already been of old time, which was before us ... *There is nothing new under the sun*" (Ecclesiastes 1:9–10). Confucius meant the same thing in saying, "I only hand on; I cannot create new things."[40] The author of the Gospel of Matthew also insisted that Jesus' message was not unique or contradictory to the accumulated wisdom of the Scriptures: "I come not to destroy the law or prophets, but to fulfill them" (Matthew 5:17–18).[41] From across the world's spiritual traditions, one finds this same insight:

> There is neither Jew nor Greek, there is neither bond nor free, there is neither male nor female; for ye are all one in Jesus Christ.
> —Christian *New Testament Bible*, Galatians 3:28

> Whatever things have been rightly said, among all men, are the property of us Christians ... We have been taught that Christ is the first-born of God, and we have declared that He is the Word of whom every race of men were partakers; and those who lived reasonably are Christians.
> —Christian Saint Justin Martyr[42]

Nothing is said to thee that was not said to the messengers before thee.

—Islamic *Quran* 041.043 [43]

It was We who revealed the law (to Moses)…And in their footsteps We sent Jesus the son of Mary, confirming the Law that had come before him…To thee We sent the Scripture in truth, confirming the scripture that came before it…To each among you have we prescribed a law and an open way.   —Islamic *Quran* 005.044–048 [44]

In varying ways the sages have described the same unvarying and essential truths; there is no real conflict twixt them all; the knowers know the way to reconcile.   —Hindu *Bhagavata* [45]

Thy truth is neither mine, nor his, nor another's; but belonging to us all.

—St. Augustine [46]

From the above discussion, one may reasonably ask, "So what, then, is the unique spiritual aspect of Taijiquan?" The answer is, there is none. There is nothing new under the sun. Every spiritual principle learned from Taiji practice can be learned elsewhere. The principles of moderation, denial of self-centered egoism, and the inner search are central to all major spiritual traditions. Some paths are just more direct than others. It's one thing to say, "I understand the idea of giving up myself and following the opponent," but quite another to actually do it when confronted with a direct physical attack, even if the attack is a symbolic or friendly exchange as in Taiji push-hands training.

It is undeniable that the *paths* that human beings follow for pursuing realization of Truth can be quite different, but each has the same end in sight:

This religion, that religion, there are various kinds but at the deepest point they are all settled on one conclusion. —Zen Buddhist Takuan [47]

Every prophet and every saint has a way, but it leads to God: all the ways are really one.   —Sufi Prophet Rumi [48]

God has never tied man's salvation to any pattern. Whatever possibilities inhere in any pattern of life inhere in all, because God has given it so and denied it to none. One good way does not conflict with another…What you get out of one pattern may be worked out in another…for not all people may travel the same road. —Christian mystic Meister Eckhart [49]

Different creeds are but different paths to reach the one God…Every religion is nothing but one of these paths.   —Ramakrishna [50]

Although certainly every spiritual tradition has its own unique history, characteristics, and proponents, different spiritual paths may be considered branches of the same trunk, all seeking balance and harmony in this world, cessation of ego toward a greater union, and inward-looking for realization of truth. The spiritual dimension of the martial arts is one of the many possible branches. The paths may indeed be quite varied, perhaps especially with regard to instruction for action in this world. The overall attitude of the Taiji path is characterized by moderation and balance. A quote from the Hindu *Mahabharata* may well express the Taiji approach to action: "Be...virtuousness, not self righteousness; devout, not fanatical;...enjoy, without elation;...speak gently, not insincerely; be brave, without boasting,...make friends, not with the ignoble; fight, not with friends; seek information, not from the unreliable;...trust, but not the evil;...be gentle, not to the mischievous; worship Deity, without display."[51] Ultimately, I believe that any path is about as good (or bad) as the intention of the person using it.

As stated in the introduction to this section, the above discussion is intended only to explain the spiritual aspects of Taijiquan by comparing theories and principles of the art to the fundamental tenets of some of the world's major spiritual traditions. By no means should you come away with the thought that you need or are expected to radically change your life when beginning Taiji. The lessons learned in Taiji are applicable to everyday life, and the way in which you live your life will affect your progress in the art. But the correct attitude for learning is one of patience and moderation. You need only approach Taiji with the attitude that you are going to improve yourself. Don't rush or overdo anything. Slowly and gradually, practice, learn, and understand the foundation of the art. There is a reason to the order and principles of different exercises. Remember the saying from *The Yang Family Forty Chapters* quoted above, "With the spiritual and the martial we must first speak of the proper timing, *for their development unfolds according to the proper sequence.*" In matters of the spiritual, consider Chen Xin's words, Taiji is a *little* dao from which one can glimpse the big Dao.

Shi
Teacher

finding a Teacher

THE EXPERIENCE OF TODAY'S EXPERT TEACHERS represents the accumulation of knowledge garnered and passed down through centuries of trial and error. It is doubtful that anyone can, in one lifetime, independently "rediscover" the complete art of Taijiquan. Those who wish to learn Taijiquan must first find a teacher who *can* and *will* share the art with them. As will be discussed below, these two are not always the same.

Your Responsibility

The first most important factor in what you learn, and therefore how you ultimately benefit from Taiji practice, is the quality of your teacher. This sounds obvious, but the counsel here is that it is your responsibility to search out and select a teacher. In China, there is an old saying that it takes three years for a student to find a teacher and three years for the teacher to decide whether he or she will accept a student (*Tu fang shi san nian, shi fang tu san nian,* 徒访师三年，师访徒三年).[1] You must find a teacher who knows the art or, at the very least, will get you started in the right direction. There are many good teachers who can do this, and there are also many who purport to teach the art but in fact know little or nothing about it. The meteoric rise in popularity of Taiji in the West over the past twenty years has inevitably been accompanied by mass commercialization of the art. Do not deceive yourself. Taiji is now big business in the West and the fundamental rule for consumers applies: "Buyer, beware." Unfortunately, there are those who care nothing more about the art than how much money they can make from it.

How far you are willing to go to study with a teacher is a question of fate, time, and environment. The more you want to study, the more you will have to search out better and better teachers, and generally the more sacrifices you will have to make. Ever since I was a child, I had heard stories of Feng Zhiqiang of Beijing, one of the greatest living practitioners of Taijiquan. For us youngsters, it was an impossible dream to meet him in person—to actually study with him was unimaginable. At that time (in the mid-1970s), Master Feng did not teach openly and could be met only via an introduction from an intimate colleague or a trusted student. Through fate and circumstance, I was introduced to Grandmaster Feng in Shanghai, and eventually was invited to study with him in Beijing. The problem was that I worked in Shanghai, and at that time I could not get permission from the Chinese government to transfer to Beijing. My solution was to quit my job and enroll in graduate school in Beijing as a law student, a move that was allowed. In order to study with the teacher I wanted, I had to surrender my career and home and move to Beijing. Even though it meant sacrificing all that I had worked for, it was possible. For me, it was an easy decision.

I realize that it is not easy to find the perfect teacher, and many beginning practitioners are not prepared to sacrifice to study from such a teacher, but in weighing the pros and cons of a prospective teacher you may wish to consider the following points.

What Style Is Best?

Do not worry about what "style" of Taiji you should begin with. The fundamental principles of Taiji movement, internal power, and self-defense applications are not different from style to style. Although each style has its own unique characteristics, the foundations are the same. Taijiquan movement is a way of moving the body and generating power. Choreographed forms are a tool to teach Taiji movement and build *gong*. After you learn these principles and have achieved a sufficient level of skill, *any* movement can be done as Taiji movement. If you don't understand this, you have not yet learned Taiji movement. When you observe partners playing free-style push-hands or free fighting, does their motion look like a choreographed form? Of course not, as the potential directions and methods of an attack, and therefore the required responses, are essentially infinite. Understanding the movement, not the choreographed form of a particular style, makes this possible. Find the teacher that best understands the principles of Taijiquan movement and let this determine the style that you study.

Do not be misled by the popular misconception that "this style is for fighting," or "that style is good for senior citizens," etc. Taiji movement is Taiji movement, period. The level of physical exertion (e.g., jumping or kicking) can easily be adjusted to suit any person's physical capabilities. I routinely teach the Chen style, commonly considered to be the most rigorous of all styles, to senior citizens in their seventies or older.

Taiji for Health or Martial Arts?

Some students spurn the thought of practicing the martial aspect of Taiji, while others want to explore the martial aspect only. Your reasons for studying Taiji are up to you, but those who are teaching should know better than to cripple the art by limiting the curriculum. Be wary of those who advertise that they "teach only the martial art," or "teach only for health," or any such restriction on the benefits of the art. The *gong* that is the foundation of the art is the source of both martial skill *and* improvements in health. If you practice correctly you will have both, and more.

Earlier I mentioned that it is true that some may discover a biomechanical principle of Taiji practice that will improve their martial skill without accumulation or nurturing of *gong*. It is also true that some measurable health benefits may be realized if one simply practices an empty form. Any reasonable exercise can improve health, and for the more sedentary, even empty, slow form movement is significant exercise. But the benefits of correct practice are exceedingly greater than what may be wrested from any narrow, incomplete approach to the art.

Whatever your personal reasons for studying Taijiquan, the foundation and the principles of practice are the same. If you practice correctly, you *can feel and will absolutely know* that you have a solid foundation upon which the "flower" of martial technique can be added, if you wish. It's like building a house: martial techniques are the ornaments in a window, while the *gong* is the (hidden) structural foundation that truly supports the house. Once your structural frame is in place, you can decorate the house as you see fit. However, if the foundation is weak or non-existent, a passerby might think "what a beautiful house," but if a storm comes…well, hopefully the homeowner has good insurance.

Even without consideration of the role of *gong* in Taiji, the interdependency of health and martial ability should be obvious. Overemphasizing and therefore overtraining any martial exercise is likely to result in an injury, and, of course, any injury will diminish your fighting capability. The more serious the injury, the less your ability to fight. This becomes a more serious issue for those who have begun to develop a foundation of internal *gong*. Those practitioners will be significantly more powerful, and can do more serious harm to themselves if they overemphasize certain martial exercises. Some have paid a very high price for ignoring this aspect of the moderation principle.

Are the Teacher's Actions Consistent?

In choosing a teacher, it is most important to observe all of that teacher's actions. Do not be impressed by a teacher's fame or title, or if they tell you they have studied with a famous teacher. Many have attended classes with famous masters, but never really learned anything. Anybody can attend a few classes with a master and parrot their teachings with claims of "discipleship," but few really *understand* those teachings. Further, just because someone is famous does not in any way guarantee mastery or even competence. In fact, many of the best Taiji practitioners are not famous at all. Fame may simply have been inherited, or what was mastered was not Taiji, but self-promotion.

There certainly is a correlation between length of study and level of accomplishment. However, some have studied for a long time and have not truly grasped the art, while others have studied for a relatively short time and are quite capable of providing quality instruction. With an open mind, watch and observe for yourself whether that teacher understands both theory and application. Observe whether what that teacher says and does is consistent. Ask yourself if his or her behavior is a model for you. In northern China, traditionally all students refer to the teacher as *laoshi* (老师). If one becomes a formal disciple, then one refers to the teacher as *shifu* (师父), which means "teacher/father."[2] Based upon your prospective teacher's actions and behavior, would you be comfortable calling him, "father" (or her, "mother")? Earlier I mentioned the saying that it takes three years for a teacher to accept a student. In China, there is an additional adage warning teachers about accepting students before knowing their true character: "Today you call me grandfather, tomorrow you will call me grandson." (*Jin tian ni jiao wo ye, ming tian ni jiao wo sun zi,* 今天你叫我爷, 明天你叫我孙子.) Clichés are clichés for a reason—they are often true. Does your prospective teacher speak respectfully and gratefully of the knowledge given by his or her own teacher? It is not possible to have truly learned the art and not feel deeply appreciative of those who have taught you.

You should not only observe the teacher's actions and behavior, but that of the other students as well. Ask yourself, "Am I comfortable in this environment?" A good teacher is magnanimous, but not indiscriminate. Although everyone learns and progresses at his or her own pace, the students on average will mirror the moral fiber of the teacher. You will know if your character is similar to that of the other students, just as the other students will recognize whether you belong in their group. The Chinese say that, ultimately, "Different spirits won't enter the same temple." (*Bu shi yi jia he shang, bu jin yi jia miao,* 不是一家和尚不进一家庙.)

Do You Get Sufficient Hands-on Instruction?

There is a saying that the internal martial arts are a gift that can only be handed down personally from teacher to student:

诀窍奥秘, 须经明师口传心授。

Jue qiao ao mi, xu jing ming shi kou chuan xin shou.

Tricks of the trade and secrets of practice must be passed on by sincere instruction from a teacher who understands the art.

It is a fact that certain aspects of this internal art are communicated only by direct contact with the teacher. You will not learn what internal power is unless a teacher demonstrates it to you, personally (i.e., hands it to you). You have to *feel* it before you can understand it. Similarly, you will not learn what silk-reeling force, "sticking," neutralizing, simultaneous neutralizing and releasing, or *ling* 灵 (lightness/agility) are unless you have the opportunity to feel them. From whomever you choose to study, you must get repeated, personal, hands-on instruction. This is closely related to the next point.

Will the Teacher Share His or Her Knowledge?

Even after you find someone who *can* teach you, you need to determine if he or she is *willing* to teach you the full art of Taijiquan. This point is exemplified in the saying, "I will teach you *quan* (form, external movements), but not *gong*." Anyone can teach a choreographed form or an "application," but the hidden gold of the art is the *gong* beneath the form. Remember the saying in the last chapter, "*kong jia zi, mei you gongfu*" (empty form, no *gongfu*)? Teachers who are willing to share their knowledge will show you how to start with the internal aspect and begin the accumulation of *gong*. However, it is possible for a teacher to be "hands-on," but still withhold the *gong*. For example, if a teacher has reached a certain level, he or she can at will "disappear" from your touch and show you only emptiness. Behind the emptiness a mountain is standing, but you will not know this unless the teacher wants you to see it.

The differentiation between "can" and "will" share knowledge may initially sound perplexing to a beginning student, but remember that this art was a secret for most of its history. There are many examples of teachers in China who taught a diluted version of the art publicly (i.e., to "outdoor" students), withholding the complete art for their select "indoor" students. An old proverb advises, "show your power to no one" (*cang er bu lou,* 藏而不露), and some teachers have taken this to heart, withholding their full knowledge and skill from potential rivals.[3] Also, as noted at the beginning of this chapter, teaching Taiji is now a business. Perhaps some believe that they will make more money if their student's practice is, to put it kindly, less than efficient.

If the teacher won't teach you, you are wasting your time. This, too, is seemingly obvious, but a few words in defense of the teacher are appropriate here. First, a teacher can only point the direction for you—it is up to you to make the journey. (*Shifu ling jin men, xiu xing zai ge ren,* 师父领进门, 修行在个人, which means "the teacher will lead you to the door, but it is up to the student to improve.") Another meaning of the saying, "I will teach you *quan,* but not *gong,*" (besides the teacher not wanting to show the student) is that the teacher cannot *give* the *gong* to the student. It depends on the aptitude of the student whether he or she "gets it." Even if the teacher wants the student to learn, he or she may not. For this reason, it is often said that it is up to fate whether one gets the *gong* of the art. If you are making progress, you will know it. If you are not, look *within* first. It is quite easy to blame others for our own shortcomings.

For a second caution in too quickly dismissing a teacher, realize that a good teacher will not waste time with wordy instruction. "One touch will penetrate" (*yi dian jiu tou*, 一点就透), according to a famous saying. When the student is ready to understand a principle, a very succinct lesson or example from the teacher is all that is needed to drive the point home. Conversely, if the student is not ready to grasp a point, all the talking in the world won't help. If the teacher is not saddling students with extensive lecturing, it may well be that he or she understands this point. A good teacher will teach and not waste time demonstrating how much he or she knows intellectually. When I began learning in China, it was traditional that the student mainly observe and follow the teacher, rather than receive spoken instruction. This traditional way of teaching evolved for a good reason.

Lastly, if a teacher is not teaching what you want, it could be that the teacher and student have different ideas of what is the best course of study for the student. At some point in time, most students develop an opinion of what they "should" be studying. Every teacher faces the problem of balancing what the student needs with what the student wants. Once you have selected a teacher, practice what you are being taught. If the teacher is good and you practice correctly, you will eventually realize that *all* aspects and benefits of the art come from the fundamental *gong*.

Is the Teacher Possessive?

A good teacher should never act in a possessive manner and should always encourage students to attend seminars and study from other teachers if they so desire. Taiji is a deep, multifaceted art, and all of us can learn from the experience and insights of others. Because of their own insecurity, however, there are some teachers who will limit their students' growth by preventing them from reaching out for different viewpoints.

In my hometown in China, it was common for teachers to encourage their students to seek instruction from other teachers. They would say, "This person is good at *qinna* 擒拿 (joint locking/controlling techniques), that person is good at push-hands, go and study from them."[4] For a while, I was fortunate enough to have private instruction from Chen Zhaokui, an 18th-generation family master of the Chen style. Even this great teacher told me that, if given the chance, I should study from his Taiji brother, Feng Zhiqiang, in Beijing. I will never forget this open-minded encouragement and kindness.

An occasional criticism of Taijiquan in the West is that it is a "cult-like" activity. Sadly, in a few extreme cases, this could be a valid charge. One characteristic of cults is that the leader closes the hearts and minds of the followers to the outside world. Lessons from outside the group are strictly forbidden, often under penalty of expulsion from the group. A true teacher would never forbid contact with or lessons from those outside of the school. On the contrary, he or she would always strive to awaken the hearts and minds of the students to the world.

A qualifier, however, is necessary here as well. Some students, especially those just beginning, are very hungry to learn and tend to want to fill their plate with as much instruction as possible. On occasion, I have had students tell me they want to attend a seminar that I know from experience will not improve their skill or knowledge. This too is okay, provided that the student is not going down a path that may be harmful. Learning how not to practice can be a valuable lesson, also. Keep in mind, however, that a teacher may have a student's best interests in mind when discouraging a certain direction.

Once You Find a Teacher

Once you find a teacher, spend as much time with him or her as you can. The more time you spend with the teacher, the more you will learn. This is another bit of advice that may fit in the "extremely obvious" category, but it has been my observation that not everyone truly understands (or believes) this simple point. Do not deceive yourself by thinking you "get it" after finishing one seminar, or that you have learned all the Level 1 lessons when graduating to Level 2. "Beginning," "intermediate," or "advanced" labels are relative. The Chinese say,

山外有山，天外有天，能人背后有能人

Shan wai you shan, tian wai you tian, neng ren bei hou you neng ren.

Beyond this mountain there is another (bigger) mountain;
beyond this world, there is another (bigger) world;
beyond a master, there is another (better) master.

Some of you may now be thinking, "Well, that's fine, but I don't have the luxury of frequent lessons with a teacher." Most of us are busy with responsibilities and do not have the time that we would like for either practice or lessons. *The key issue is to practice as efficiently as possible.* Do not waste your time with extraneous or tangential exercises. To accomplish this, a good question for your teacher is always, "What should I be practicing, and what percentage of my time should be spent on each different exercise?"

Once you have taken the time to select a teacher and school, respect and practice what you have been taught—even if at first you don't understand it. It's human nature to think that "the grass is greener on the other side." The Chinese say, "The faraway monk is the smartest" *(Yuan lu de he shang hui nian jing,* 远路的和尚会念经)*,* which has the same meaning as, "A man is not a prophet in his home town." True, to continue advancing, you may need to search out better teachers. But start by respecting, appreciating, and truly learning what you already have.

The art of Taijiquan is continually evolving. If a teacher is good, the younger students will likely reach a higher level than the teacher. Why? Because a good teacher will allow the students to benefit from his or her experiences and mistakes, and their practice will therefore be that much more efficient. Once you know what to look for, finding a good teacher is feasible and worth your effort. As the Chinese say,

苦练十年，不如名师一点。

Ku lian shi nian, bu ru ming shi yi dian.

One word from a knowledgeable teacher
will save ten years of hard practice.

Jing
Tranquility

Chapter Four

Wuji Meditation

WHAT IS REFERRED TO AS STANDING OR SITTING MEDITATION in the West is what we call *wuji* practice in China. Along with Taiji form movement and push-hands exercises, *wuji* practice is one of the three essential "pillars" of Taiji training. As mentioned in Chapter 2, all practices of Taiji are *qigong*, or energy gathering/nurturing exercises. *Wuji* meditation is the most fundamental, and therefore the most important, of all *qigong* exercises.

"*Wuji* is the Mother of Taiji"

Wuji may be translated as "no extreme," as opposed to Taiji, which means literally "grand extreme." *Wuji* is a void or abyss. In *wuji* there is no differentiation between yin and yang. It is neither "this" nor "that"—it is "no thing" (nothing). But even in the stillness of *wuji*, there is the possibility of movement, and when that critical movement happens, yin and yang separate from within *wuji* to create Taiji.

So it is said that Taiji comes from *wuji* (*wuji sheng taiji*, 无极生太极). Without *wuji* there is no Taiji. Acquiring the fundamental *gong* for Taiji therefore begins with *wuji* practice, or standing and sitting meditation. This chapter will explain how to do the *wuji* meditation practices and address common errors in these practices. Importantly, it will also discuss, from both traditional and Western scientific perspectives, why these practices are considered a foundation of the internal martial arts.

In China, it is well known that *wuji* is the starting point for Taiji practice. Although the different internal martial art styles evolved from various philosophies and therefore may use different terms, meditation practice is the essential foundation for all of them. That *wuji* is primary is evident in a famous saying from the internal martial arts tradition:

不静不见动之奇。

Bu jing bu jian dong zhi qi.

If you don't have quiet or tranquility,
you will never see the miracle of moving.

Traditionally, there were two contrasting schools of thought regarding teaching *wuji*. Because it is the essential *gong* practice, many teachers kept it as a very closely guarded secret and taught it only to trusted (i.e., "indoor") students. By not openly teaching *wuji*, teachers ensured that the fundamental *gong* was withheld from those they believed were undeserving. Often this secret was reserved for select family members. At the opposite extreme, other teachers would demand that the beginning student start with long hours of standing meditation practice for an extended period of study. This was done primarily to test the mettle of the prospective student. At first, *wuji* practice may seem boring to beginning students, and they, not fully trusting the teacher, may doubt that they are learning anything and quit. If students do not persevere with the fundamental *gong* practice, the teacher knows that they will not truly learn the art, and thus this "test" saves the time of everyone involved.

Whether for selfish reasons or from the belief that it is better not to "cast your pearls before swine," there are still some who practice, but do not teach, *wuji*. In my opinion, it is not necessary to withhold the *gong* from anyone. Those who do not practice moral virtue will always be afflicted with a "monkey mind" racing to their desires and therefore will remain unable to truly enter the quiet contemplation of *wuji* practice. They will never find peace or be able to realize and understand the fundamental *gong*. You cannot fool this natural law.

The standing and sitting *wuji* practices are different and yield different benefits, so we will address each one separately. One commonality of both, however, is that *how deeply you can "enter quiet" determines how much benefit you will get from the practice*. As we discussed in Chapter 2, how deeply you can go into quiet is ultimately a personal, spiritual issue. You cannot live your life in a manner antithetical to spiritual well-being and expect to truly enter quiet during an hour or so of *wuji* practice each day. This is why my teacher said that a Taiji practitioner must start with *"xiu lian"* (修炼), a Chinese term that embodies morality and purity of thought and behavior. This same point is echoed in the well-known saying: *"taiji tai he"* (太极太和), which means that peacefulness is a requisite of Taiji. Remember Grandmaster Feng's words: "Taiji is the *gongfu* of *xujing* (emptiness and tranquility)...this is the most important principle of all."

Wuji Zhuang (Standing Pole)

Wuji zhuang (无极桩), or standing meditation, is translated as "standing pole" exercise and is the basis for Taiji movement. In fact, the Taiji form movement is often referred to as "moving pole" (*huo zhuang*, 活桩), highlighting that Taiji movement evolves from practicing standing *wuji zhuang*.[1] Both the classical literature of Taijiquan and the oral tradition of the internal martial arts repeatedly emphasize that *wuji zhuang* precedes Taiji movement. Chapter 7, "Training Methods for Sparring," of *The Yang Family Forty Chapters*, begins with this point:

> In central equilibrium (what is commonly called "standing pole"), the feet develop root, and then you may study the four sides and advance and retreat.[2]

Well-known sayings within the internal martial arts community further assert:

练拳不站桩, 吃饭没粮仓。

Lian quan bu zan zhuang, chi fan mei liang cang.

Practicing form (external movement) without practicing standing pole
is like eating food with no grain in the storage bin.

百动不如一静, 百练不如一站。

Bai dong bu ru yi jing, bai lian bu ru yi zan.

One hundred movements are not as good as one stillness;
One hundred practices are not as good as one standing (pole).

The following discussion of *wuji zhuang* addresses various aspects of standing meditation in the order in which a practitioner would generally encounter them. First, one must be aware of correct posture. Once postural principles are understood, the practitioner can focus on learning to relax and to experience and internalize "central equilibrium." A section of practical "do's and don'ts" includes answers to common questions, followed by a description of common sensations and experiences. Lastly, we look at the deeper goal of "nurturing *qi*."

Posture

Many different stances are used for standing meditation practice, and yet all are fine so long as the fundamental tenets of *qigong* posture are maintained. Many available sources discuss posture, and your teacher can best correct your individual posture, so I will not dwell on this topic other than to provide a summary of postural principles and some of the rationales behind them. For more information on this topic, see in particular the book by my Taiji brother, Wang Fengming, entitled *Special Daoist Taiji Stick and Ruler Qigong*,[3] from which the following is taken.

✦ **Head.** The head should be held straight, not tilting forward or back or from side to side. The chin should be tucked under while simultaneously slightly "lifting" the *baihui*[4] point at the crown of the head, thus straightening the head and upper spine. To maintain this posture, it is helpful to imagine that you are holding a light object (for example, a piece of paper) on top of your head, or that you are suspended from an imaginary string attached to the *baihui* point. Still another visualization technique to assist with this posture is to imagine that you grow an inch while standing.

The upper *dantian* (called the "house of primary vitality") is located in the center of the head between and behind the eyes. Traditional Chinese medical theory explains that keeping the head straight helps induce blood to ascend to the head to nourish the brain, and allows *qi* to ascend to the upper *dantian* to nourish vitality. The correct posture of the head also plays a significant role in regulating body structure and balance.

✦ **Face, mouth, and eyes.** The muscles of the face should be relaxed, and the mouth should neither frown nor grimace. The Mona Lisa's smile is an image of a relaxed face. Traditional Chinese medical theory believes that the internal organs are connected to the face via meridians and collaterals, so to make the *qi* and blood flow smoothly, the face must be relaxed and natural.

The mouth should be closed lightly and the tongue should be raised with the tip touching the upper hard palate. Traditional Chinese medical theory asserts that touching the upper hard palate with the tongue connects the *ren* and *du* meridians of the "small heavenly circulation." Touching the tip of the tongue to the upper hard palate of the mouth also serves to promote generation of saliva, which is beneficial to digestion.

The eyes should be relaxed, and may either be closed or open. Since vision is one of the three components of balance,[5] some may initially find it difficult to close the eyes and maintain balance while standing quietly. Whether the eyes are closed or open, the key point is that the practitioner should relax, focus inward, and not allow the mind to be distracted by thoughts or external events.

+ **Neck.** The neck should be held straight and relaxed so as not to adversely affect the passageway of nerves, blood vessels, meridians, and collaterals connecting the head and trunk.

+ **Shoulders.** The shoulders should be directly above the waist to maintain a straight and balanced posture. Dropping and relaxing the shoulders is very important in relaxing the whole body, sinking *qi* to the lower *dantian* (the center of the body behind the navel), and realizing the natural posture of hollowing the chest and rounding the shoulder blades. Relaxing the shoulders is also helpful for the smooth flow of *qi* and blood to the hands.

+ **Chest and upper back.** With the shoulders dropped, the chest is naturally and slightly concaved (i.e., "hollowed") and comfortable. The thoracic cavity will then allow the smooth and unrestricted descent of the diaphragm, thus affording deep and relaxed respiration. The hollowing of the chest will also help the body weight to descend, and will reduce the pressure on the heart and lungs and favor their function.

With all of the above postures at work, the upper back and shoulder blades will be slightly rounded and the upper vertebra will have a slight erect or raised feeling. This is the upper portion of the "spinal bow." (See Chapter 5 for a discussion of the "five bows.") Traditional Chinese medical theory believes that hollowing the chest and erecting the back will help raise the *qi* upward through the *du* meridian. Also, acupuncture points on the back are general convergence points for the *qi* and blood, which allow communication between the meridian *qi* of the internal organs; therefore, exercise of the back helps regulate *qi* and blood.

+ **Elbows and knees.** The elbows and knees should be slightly bent and should neither be locked in position nor bent too much. If the arms are held extended and relaxed, the elbows will naturally drop toward the center of the body. Knees should always be aligned naturally with the direction of the feet, and as a general rule to maintain balance and mobility, the knee should never protrude beyond the foot.

+ **Pelvis and lower spine.** The tailbone should be tucked under slightly to further straighten the spine. In so doing, the buttocks will be slightly drawn in and will not protrude, and thus will allow the hips and waist to further relax and will assist with lowering the body weight and sinking the *qi* to the dantian. In combination with the inhaling phase of reverse breathing (discussed in Chapter 5), this is the lower portion of the "spinal bow."

This adjustment is perhaps the most difficult to describe in words—it is a subtle and relaxed adjustment called "sinking the *kua*," where *kua* (胯) basically refers to the hip joints. The motion for positioning the pelvis is similar, but not identical to, what is known in the West as a "posterior pelvic tilt." In a posterior pelvic tilt the lower spinal curve is flattened, but it is comparatively a more forceful motion that tenses the muscles, especially the gluteus maximus and hamstring hip extensors. Sinking the *kua*, however, results in a relaxed hip, waist, and legs, a gentle straightening of the lower spine, a lowering of the center of mass, and in combination with the other postural principles above, a gentle stretching of the torso.

✦ **Foot stance**. The actual posture being practiced will determine the width of the stance. Different schools have different standing meditation postures that they like to practice. For simply standing with the arms at the side, the stance should be natural with the feet at shoulder width or slightly greater apart. In other postures where the arms are held in front and/or the stance is staggered, the stance may be slightly wider and the knees slightly more bent.

Much of the available Taiji literature spends considerable time discussing posture—so much so that it is not uncommon for some to make the mistake of equating posture with technique. Posture alone is *not* technique—don't rely on it as a means of self-defense! The basic internal Taiji force, *peng jin* (掤劲), is not a simple postural trick that can be done by anyone who can adjust the body in a magical alignment to ward off an attack. *Peng jin* is pure *gong*, the foundation of which is built in *wuji* practice. It is not a technique or trick that is performed and then finished—it is always available to those who have practiced correctly.

Photos 1 and 2. Yang Yang in *wuji zhuang* meditation posture.

Photos 3 and 4. Alternate standing meditation posture called *"santi."*

Here's one angle from which to view the relation between posture and application. All of the martial applications of the art fundamentally rely upon and seek to defend mental and physical central equilibrium (*zhong ding*). For many reasons, improving your posture is integral in developing and practicing mental and physical equilibrium. But mental and physical equilibrium is not a technique that is turned on or off—it is part of the *gong* developed and internalized over the course of practice. Martial application, in turn, depends mostly upon the *gong*. Attention to posture is one facet of how to practice correctly and accumulate *gong*, but posture itself is not technique.

The First Task—Learning to Relax and to Experience and Maintain Central Equilibrium

The first step of standing *wuji* practice is to consciously relax the body, and employ only those muscles that are required to hold the position (more about this later). Relax the shoulders. People always hold some unnecessary tension in their body. Even now, as you are reading this book, can you relax your shoulders more? Check your structure, adjust your pelvis to keep the lower back straightened and hips slightly bent or "sunken," tuck in the chin and slightly raise the top and back of your head, relax the shoulders again, let go of any unnecessary tension—you get the point. While keeping the height of the head a constant and maintaining a straight spine, sink the weight. There will be a feeling of the spine and internal torso stretching slightly. Feel as though you are being suspended from above by a string attached to your head. Feel you are sinking the *qi* to the lower *dantian*, while at the same time, "raising the spirit" to the *baihui* point on the top of the head.

"Sinking the *qi* to the *dantian*" and "relaxing the body" are essentially synonymous. When you are nervous or tense your *qi* will rise. The next time you are angry, tense, or nervous, stop for a moment and become aware of your body. You will feel your breath floating up. When the *qi* floats up, it affects the physical body. The center of mass will seem to rise, which in the martial arts is referred to as "floating." High shoulders are another physical manifestation of the *qi* floating upward. With concentrated awareness in standing meditation practice, the sensation of sinking or rising *qi* will soon become obvious. When you can relax and sink the *qi*, this then is practice of "rooting the body," an essential skill for the self-defense strategies of Taijiquan.

Note that "relax" does not mean "collapse." You cannot collapse if you are maintaining the proper body structure (including holding the arms extended in different positions). To relax (in the physical sense) means to loosen all tension, and "turn off" all muscle groups that are not necessary for the task at hand. Ponder again the meaning of *wuji*. This is the physical and mental state you are practicing. In standing meditation, the body is neither yin (limp) nor yang (stiff), but in a balanced stillness from which movement is possible.

As you learn to relax, you can then proceed to look inward and improve body awareness and balance. From this awareness, you will naturally learn to identify and correct poor posture. Awareness of body structure and balance is a fundamental component of any martial art. It is also of immediate benefit to daily activities in terms of reducing the probability of accidents/injury.

And so beginning *wuji zhuang*, or standing meditation, is the practice of learning to relax, sinking the *qi* to the *dantian* and rooting the body, improving body awareness, and nurturing body structure. All of these components may be summarized by saying that *wuji zhuang* practice is "learning to experience and maintain central equilibrium."

Some Do's and Don'ts

To practice *wuji zhuang*, wear loose, comfortable clothing and practice in clean air—outside if possible. In China, people traditionally practice under a tree. One reason is that, in urban environments, the air is noticeably fresher under a mature tree. It is also traditionally held that you can gather energy from the natural environment—trees, oceans, mountains—all of nature is a source of *qi*. If you do practice seriously, you may generate heat while standing, and may sweat. Traditional Chinese medical theory believes that wind is a pathogen, and that one is more susceptible to wind entering the body after sweating. It is therefore important to avoid exposure to wind during and after practice. This recommendation is the subject of another famous saying:

练后满身汗, 避风如避箭。

Quan hou man shen han, bi feng ru bi jian.

After sweating, you should avoid wind as you avoid arrows.

There is considerable debate among the internal martial arts as to how long one should practice standing. Beginners can start with ten to fifteen minutes of practice every day. I was taught to stand for about 45 minutes or more. Of course, how long you stand is a function of your age, physical condition, and skill level. As with any exercise, you should listen to your body, and feel what is right for you. Nurturing is the key to efficient practice. It is better to practice ten minutes every day than to practice one hour once a week. It is better to practice one hour every day than to spend six hours practicing only on the weekend. When standing with the arms extended, as demonstrated in Photos 1–4, a frequent question is, "How long do I have to endure the pain?" In accordance with the moderation principle, you should neither stand struggling in pain nor quit at the first sign of discomfort. Learn to relax so that you don't rapidly accumulate intolerable levels of lactic acid, but if you are tired, lower your arms and relax. When you feel more comfortable, raise them again and continue practicing. Also, to relax during standing, do not attempt to stand too rigidly. Allow yourself to sway very gently in whatever pattern your body naturally adopts.

Traditionally, one school of thought held that meditation practice should be done in the evening and movement practice should be done in the morning. Most of us do not have such leisure time available. Practice when you have the time, but set a routine and practice at the same time every day. After a while, those who practice correctly and routinely will begin to feel the *qi* accumulating in the *dantian* before starting practice—the body will know it's practice time.

Although we should not be too lackadaisical and look for excuses not to practice, there are times when one should not practice *wuji* (or Taiji, for that matter, since all Taiji practice is *qigong* practice, and the following advice applies to any *qigong* exercise). If you are emotional, angry, or upset in any way, do not practice. Take a break and calm down. If you are physically—as opposed to mentally—tired, take a break and rest. A physically tired person will tend to enter a dull sleep-like trance, a state contrary to the quiet awareness of meditation. When tempted to push past physical tiredness, remember the moderation principle, and do not feel as though your practice is a job that you must do regardless of your condition. As a general rule, you should continue practicing if you are mentally tired, as correct practice will rejuvenate the practitioner. The Chinese say that the meditation will restore the *qi* and *shen* (spirit) that have been depleted in a mentally tired person.

Also, you should never practice with a cold or flu. (This is even more serious with sitting *wuji* practice.) The Chinese say that the cold will be driven "deeper" into the body during meditation, and I can assure you from experience that this is so. The more advanced your practice, the worse off you will be if you practice meditation at the onset of or during a cold. Lastly, do not practice meditation immediately prior to or after sex.[6] There is no definitive limit here—the appropriate time interval between sexual activity and meditation practice is unique to the person and level of practice. The instincts of propagation and self-preservation are perhaps the greatest of all animal instincts, and by no means do I recommend that sexual desire be totally suppressed. When in doubt about the appropriate quantity of anything, it's always safe to go back and again consider the moderation principle. Practice unswervingly and let everything happen naturally. Over time, the importance of sexual moderation will be obvious to anyone who perseveres in practice.

During a practice session, it is okay to do only standing meditation. Another good routine is to alternate standing and form (or simple, repetitive *qigong* drills). Stand for a while, then do form, stand some more, do another form. That is an excellent way to nurture and develop your *qi.*

Common Sensations

There are many sensations that may arise in *wuji* practice. Do not look for these as "signs," or think you are not making progress if you do not feel a sensation as reported by a fellow student. You are different from everyone else, and such thoughts amount to nothing more than a distraction from going into quiet. I would recommend talking about sensations in meditation only with your teacher. Most often, the correct advice will be to forget about it and go deeper into quiet. *Wuji* practice works for everyone to the extent and degree that the practitioner can enter quiet. Everyone has the same problem of overcoming a noisy mind and entering quiet. The greatest master in the world once had the same difficulties you have when practicing meditation. The single difference is that, regardless of the obstacles, the master persevered in practice.

That said, there are some sensations that are fairly common. The sensations may occur anytime—before, during, or after practice. For example, in the beginning stages of learning to relax, the legs may start to tremble. Numbness, tingling, and warmth are common. It is also common for the practitioner to pass gas. The digestive system is regulated by *qi*, and growing *qi* will make the digestive system work more vigorously. Regularity is a side benefit of *wuji* practice reported by many, as is deeper and better quality sleep. Many other sensations described below are related to the accumulation of *qi*, which is the primary objective of standing meditation practice once one has learned to relax and become aware of the body.

Nurturing Qi

Once the practitioner can relax, sink, and hold central equilibrium without constantly thinking about posture, the goal is to go into quiet and nurture *qi*. There is no one "right" way to enter quiet. What works for you is the right way. Some can stand and repeat a simple one-word mantra, for example, "quiet…quiet…quiet." Others may focus on body sensations, either internal or external. Still others use an image to relax and feel comfortable, such as imagining that the feet are standing on cotton, or that the body is immersed in water up to the neck. Countless other techniques for quieting the mind have been used successfully. As you are standing, you will find that your mind will jump back to daily affairs, but that is to be expected. This is the time you are practicing going into quiet. Just let disturbing thoughts go, using whatever technique you prefer, and go back to practicing going into quiet. "Let it go" is a good reminder. The most important principle of practicing quiet is to *be completely natural*. Don't try to force anything. We'll talk more about this below in the discussion of sitting meditation.

At the stage that you enter quiet, the feeling of *qi* will start to be readily apparent. You can sense the *da zi ran qi* (大自然气), or "environmental *qi*," and can feel it mix with your body as you breathe in and out. You can feel the *qi* accumulating and expanding in your body. At this point, just focus on going deeper into quiet awareness. You are now "building" your *qi*. Eventually, the feeling of growing *qi* will be obvious. You will get an expanded "full" feeling, first in the *dantian* and later throughout the rest of the body. It may feel as though the body is being "pumped up," just as a ball is filled with air. Now you are nurturing the fundamental internal force that is *peng jin*.[7] At some point, it is common to feel as though your energy is bursting. During the day, you may feel like hitting something just to express your energy, or feel as though someone could hit you and it wouldn't matter in the least. You may feel as though you could walk through a wall. You may feel a sense of physical lightness, and you may walk around thinking, "Wow—this feels really good!" At any time, you may experience a "fluttering" vibration in the *dantian*.[8] Your confidence will improve, and you will be calmer and less afraid or intimidated by any situation.

Don't get overconfident, however, as this is yet a beginning stage of development. Although some sensations may be quite alluring, for the most part, forget about them. Never develop an attachment to a particular sensation. Focusing on these feelings will only stall your progress. Just keep practicing entering quiet, and let everything happen naturally. Your *qi* and internal force, or *peng jin*, will continue growing in proportion to the time you spend in quiet standing meditation. By dedicated and correct practice, you can nurture and increase your *qi* and thereby truly experience how "extreme hardness is accumulated through softness."

Sitting *Wuji* Meditation (*Da Zuo*)

Although much of the advice given above for standing practice applies to sitting meditation as well, in sitting meditation we go even deeper into quiet, and for this reason it is a very serious exercise that must be done correctly. Unresolved mental or emotional issues should be addressed before practicing sitting meditation.

Sitting meditation can be done on a chair or cross-legged on the floor. The spine and head should be held straight and erect, and the body should be "relaxed" but not collapsed. If using a chair, sit as far toward the front end of the seat as possible. If you prefer to sit on the floor, I recommend that you sit on a cushion. This will help to keep your back straight and relaxed and therefore help the energy to flow smoothly. If you do need additional back support, it is okay to begin with the back lightly supported (for example, against a chair backing). Gradually, as you get stronger, you will want to withdraw this support.

For sitting cross-legged on the floor, some schools hold that the "lotus position" is the easiest for keeping the back straight. This requires great flexibility in the knees. Some will be able to train their body to sit in the lotus position, and others may seriously hurt their knees if they try. Sit in the position that is comfortable for you.

From the start of sitting, the task is to look inward and enter quiet contemplation. Except for a few rare souls, we all need a technique to calm our "monkey minds" and slowly experience true quiet. Again, countless techniques have been successfully used. As mentioned above in the discussion on standing meditation, mantras are a well-known way of quieting the mind. One may

Photos 5 and 6. Sitting meditation in a chair.

simply repeat, "quiet…quiet…quiet." Some prefer an overtly spiritual theme, such as repeating a line from a prayer. Another category of meditative tools is the use of breathing techniques. Recognizing the direct relation between the breath and a calm mind, some consciously count the breaths in an ever slower, steadier, breathing pattern. Another tool from the Zen Buddhist tradition is to allow the mind to focus on and experience only the present. This is a deceptively direct way of arresting the ego, which, with its insatiable appetite, constantly pulls the mind to either revisit past experiences or ponder future desires or worries. Focusing awareness on bodily sensations is yet another widely used category of meditation techniques. In becoming aware of bodily sensations, one can start with the more obvious feelings on the body's extremities and proceed to more subtle "inward" sensations that can only be felt with an increasingly quiet mind. The Daoist meditation techniques of focusing on *dantian* and circulating *qi* are an example of this category of technique.

Ultimately, the techniques that you use for beginning sitting meditation practice are entirely a personal choice. The methods and thoughts that I used to learn to experience quiet contemplation may not work as well for you as

Photos 7 and 8. Sitting meditation on the "floor."

other methods, and for this reason I only lightly touched upon some of the possible techniques. The key point is that the goal of sitting meditation is to enter deeply into quiet contemplation, where *feeling* and *awareness of being* replace the incessant thought stream produced by the ego, and that the myriad techniques available are simply tools for doing this. A Jesuit priest, Anthony de Mello (1931–1987), wrote an excellent book on meditation entitled, *Sadhana: A Way to God*, in which he repeats a story confided by a fellow monk. After a lifetime of practice, the monk admitted that it didn't seem to matter at all whether he repeated a religious mantra or sat quietly counting to himself "1 … 2 … 3 …"—both techniques led to the exact same state of quiet contemplation. The reality of quietness is the same, regardless of the path one uses to get there.

Three Common Errors

There are three common errors or misunderstandings of sitting *wuji* practice. The first we have already intimated, and that is mistaking the path for the goal. This is akin to the old parable of the teacher pointing to the moon but the student seeing only the finger. There are as many examples of this error as there are different techniques, but (since this is a book about Taiji) we shall limit our example to the popular meditation technique of "circulating *qi*." Some beginning Daoist meditation exercises focus first on sensing the *qi* and then "moving" the *qi* in various orbits within the body. This "works" for any beginning practitioner simply because in order to feel a sensation at any point within the body, we need to relax and single-mindedly focus our attention on that point (i.e., quiet the "monkey mind"). The nervous system, which relays sensory signals to the brain, pervades all of the body from the skin surface to the internal organs. From the macro scale of blood pulsing in arteries and veins to the micro cellular level, the body is in constant activity. It is astounding how much of that activity one can feel with an aware, focused, undistracted, and quiet mind. From the Eastern perspective, we can say that *qi* is everywhere and flowing everywhere, so it's kind of hard to miss. (According to traditional Chinese medical theory, if the *qi* isn't flowing in the body, you have a serious problem.)

Focusing on bodily sensations can be a very effective way to lead the practitioner to gradually experience quiet contemplation, but depending upon the way in which a student is taught, it is an easy mistake for the beginner to believe that "circulating *qi*" is the purpose of sitting meditation. At the extreme of this error, the practitioner is convinced that he or she must pass through higher and higher levels of "*qi* circulation." In search of this goal, he or she then makes the serious error of falling into the habit of using mental force to "move the *qi*" in the desired path. At this point, the practitioner's mental attitude is absolutely contrary to that required for entering the quiet of *wuji*. The "noise" of such a desire is no less distracting than any other mental noise. Depending upon the force used and overall aggressiveness or stubbornness of the person, such an attitude in sitting meditation practice can be quite dangerous. The *Dao De Jing* clearly advises against using mental force to control *qi*:

> For the mind to dictate to one's *qi* is called *violent* [emphasis added].[9]

The way to avoid this error is to *always let everything happen naturally*—do not use your will to try to force any particular result that you think should be occurring. *Wuji* is nothing. Sit still and *do nothing* to realize *wuji*. With unattached awareness, decrease and decrease again—that is the correct attitude for entering the true quiet of sitting *wuji* meditation. With practice, you will come to understand the meaning of the oft-quoted passage from the *Dao De Jing*, "The way to do is to be."[10]

A second very common error for beginners is to let the imagination run wild. Whether due to recalling stories about what could or should "be happening," or simply because of a creative imagination, some can spend their time in sitting meditation daydreaming or following a fantasy. To prevent this, some teachers recommend that the eyes be kept slightly open during sitting meditation practice. Again, what works for the practitioner is the correct way. Some students may have to keep the eyes open to remain grounded, while others are a bit less prone to fantasizing and find that closed eyes better facilitate the quieting of the mind.

A third common error is for the practitioner to develop an attraction to the sensations or experiences encountered during meditation. Generally, this caution is more applicable to those who have advanced in their practice. Whether physical or spiritual, the sensations, manifestations, or feelings experienced can be gratifying, even joyous. But an attachment to these experiences is no less disturbing to the mind than ordinary physical desires. Some masters caution that spiritual greed or attachment is an even greater pitfall than "ordinary" covetousness. Again, the way to avoid this error is to sit quietly and *do nothing*. Experience *wuji* for what it is and not for what you think or want it to be.

More Do's and Don'ts

All of the do's and don'ts mentioned above for standing meditation apply even more to sitting. Sitting meditation is a powerful exercise, physically and mentally, and should be approached with sincerity. I will repeat that personal mental or emotional issues should be resolved before practicing, or at the very least, those with such issues should practice under the close guidance of an instructor.

If you do enter into quiet, it is important that you are not suddenly disturbed. Let your family know that this is your practice time and that you should not be interrupted. It is not necessary to practice in a soundproof room, as background sounds can easily be ignored. But in deep meditation, slight sounds can be "felt" strongly, and unexpected, sharp sounds (such as a knock at the door or telephone ringing) can startle you significantly. In my experience, a sharp, unexpected sound can almost feel like a shot going through my body. If you are startled during practice, stop and take a break until you have calmed down. You will know how long you should rest—maybe only for a few minutes or maybe for a day or more.

As with standing meditation, beginners can start with ten to fifteen minutes of practice. The time you sit will increase naturally, in direct proportion to the depth of quiet realized. As you first enter quiet, you may not be aware of the time passing—one hour can seem like ten minutes. Also, as mentioned above, the benefits derived from standing and sitting meditations are somewhat different. My advice is to separate the times that you practice sitting and standing (i.e., alternate the practice each day, or do one in the morning and the other in the evening—whatever fits your personal schedule). In so doing, you will get a better feeling of the *gong* derived from these exercises and therefore better understand *why* you are doing them. If you understand why you are doing the exercise, you will be better able to efficiently adjust your practice as needed in the future. (But it's not going to hurt a thing to sit immediately before or after standing.)

At some point, the practitioner must cast aside the method that is used to enter quiet and just simply sit in *wuji*. Only you will know when you have reached this stage. If the technique is discarded too early, you likely will not be led to experience deep quiet. If the technique is held too long (or too dearly), then again this is the common error of mistaking the technique for the goal.

The feelings, sensations, and experiences of deep quietude are unlike anything experienced during everyday life. For this reason it is extremely difficult, if not impossible, to describe them in words. There are stages of development, but every description that I have read or been taught of these stages is different—most likely because of the difficulty in expressing the feeling and simply because everybody is different and will progress at differing rates. Worrying about what stage of development you are at is just another distraction, so I am purposely omitting trying to name and describe levels of quietude. Without exception, if you are progressing in sitting *wuji* you will feel an increasing sense of lightness, peace, calmness, and tranquility.[11]

Each episode of sitting meditation will likely be different. In whatever sitting position, eventually you will be uncomfortably numb or sore somewhere. Some schools believe that enduring such pain is good practice for quieting the mind. I believe that the principle of moderation applies here as well. One should not quit at the first sign of discomfort, nor is it necessary to endure significant pain for long periods of time. If you are numb or sore after a while, stretch out, and then go back even deeper into quiet.

The *Gong* of Sitting

Sitting *wuji* is also the practice of nurturing and accumulating *qi*. As with standing, when you begin to truly enter quiet, the feeling of nurturing *qi* will be quite obvious. If you practice earnestly and allow, rather than force, yourself to enter quiet, you will ultimately understand the meaning. Of course, sitting *wuji* is also one facet of the spiritual aspect of the art of Taijiquan, as discussed in Chapter 2.

Equally important for the development of Taiji skill, sitting meditation is considered an essential practice for realizing the *gong* of *ling* (灵). Authors usually translate *ling* as "agility," but it means much more than that. *Ling* is light, nimble, flexible, and effortless. It is also instantaneous, with no delay between thought and action. *Ling* refers to the mental as well as the physical; it is the agile movement of a coordinated mind and body. From a purely mental aspect, *ling* is a calm and penetrating awareness, the ability to anticipate or foresee an opponent's movement. With *ling*, one can move with lightning quickness before the opponent moves. Just as standing meditation is imperative for developing a foundation of internal power and therefore was often guarded as a secret, the importance of sitting *wuji* practice for the development of *ling* was long withheld from public teaching.

Just how does sitting *wuji* practice contribute to the accomplishment of *ling*, you may reasonably ask? That's a valid and interesting question and one that I believe can be answered partly by scientific research. My teacher, Master Feng Zhiqiang, provided an interesting clue—he has taught that sitting *wuji* practice is specific exercise of the nervous system. I would further this with the hypothesis that *all* Taijiquan practices may be specific exercises of different aspects of the nervous system.

The Nervous System and *Wuji*/Taijiquan Practice

Taijiquan is the art of efficient movement and power. From a Western scientific perspective, all voluntary movement is governed by the nervous system. It therefore stands to reason that many of the mechanisms of Taijiquan may be explained, at least in part, by future research focusing on the nervous system. Such research will surely improve our understanding of the art. At the same time, the unique training systems of internal *gongfu* may likewise extend Western scientific knowledge of the human body and its capabilities.

Throughout the remaining chapters, I suggest ways in which Western perspectives on the nervous system may be integrated with the concepts and processes of Taijiquan to better understand both the complexity of the art of Taijiquan and its recognized medical benefits. As discussed below, established principles of neural science may help to explain mechanisms of *wuji* meditation practice. Subsequent chapters offer hypotheses of how neural science may help to explain mechanisms of form and push-hands training, as well. Finally, Chapter 7 summarizes this integrated approach with a model of links between Taiji practice and the functioning of the nervous system.

Before we jump into a discussion of the relationship between nervous system function and *wuji* practice, however, a brief synopsis of the nervous system and its parts may be helpful. Understanding these functions of human anatomy should enable us to better understand how and why Taiji works. The nervous system is composed of two anatomically distinct, but functionally intertwined networks: the *central nervous system* and the *peripheral nervous system*.

The Central Nervous System

Comprised of the brain and spinal cord, the central nervous system is the commander of all behavior, including voluntary movement. In contrast to reflexive movement, which can happen without direction from the brain, all voluntary movement begins with electrochemical signals from the brain that travel through the spinal cord and out to the target muscles required to generate the movement.

The central nervous system is organized in a hierarchy, with different regions located at different levels. At the top of the hierarchy is the *cerebral cortex*, which is responsible for higher-level cognition, including motor planning, attentional control, conscious awareness, intention, and emotional and social judgment and understanding. Tucked underneath the cerebral cortex are a variety of subcortical areas such as the medulla, pons, midbrain, cerebellum, and diencephalon. Information processed in these regions does not necessarily reach conscious awareness. Electrochemical signals travel along nerve pathways between the cerebral cortex and these lower levels of the hierarchy, all the way to the spinal cord, where the peripheral nervous system will carry them to the parts of the body involved in movement. The nerve pathways stop at different "relay stations" in the brain where clusters of cell bodies bring together different types of information to influence the messages that go out. Some of these relay stations include the medulla, the pons, and the cerebellum, all of which are engaged in sensory and motor processing. The thalamus and hypothalamus, centrally located in the diencephalon, are also critical relay stations where information about movement is integrated and transferred.[12] In Chapter 5, we will discuss in greater detail how these different regions of the brain contribute to motor programming and how communication between the cerebral cortex, the cerebellum, and a part of the midbrain known as the basal ganglia is essential for smooth, coordinated, and efficient movement, like that practiced in Taiji forms.

The Peripheral Nervous System

The peripheral nervous system, which carries electrochemical messages to and from the central nervous system, is subdivided into the somatic sensory system and the autonomic system.

✦ **Somatic sensory system.** The somatic sensory system is composed of cranial nerves in the brainstem and diencephalon that relay sensory input to the brain, and spinal nerves that govern voluntary muscle contraction. Messages from the somatic sensory system tell the brain about the body and its environment, and messages from the brain travel via the somatic sensory system to calibrate the movement of the body to respond appropriately to that environment.

All human motion is accomplished by nerve signals causing musculoskeletal contraction that moves the body joints. For example, bending the elbow is accomplished by nerve signals that "tell" the biceps to contract. However, every joint is connected to opposing muscle groups (e.g., flexers/extensors or adductors/abductors). To move a limb, not only should one muscle group be told to contract, the opposing muscle group must be allowed to relax.[13] In the example of bending the elbow, the biceps (flexor muscles in this case) must contract, but if the triceps (the extensor muscles in this case) were also contracted, the elbow would not bend. Nerve impulses are responsible for both contracting the necessary muscle group and relaxing the opposing muscle group to allow the desired motion to occur.

Each nerve is connected to a specific number of muscle fibers, which are referred to as a "motor unit." When an impulse is sent via a nerve, all connected muscles in that motor unit contract (or relax). Depending on the motor unit's function, the number of muscle fibers per nerve varies greatly. Finely controllable movement (such as eye movement) results from single nerves controlling a small number of muscles, whereas motor units used for larger movement (such as in the back) have a larger number of muscles per nerve. The number of motor units activated at any given time determines the strength of the muscle contraction. In other words, the more motor units activated, the more muscle fibers that will be involved in the contraction, and therefore the stronger the force will be. The role of the somatic sensory system in Taiji movement may already be implied here, but it will be especially relevant in later discussions of standing meditation, as well as Taiji movement and push-hands.

✦ **Autonomic system.** Unlike the somatic sensory system, which governs voluntary movement, the autonomic system controls the involuntary muscle movements of the internal organs and glandular secretions. This system is further subdivided into sympathetic, parasympathetic, and enteric divisions. The enteric division is largely an independent, intermittent system that controls only digestive reflexes. However, the parasympathetic and sympathetic divisions, regulated by the hypothalamus in the brain, maintain constant signals to target areas and operate in conjunction with each other. As will be obvious from the description below, the parasympathetic and sympathetic divisions correspond respectively to "yin and yang" characterizations of the autonomic nervous system.

The sympathetic system, the yang aspect of the autonomic nervous system, increases awareness and prepares the body to respond to challenging or dangerous situations. The extreme of sympathetic activity is the stressed "fight or flight" response. The parasympathetic system is the complementary opposite, or yin aspect, which restores the body to a resting state. For example, the sympathetic system can increase the rate and strength of the heart's contractions and can raise blood pressure by constricting small arterioles; the parasympathetic system, on the other hand, slows the heart, decreases blood pressure, and expands the capillaries. Sympathetic nerves dilate the pupil of the eye to receive more sensory input; parasympathetic nerves constrict the pupil to reduce sensory input. Sympathetic activity generally decreases glandular secretions, whereas parasympathetic activity generally increases glandular secretions. After explaining research findings on the effect of meditation on autonomic nervous system function, we will then consider why the regulation of the sympathetic and parasympathetic systems, realized by meditation practice, is essential for Taiji movement.

Research Findings and Areas for Research on *Wuji* Practice and the Nervous System

Having quickly reviewed the terms and functions of the nervous system, we can now return to the question of how this is relevant to *wuji* and Taiji practice by looking again at sitting and standing meditation, but in a new light.

Sitting meditation. Recent scientific studies have documented the physiological changes induced by meditation.[14] By measuring specific physiological responses, such as cardiovascular and pulmonary functions, hormonal and neurotransmitter levels, brain wave activity, cerebral blood flow, and skin moisture content, studies have repeatedly characterized the physical state induced by meditation as a reduction of sympathetic activity and increase in parasympathetic activity.

Even without these scientific measurements, the experience of the shift from sympathetic to parasympathetic dominance is easily identifiable by the typical sensations felt in standing and sitting meditation. For example, the parasympathetic cycle is associated with increased glandular secretion, including copious, watery saliva production and increased gastro-intestinal activity. These characteristics are classic symptoms of beginning meditation. As described earlier in this chapter, *wuji* practitioners commonly experience increased saliva production and gastro-intestinal activity (manifested by belching or passing gas). Expanded capillaries and increased blood flow near the skin's surface during the parasympathetic cycle also may explain the sensations of warmth and tingling on the skin's surface reported by many practitioners.

As pointed out by Young and Taylor (1998), the physiologic pattern of the initial stages of meditation is consistent with parasympathetic activity— a drop in sympathetic nerve hormone and neurotransmitter levels, decrease in skin moisture, increased cerebral blood flow, respiration decrease without significant changes in arterial oxygen and carbon dioxide concentrations, and a marked decline in blood lactate. This pattern is so consistent that it is now commonly known in the scientific community as the "relaxation response."[15]

Young and Taylor, however, additionally point out that in advanced meditators there is also evidence of enhanced control over sympathetic activity. For example, they note that in advanced meditators increased adrenaline (indicative of sympathetic nerve stimulation) has paradoxically been observed in the presence of a decreased heart rate (indicative of parasympathetic dominance overriding the ability of adrenaline to increase heart rate). The authors note that this "reflects a coupled modification of both sympathetic and parasympathetic activity rather than simply reduction or increase of sympathetic activity alone."[16] These authors conclude that, while parasympathetic dominance characterizes the initial stages of meditation, it is also a doorway to enhanced control over all autonomic activity.

The word "control" is the key point in this last argument. The extreme, involuntary sympathetic activity of "fight or flight" is the ordinary response to danger. This, however, is a tense and nervous state in which rational thought is bypassed and fear dominates (hence the term "scared stiff"). Through sitting meditation, the Taiji practitioner gains greater control even over the body's autonomic system and therefore greater control over how the body responds to imminent danger. It is evident that sitting meditation calms the body, improves control of involuntary reactions, and restores the yin/yang balance of the autonomic nervous system. Through greater control of both parasympathetic and sympathetic functions, sitting meditation practice enhances the ability of the practitioner to remain calm and relaxed, yet maintain ultimate vigilance and alertness when faced with imminent danger. The ability to remain calm and relaxed, yet alert, is also an obvious requisite for the light, instantaneous, and agile movement of Taiji characterized as "ling."

Another possible explanation for how sitting meditation improves agility and motor skills is suggested by studies on the neurotransmitters of meditators. Neurotransmitters are chemicals that communicate electrochemical signals between nerves. Some neurotransmitters are essential for motor functions. For example, the neurotransmitter dopamine, long believed to cause a pleasurable "reward" experience in the brain, is now known to also be important in motor function. (A loss of dopamine neurons is the cause of Parkinson's disease, a debilitative condition characterized by tremors, rigid movements, and difficulty initiating movements. The famous boxer, Muhammad Ali, was diagnosed with Parkinson's.) Interestingly, recent research has found significantly increased dopamine production in the striatum (a subcortical region of the brain) in meditators.[17] Perhaps sitting still in deep quietude restores the neurotransmitters necessary for smooth and coordinated movement.

Another traditionally ascribed benefit of sitting meditation is the improved quality of sleep enjoyed by Taiji practitioners. Good quality sleep is absolutely necessary for both health and martial skill—if you don't accept that, just pay attention to how poorly you function, both mentally and physically, after a night of poor sleep. One possible physiological explanation for how meditation helps sleep was reported by Tooley, et al. (2000). These researchers found "significantly higher plasma melatonin levels in the period immediately following meditation compared with the same period at the same time on a control night."[18] Melatonin, secreted by the pineal gland in the brain, is a hormone that promotes sleep.

At present, Western medical research is increasingly focusing on the physiological and neural effects of meditation. Using a variety of sophisticated instruments, researchers are now capable of capturing precise images of the brain and can therefore identify changes in brain activity during meditation practice. Whereas in the past, scientists largely believed that neural connections were genetically fixed and developed only during the first few critical years of life, today it is recognized that the brain has neuroplasticity, or is capable of forming new neural connections throughout life. The relaxed but focused attention characteristic of sitting meditation provides researchers with an excellent means to monitor consciously invoked changes in neural activity.

Standing meditation. I previously mentioned that one of the goals of standing *wuji* practice is to learn to relax and use only those muscles necessary for the task at hand. We can now explore this in more depth using the insights of Western medical research. It is entirely false to believe that a Taiji practitioner strives to "avoid muscle force." Musculoskeletal action is necessary for any movement and for posture control. You couldn't even stand if you didn't use your leg muscles. A more accurate description is that the Taiji practitioner strives to improve the overall efficiency of muscle contraction. For example, in holding a standing posture, one practices relaxing all opposing, or antagonist muscle groups, which allows the effective, or agonist muscle groups to work much more easily and efficiently. It is not always an easy job to relax opposing muscle groups—as anyone who has tried standing meditation can attest! For example, in the posture commonly called "holding the urn," the arms are held rounded in front of the body at chest height. Only a limited number of muscles are required to hold the arms in this position. This is not, however, intuitive. Anyone just beginning practice will simultaneously contract opposing or other unnecessary muscle groups and therefore will expend excessive energy and quickly tire. The advice to drop the shoulders and slightly "round" the back across the shoulder blades helps the practitioner to consciously relax the opposing or unnecessary muscle groups. (However, if done excessively, this too will contract different, but just as unnecessary, muscle groups.)

In fact, it is common for the untrained and/or excited body to overreact to any situation or task and stimulate unnecessary (and frequently opposing) muscle groups. The extreme of this is the example of the person who, when confronted with some perturbation, tenses all muscles and becomes rigid. The technical term for this is called "global contraction"—in Taiji, we call it being stiff. From the musculoskeletal perspective, such a reaction:

+ Tenses opposing muscle groups, which significantly decreases the overall effectiveness of a potential counter response,

+ Consumes exponentially greater energy than is required for the situation, and

+ Debilitates the somatic sensory system's control of balance.

In Taiji, we just say that it makes them easy to push. To variable degrees, we are unnecessarily tensing our muscles and expending excessive energy all the time—even now, can you relax your shoulders again?

So one goal of standing meditation is to consciously train the body to perform a musculoskeletal task as efficiently as possible. In more technical terms, practitioners of standing meditation learn to adopt the ideal pattern of contraction and relaxation of agonist and antagonist muscle groups. Note that, even in standing meditation, this is a dynamic process. For example, the act of breathing alone will cause changes in one's center of mass, and these changes must be met with an accompanying change in the leg muscles employed to maintain balance and posture. Also, even very slight changes in arm position will necessitate a change in muscle groups necessary to hold the desired posture. The quiet, meditative state allows efficient processing of the continual flow of sensory information necessary for balance (visual, somatosensory, and vestibular) and use of this stream of sensory information to constantly adjust and efficiently employ effective muscle groups. Gradually one learns to complete the standing meditation task while maintaining an energy-conserving and ultimately an energy-accummulating state.

In progressing from static sitting and standing meditation to dynamic *qigong* breathing exercises and Taiji form, Taiji practitioners can learn relaxed movement. If you can't relax unnecessary muscle groups when standing still, how can you do it when moving? If you can't relax during movement, how will you relax when confronted with a perturbation (e.g., push-hands or an attack)?

Besides relaxing, another essential aspect of moving qigong (and some static exercises) is intention. Intention is imperative for the development of strength in relaxed movement. For pure strength training, some internal gongfu exercises are very simple repetitive motions but are done with a focused mind. For example, in some exercises the practitioner just stands with a relaxed body and imagines exerting a great force (for example, pulling a tree from the ground, or pushing a very heavy object). The question is, how does this improve strength? From the neurobiological perspective, we know that the number of motor units activated is a major determinant of the strength of the response of a muscle contraction. Does the conscious use of intention, coupled with a relaxed body, affect the ability to activate more somatic sensory motor units in target muscle groups?

A study at the University of Iowa conducted in 1992 documented the effectiveness of intention in increasing strength. During this study, finger strength of three groups was evaluated—one group exercised by performing a training program of a repetitive maximal isometric muscle contractions, one group only imagined that they were producing maximal isometric contractions without actual muscle activation, and the third group did not train at all. The average strength of both the first and second groups increased significantly more than that of the control group—the first group improved by 30%, while the second group (using intention only) increased by 22%. Of course, Taiji movement is infinitely more dynamic and complex than the limited action of isolated isometric contraction, but this early study does demonstrate the potential for strength increase through intention only.[19]

Exactly what muscle groups are beneficial to the task is another issue. It is possible that, through conscious relaxation and the use of intention instead of habitual "external" muscular force, the internal martial arts train us to use effective but largely ignored "internal" muscle groups. The core musculature of the trunk and pelvis, I believe, is especially strengthened in Taiji training. These core muscles—the transverse abdominus, internal and external obliques, quadratus lumborum, multifidus, and illiopsoas, to name just a few—are responsible for maintaining the stability of the spine and pelvis and are therefore critical for the maintenance of balance and posture. Maintaining correct posture in standing meditation may be a direct, and gentle, strengthening mechanism for these core muscles. The core muscles are also critical for the transfer of energy from large to small body parts.[20] Because the peripheral muscles of the shoulders, arms, and legs are anchored to the spine or pelvis, all power is either generated from or transferred through the core of the body. Greater strength of the core not only yields a greater power output, but also increases the neuromuscular efficiency of peripheral muscles—with a stronger core, less forceful contractions of the peripheral muscles are required to produce a given amount of power.[21] Through a combined emphasis on relaxation of peripheral muscles and intention of movement, Taiji form practice may be a mechanism to both "teach" the body to use, and significantly strengthen, the core musculature.[22]

Much of the above discussion of the relation of the nervous system to *wuji* practice is still conjecture, but it seems to be an area rich in research potential, given interested scientists and available grants. To conclude our brief discussion of the nervous system and internal *gongfu*, I will share a traditional saying that, to me, most directly suggests the relation of these two. The Chinese say that, in practicing Taiji, one is trying to, "Let your body listen to your mind." Is this not a description of the function and purpose of the nervous system?

Finishing Exercises

We should end our discourse on *wuji* practice with a discussion of the very important massaging finishing exercises with which practitioners should consciously and deliberately end each meditation session.

The purpose of finishing exercises is to slowly and gently "wake up" to the outside world and to massage and promote circulation throughout the entire body. Traditional Chinese medical theory believes that massaging helps prevent stagnant *qi*. There are many different methods or ways to perform finishing exercises. Different schools have and prefer different finishing exercises but in general all should massage the head, ears, arms, trunk, kidneys, and legs. Gently slapping, hitting, or rubbing acupressure points on the body are excellent ways to do the massage, and you can use this time to learn and experience where acupressure points are on the body.

For Taijiquan practice, another important finishing exercise is to "rotate the *dantian*." In this exercise, one places the hands over the *dantian* and "thinks, looks, and listens" inwardly while rotating the *qi* in the *dantian*. The hands and arms externally trace the internal *qi* movement. It is traditionally taught that men should begin at the bottom of the *dantian* and rotate upward to the left and downward to the right in a circular motion, with increasing circumference on each rotation. After 36 rotations, they should reverse direction and perform 24 rotations, each decreasing in circumference until finishing at the *dantian*. Traditionally for women, the practice is the same but begins in the opposite direction.

This exercise can greatly advance your Taijiquan level by helping to coordinate the whole body movement with the *dantian*. At first, while making the circles the external hand and arm movement will lead and the energy in the *dantian* will follow. Gradually, you will begin to feel that the energy in the *dantian* is leading and that the hands and arms are following. Eventually, *dantian* energy leading the external movement will become an obvious and distinct feeling and you will naturally carry over this accomplishment into moving exercises. The energy and state of relaxation, calm, and awareness accumulated in *wuji* practice greatly enhances your ability to reach the level where the inside leads the outside.

Taking Stock

Before proceeding with the discussion of Taiji form in the next chapter, let's take stock of how things are going for you. If this book's advice has worked, you have found a teacher and school that you are comfortable with. You have started your practice with the internal aspect of *xiu lian* (morality/character/spirituality) and have learned to quiet your mind. This attitude allowed you to begin the fundamental *gong* practices of standing and sitting meditation, and, reciprocally, the standing and sitting practices taught you how to further quiet your mind. To the extent that you could quiet the mind, you have learned how to relax and have begun to nurture your *qi*. Sometimes you felt encouraged and motivated, and sometimes you wondered, if only very secretly to yourself, whether you were just wasting your time. But if you persevered in daily practice, you eventually began to truly build and feel your energy and strength increasing. You may not know what internal power "is" intellectually, but that doesn't matter in the least, because you have started to feel it. You feel stronger and more vital. You have begun to feel, understand, and internalize mental and physical equilibrium. You may have noticed another interesting thing, and it is very comforting—you are not nearly as fearful as before. This has nothing to do with fighting. Rather, it is a feeling of calm confidence and peacefulness. You no longer fear the boss at work (or any authority figures), losing material possessions or position or status, or what other people "think" about you (at least not nearly as much as before). In short, you have truly begun to build a foundation of *gong*, and because of this, the potential for martial application of the art is already very obvious to you—and you haven't even done any form yet![23]

Dong
Movement

Chapter Five

Taiji form Movement

BEFORE WE DISCUSS THE CHARACTERISTICS AND PRINCIPLES of Taiji form movement, I would like to begin with the simple and perhaps most often asked question—why practice form?

Why Practice Form?

There are, of course, many potential benefits of form practice, and people practice for different, yet equally valid reasons; however, the principles of form movement originated to serve three fundamental purposes:

1. To nurture and build energy

2. To exercise and continually improve the mind/body connection

3. To teach the practitioner the mechanics of efficient body movement.

The first two of these purposes further develop what was begun in *wuji* sitting and standing meditation practices. In practicing slow movement, we build upon this foundation and emphasize motor and sensory system development and integration. The product of energy, mind/body connection, and mechanical aspects of form movement is, in a word—power.

As we are reminded in the classic poem *Treatise on Taijiquan*, Taiji was initially created as a martial art. Here the author compares Taiji to other martial arts, concluding that they are all different from the "science of power" that is Taijiquan:

> There are many other styles of martial arts. Although the forms are different, they are all the same in that, ultimately, they are nothing more than the strong beating the weak and the slow yielding to the fast ... All this is inherited natural ability. It is not related to the science of power.[1]

77

By design Taiji movement is powerful, and as this poem implies, this power has to be learned. Taiji form is the tool for learning the mechanics of efficient movement and power. Knowing that its original purpose was to achieve this powerful movement is necessary to truly understand the form.

There are two requisites for powerful movement. First, one must be able to generate the power. Technically, "strength" is a measure of force, and "power" is the force generated per unit time—the shorter the time in which you can express a force, the greater the power of that force. Taiji practice increases both strength and power by uniting the energy gathered from *wuji* and Taiji form practice with the learned mechanics of Taiji movement. Second, to accomplish powerful movement one must be able to efficiently express the power in the intended direction. By focusing the direction of the movement, the power of that movement is maximized. The ability to move with precision in an intended direction is a function of the efficiency of the mind/body connection combined with the learned mechanics and motor skills of Taiji movement. These conditions necessary for powerful movement are merged in a famous traditional saying:

周身一家, 力发一点, 点点透骨。

Zhou shen yi jia, li fa yi dian, dian dian tou gu.

The whole body is one family; the released energy focuses
on one point; [then] every touch can penetrate the bone.

The "whole body is one family" refers to the efficient, coordinated, synergistic movement learned from form practice. "The released energy should focus on one point" refers to the necessity of being able to focus and express the movement or force in a specific direction. The Taiji form ultimately teaches you to move (and therefore express a force) in any direction, with any part of the body. The duration, distance, and magnitude of potential forces are also variable. For example, a force can be longer in duration and distance, as in a push, or can be short and explosive over a short distance, as in the "inch force" commonly mentioned in martial arts. The *ba fa* (八法), or "eight forces" of Taijiquan (*peng, lu, ji, an, cai, lie, zhou, kao*, 掤, 捋, 挤, 按, 採, 挒, 肘, 靠) are simply descriptions of direction, duration, and distance of forces. The "five steps" (*wu xing*, 五行) refer to achieving dynamic motion in any direction, while maintaining balance, body structure, and footwork.

When a skilled practitioner reaches the level where his or her "body will listen to the mind," every part of the body becomes a potential mechanism for self-defense. When the whole body is one family and you can focus and express force in any direction, at any time, with any part of the body, then you can then react to the infinite situations presented in a combative situation with efficiency, power, and agility. This requires a high level of skill and involves mechanisms of movement that are foreign to the average person.

I realize that some of you may be confused, or perhaps even a bit disillusioned, at this point. Taiji, as you have been led to think by popular myth, is about the weak defeating the strong. Those of you who have studied the classics may remember the famous phrase in the *Taiji Treatise* immediately following the passages quoted above:

Four ounces are used to deflect a thousand pounds.

The question to ask here is, "four ounces of what?" The "thousand pounds" in the *Treatise* symbolizes natural strength, or "brute force." More generally, it symbolizes a high level of natural athletic ability, which in the preceding passage of the *Treatise* is recognized as the foundation upon which other martial arts ultimately rely. Of course, four ounces of natural strength and athletic ability cannot defeat a thousand pounds of the same. The "four ounces" symbolizes the power *that has to be learned and accumulated* from Taiji practice, something that is quite different from natural strength and ability.

In Chapter 4, I noted that it is incorrect to think that Taiji does not use "muscle force." All human movement, and even all postural control, relies upon muscular contraction. But the mechanisms of postural control and movement learned from Taiji ultimately allow for more efficient movement, and therefore more efficient exertion of force. That is why a lower "unit" of Taiji movement or force can defeat higher levels of "brute force." The "four ounces" and "one thousand pounds" do not refer to total force output, but rather to the expenditure of energy required to produce the force. Again, look to the standing meditation practices as a simple example. Strong, muscular persons, such as body builders, often cannot hold a static standing meditation posture as long as a trained, elderly, seemingly frail grandmother, because they have not learned the relaxed, synergistic, and optimally efficient pattern of agonist and antagonist muscle contraction necessary to hold the posture.

The learned, synergistic power of Taijiquan is often categorized as "internal," to distinguish it from the familiar "external" strength of locally contracted muscles that everyone knows and employs instinctively. In traditional terms, the physical aspect of internal Taiji power is described as a combined soft and hard power, where the softness is a soft, light, smooth, and elastic energy (but not weak, limp, or broken), and the hardness is a strong, powerful, solid energy (but not stiff, clumsy, or excessive). So do not make the mistake of interpreting "four ounces" to mean that little or no tangible force is used in Taijiquan. Just as water is soft but the power of a wave can be exceptionally strong, Taiji movement is relaxed but purposely and tangibly powerful. The masters that I have been fortunate to study with have been exceptionally powerful men.

It is also traditionally recognized that the relative degree to which one can improve internal power is much greater than the degree to which one can improve natural physical strength. The internal energy and power built from standing and sitting meditation and form practice will feel very strong indeed, and the difference between this internal strength and localized muscle strength is easily perceptible. Anyone who practices Taiji correctly, no matter the age, sex, or natural ability, will significantly improve power.

With a clearer understanding of why we practice Taiji form, we can now turn our attention to the characteristics and principles of correct practice. Through generations of experience, the principles of Taiji form practice evolved as rules by which the primary goals of nurturing energy, improving the mind/body connection, and learning the mechanics of powerful movement can most efficiently be realized. All other benefits of form practice are a by-product of practicing in accordance with these principles.

Universal Criteria for Taijiquan Movement

As we discussed in Chapter 2, yin and yang are united in stillness and separate in movement. When yin and yang separate in movement, Taiji is created. The art of Taiji movement seeks the balance of yin and yang, both for health and martial arts. When yin and yang are balanced, the body will be healthy and strong. When you understand yin and yang and incorporate them into form, you are beginning to truly learn the art of Taiji movement.

According to Chinese philosophy, yin and yang are equal and opposite manifestations of the same phenomena. They are mutually dependent; without one, the other wouldn't exist. Hence the simple observation in the *Dao De Jing*:

> Being and nonbeing give birth to each other
> Difficult and easy complete each other
> Long and short form each other
> High and low fulfill each other
> Tone and voice harmonize with each other
> Front and back follow each other—
> It is ever thus.[2]

The interplay of yin and yang is cyclic; they constantly transform into each other. The extreme of one is the birth of the other. To achieve one, start with the other:

> If you would have something shrink,
> you must first stretch it;
> If you would have a thing weakened,
> you must first strengthen it;
> If you would desert a thing,
> you must first be its ally.
> If you would take from a thing,
> you must first give to it.[3]

Taiji movement is characterized by its use of this interdependence of yin and yang. If you want to go right, first you have to move left. If you want to release, first you have to store. If you want extreme quickness, first you have to practice slowly. If the left is attacked, you yield on the left and counterattack on the right. If the opponent attacks with the upper body, his or her lower body is undefended. If you want extreme hardness, you start with extreme softness. The standing meditation practice gives us our first concrete example of this—the softness in *wuji zhuang* gives birth to a hardness that is superior to external or "ordinary" strength.

Besides utilizing the interplay of yin and yang, there are three other main characteristics of Taiji movement. First, as we have stated, Taiji movement is a *qigong* or energy gathering/nurturing/circulating exercise. Second, all Taiji movement is exercise of *xin yi* 心意 (mind/intention) and *qi*, rather than natural athletic ability and external strength. As the saying from the *Taiji Treatise* quoted at the beginning of this chapter indicates, Taiji movement must be learned—it is constant exercise of one's cognitive function as well as physical exercise. In Taiji form, *xin yi* is emphasized at an early stage of a practitioner's development, as we will discuss below. Third, Taiji movement is characterized by the spiraling silk-reeling energy (*chansi jin,* 缠丝劲). This silk-reeling is not the result of conscious effort, but rather is what happens naturally when movement is performed correctly in accordance with Taiji principles. We will talk more about silk-reeling later in this chapter as a relatively advanced stage of a practitioner's development and then again in the next chapter on push-hands.

Despite the plethora of moving *qigong*, Taijiquan forms, and individual silk-reeling exercises, these four characteristics remain true of all Taiji movement. True, different exercises have been developed to emphasize and therefore train specific aspects of the art, but all Taiji movements are based upon and seek the balance of yin and yang. All are *qigong*; all are exercise of *xin yi* and *qi*; all generate silk-reeling energy. They are all of one family and can produce the same results if practiced correctly. Although the remainder of this chapter primarily discusses the Taiji form, the principles for form practice discussed below apply to any Taiji movement exercise to some degree. We will start by addressing basic principles of posture and breathing. Next, we will look at the different stages of development in form practice in the order in which I would generally teach them. Lastly, we will discuss the practice of *fajin* (quick releasing energy).

Posture

The principles of posture and body alignment for Taiji form practice are fundamentally the same as for all *qigong* exercises. Thus the principles of posture mentioned in the previous chapter for standing meditation apply to form movement, as well. The following principles are additional considerations in practicing Taiji form movement:

1. Keep a relaxed, natural posture

2. Keep the "five bows"

3. Keep central equilibrium and straight and centered

4. Avoid an excessively low stance, and

5. Understand the importance and function of turning the waist.

Always Keep a Relaxed, Natural Posture

"Natural" is the key word here. It is not possible to relax if the body is held in an unnatural position. What is an unnatural position? Here we are primarily referring to the orientation or angle of the body joints relative to the direction of movement. For every Taiji form, there is a specific direction of movement (and therefore a specific direction of force exerted). If the body's joints are not naturally aligned with the intended direction of movement, two outcomes are certain: the force exerted will be weak (or even non-existent), and the unnatural alignment will eventually result in injury. This simple principle of posture is the subject of the following verses from Chen Changxing's *Important Words on Martial Applications*:

> Moving body first take clever (e.g., favorable) place (position), this is called important formula of tactics. Joints of bones should be adjusted (*dui*), otherwise there is no strength.[4]

To maintain natural alignment throughout the form, especially with regard to the orientation of the knee joints, it is necessary to constantly make slight adjustments in the stance. The knee joints should always be aligned with the direction of the feet. This may seem obvious, but in my classes I constantly observe people failing to adjust their stance and attempting to contort their bodies in all sorts of unnatural positions—effectively applying *qinna*, or joint locking/controlling techniques, on themselves. Apparently the simple rule of maintaining natural alignment is not always intuitive. When teaching form, I have learned to emphasize all necessary footwork, however minor. Eventually, as one learns to automatically adjust stance to maintain natural alignment, the adjustments occur smoothly with the form movements and are not perceptible as separate, distinct motions. Of course, the principle of natural alignment applies not just to the knees, but to all joints. All joints should be relaxed and should not be rotated beyond a position of comfort and strength.[5]

In practicing repetitive motions, we are trying to instill habit (and therefore also decrease reaction time). Through first standing meditation and then slow form practice, one should develop *awareness* of the body structure and balance and develop the habit of constantly making adjustments where appropriate. The jumping motions of the second routine (*er lu*) of the Chen style (also called *pao cui* or "cannon fist") provide additional training for postural adjustment. In practicing the jumping motions, one learns how to instinctively land in a position of natural alignment and strength during fast movement. No matter how high the skill level, at times one will land in an imperfect position and must intuitively and immediately adjust the stance to proceed with the next movement in the form. To graduate from form to self-defense application, one must have thoroughly instilled this habit of sensing the body's alignment and balance and instinctively correcting poor posture. In fighting applications, one must be prepared to exert force in any direction at any time with any part of the body—sometimes explosively using *fajin*. To do so, it is necessary to always maintain a natural stance.

The simple rule is that if the body position feels unnatural or contorted, the posture is wrong. This principle of natural stance is common to many martial arts and was eloquently and concisely stated by Gerard Thibault d'Anvers, a late 16th- to early 17th-century master swordsman:

> I have seen that people are accustomed by all of these styles to strange postures; the body bent in several angles with feet and legs put out of their natural proportion, and in postures wholly repugnant to the ordinary way one walks or stands. Instead of showing any great courage by these postures, in fact, those who use them inconvenience themselves and lessen their own force.[6]

The awareness that we develop through standing meditation and form practice will eventually carry over into our everyday life, until it becomes easier to recognize poor structure in any daily task and correct it.

Keep the "Five Bows"

The "five bows" refer to the five curves provided by arms, legs, and torso. To accomplish this, the arms and legs should be rounded, with a slight bend in the elbows and knees. To keep the bow of the torso, it is necessary to rotate or tuck the buttocks in slightly and "sink" and relax at the hip joints, thereby straightening the curve in the lower back. At the same time, the shoulders should be sunken and relaxed, the shoulder blades slightly rounded, and the head held straight and level by slightly tucking in the chin and "suspending" the top of the head from the *baihui* point. In combination, and if central equilibrium is maintained, you will feel a slight stretching of the spine and torso. (Note that I said "slight" in all descriptions—don't try to force or overdo any posture.) You may also feel a warm or tingling sensation in your hands, as the posture will immediately improve circulation. As you proceed with the form movements, you will begin to feel the flexing of the spine bow and the cyclic storing of energy in the torso. The Chinese describe the feeling of the cyclic stretching and folding of the torso as "kneading the dough." It provides a gentle massaging—tensing and pulling—but at the same time maintains a connected, almost sticky, feeling. It is difficult to describe, but once you recognize it in your practice, you will understand it.

The utility of the five bows is easily understood from biomechanical and structural/mechanical perspectives. The maximum potential force of the arms and legs is afforded when a muscle is in midrange—that is, bent.[7] According to the "crossbridge" theory, muscles generate force by the molecular energy of thin actin and thick myosin filaments sliding past each other. Contrary to popular opinion, the muscle fibers do not actually shrink upon muscle contraction. Instead the myosin filaments, utilizing the walking action of contacting points (i.e., crossbridges) between the myosin and actin, push the actin filaments past them. The relative position of the actin and myosin muscle filaments is determined by the length of a repeating contractile unit, termed a sarcomere. (The length of the sarcomere changes during concentric or eccentric muscle contraction.) The optimal position of the actin and myosin filaments, from which the maximum, or most efficient, output of force is possible, will correspond to the muscles being in a more or less mid range or bent position.[8] Thus, in the five bow position, the arms and legs are in optimal position to generate maximal force.

A second biomechanical rationale for the five bows is that slightly bending the elbows and knees will provide better mobility and maneuverability in response to a disturbance. Translated into Taiji terms, this means that when the elbows and knees are slightly bent you have more options for movement in response to an attacking force. For example, it is easy to understand how slightly bent knees are integral to maintain balance. If the knee joint is locked, you can maneuver around only two levers in the lower body, instead of three, and so the capability to respond to a perturbation is diminished.[9] Yet, if the knees are bent too much, you debilitate yourself by removing the option of using downward energy to neutralize an attack. (The downward energy is called *an* 按, and is one of the eight forces of Taijiquan discussed in detail in Chapter 6.) Perhaps the most important benefit of maintaining a position of maximum maneuverability is that the potential for injury is minimized. The potential for injury is greatest when the elbow or knee joints are locked, or when the knees are bent at severe angles.

A third and final consideration is that the slight, natural curving of the body with the five bows yields the simple mechanical benefits of an arched structure. The natural curve of an arch dissipates force outward along the curve. Instead of pushing directly inward, a force acting on an arch is dissipated out to the ends of the structure.[10] When the five bows are attached as one and the body is linked as one unit, the "end" of the curve may be the ground surface, or it may be the other, "counterattacking" side of the defender's body. Either way, the force is dissipated away from its target.

Keep Central Equilibrium (*Zhong Ding*) and "Straight and Centered" (*Zhong Zheng*)

A major goal of the Taiji form is to learn to move the body with maximum agility and strength while always maintaining central equilibrium. As mentioned in the previous chapter, maintaining central equilibrium is first practiced in standing meditation, or "standing pole," exercises. Taiji form applies movement to that practice and so is often referred to as a "moving pole." We will discuss central equilibrium further in the next chapter on push-hands, because all of the martial applications of the art fundamentally rely upon and seek to defend mental and physical central equilibrium (*zhong ding*). Identifying and maintaining central equilibrium during form movement is necessary practice for these martial arts applications.

Central equilibrium and the five bows are related in the concept of *zhong zheng* (中正), or "straight and centered." It is *zhong zheng* when the upper, middle, and lower body are linked together as one unit and the five bows are combined into one. Traditional Taiji theory asserts that when the body is *zhong zheng* the *zhong qi* (中气) will circulate smoothly up and down the body.[11] To realize *zhong zheng*, the head should be suspended, the waist loose, the hips sunk, the tailbone kept in, and the spine straight. Finally, the *baihui* point on the top of the head should be centered over the *huiyin* point between the anus and genitals.

Height of Stance

As you may have already inferred, I am an adamant opponent of practicing the Taiji form (or push-hands) in a continuously low posture, for practical, biomechanical, and medical reasons. From a traditional perspective, Taiji is exercise of *yi* and *qi*; it is not exercise of the brute force of the leg muscles. When the knees are bent too low, the *qi* and the silk-reeling energy are cut (silk-reeling is discussed below and in Chapter 6). Yin and yang require possibilities both up and down; however, there is no balance of yin and yang when the leg muscles are constantly contracted in a low posture. It is not Taiji movement if there is no smooth flow of *qi* and silk-reeling force; it is not Taiji movement if there is no balance of yin and yang. A constantly low posture hinders this flow and balance necessary for Taiji movement.

Biomechanical argument against excessively low postures. From a biomechanical perspective, the body is in a considerably weakened and less agile position when the knees are bent too far. (The quote attributed to Gerard Thibault d'Anvers above applies perfectly here as well.) Also, the structural benefit of the "bow" is destroyed when the knees are bent beyond a certain degree, so that force acting above the knee cannot be efficiently transmitted to the ground.

Lowering the body too far also inevitably violates the postural principles of Taijiquan. Before we get into a biomechanical explanation of why this is so, we need to define two simple terms:

+ **Base of support**. The base of support is the area above which a weight can be supported. In human posture, it is simply determined by the position of the feet.

+ **Center of mass**. The center of mass is a point around which the body's mass is equally distributed. In other words, the body is balanced at the center of mass in all directions.[12]

The relation of these two terms to balance is straightforward—to maintain balance, a point projected from the center of mass to the ground must fall within the range of the base of support. It is not possible to stand if the body's center of mass falls outside of the base of support. With the help of these biomechanical terms, we can further explore the possible strategies for lowering posture, and the effect of these strategies on balance.

In the vernacular, when we talk about lowering the posture (and therefore center of mass), we often refer to "bending the knees." Technically, however, it is a combination of hip, knee, and ankle flexion that is necessary to lower a stance. Actually, many scholars speak primarily of hip flexion, since that is the biomechanical action necessary to lower a stance to any significant degree. This point is illustrated in Figures 1 and 2. Figure 1 demonstrates what happens if only the knees are bent. If the ankles and waist are not bent with the knees, the center of mass will quickly fall behind the feet and the person will fall backward. If the knees and ankles are bent (but not the waist), the center of mass will soon be in front of the feet, and the person will fall forward (Figure 2).

To lower the center of mass and stay "straight and centered," Taiji teaches us to slightly bend at the hip and moderately bend the knees (and ankles). The method for bending the hip is referred to as "sinking the kua." As explained in Chapter 4, this motion is similar to a "posterior pelvic tilt," but is more relaxed. Sinking the kua results in a slight straightening of the lower spine and gentle stretching of the torso, but if done correctly, the buttocks, hamstrings, and hip remain loose and relaxed. Figure 3 illustrates this basic Taiji method of lowering the center of mass while maintaining a balanced, straight, and relaxed posture. As the knees are also slightly bent, the "two bows" of the legs are maintained as well.

However, if the hip is bent too far, the center of mass will again fall behind the feet and the person will fall backward, as illustrated in Figure 4. To continue lowering the posture without losing balance, one (or both) of two things must happen. Either the person must bend forward at the waist (as shown in Figure 5), or he or she must bend the knees to the extent that the knees pass beyond the front of the feet (as shown in Figure 6). Both of these strategies are effective in maintaining the center of mass above the base of support, but both also breach the structural principles of Taijiquan. Bending forward at the waist violates the Taiji principles of "central equilibrium" and "straight and centered." Placing the knees beyond the feet, of course, results in a considerably weakened stance in which balance is easily disrupted.

The above discussion is not to say that one should never enter a low stance, but rather that it is quite incorrect to practice in a continuously low posture. In the Chen style, for example, there are a select few movements that require the practitioner to temporarily achieve a lower stance.[13] These postures, however, are not held continuously. Upward motion always follows downward motion. It is not important that a beginning practitioner should have or quickly develop the strength and ability to perform the low postures. The

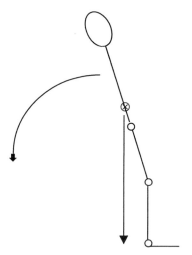

Figure 1. When you bend only at the knees, your center of mass will fall behind the base of support, and you will fall backward.

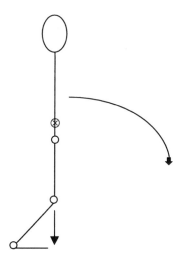

Figure 2. When you bend at the knees and ankles, your center of mass will soon be in front of the base of support, and you will fall forward.

Figure 3. When you bend slightly at the hip (i.e., "sink the *kua*") and at the knees and ankles, your center of mass is lowered but remains well within the base of support. You remain relaxed, balanced, and "straight and centered"; therefore, the Taiji principle of *zhong ding* is maintained. This is the fundamental Taiji stance for standing meditation, form, and push-hands.

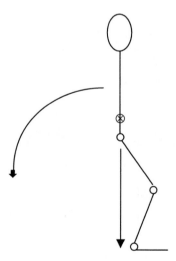

Figure 4. However, if you lower your posture by further bending at the hips, knees, and ankles, your center of mass will fall behind the base of support, and you will fall backward.

Figure 5. To maintain balance in a low posture, you must either bend forward at the waist (forfeiting Taiji postural principles of "central equilibrium" and "straight and centered"), and/or...

Figure 6. ... your knees and ankles must be bent to a degree where the knees extend beyond the feet. The postures depicted in Figures 5 and 6 are effective in maintaining the center of mass above the base of support, but both violate Taiji postural principles.

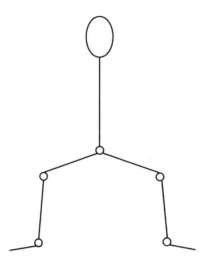

Figure 7. (Front view.) If the feet are rotated outward, it is possible to avoid bending forward at the waist in a low posture. However, the low posture and position of the feet greatly diminish the potential directions and magnitude of force that can be exerted (negating the martial value of the posture), and, because the kneecap is pulled laterally, the strain can result in injury (patella femoral pain syndrome).

critical point is that the practitioner should know and apply the correct *intention* for each form movement. (The precedence of the mind in Taijiquan is addressed in the *xin/yi* discussion below.) If the primary direction of force in a form is downward, it is enough to have the intention of "down" in the movement. In this way, one can gradually increase localized, external muscle strength and achieve lower postures while at the same time (and most importantly) learn and experience how to move with internal power.

Medical argument against excessively low postures. Finally, and perhaps most importantly, if the posture is excessively low, the risk for knee injury is greatly magnified. Here are two possible explanations why.

First, if the knees extend beyond the toes, the pressure on the kneecap will increase drastically. The cap will push inward on the knee, resulting in abnormal rubbing and pain. Second, in low postures with a wide stance, the toes necessarily rotate outward. This posture is illustrated in Figure 7. In this stance, the kneecap will be pulled laterally, possibly resulting in patella femoral pain syndrome. It is true that, with the feet positions depicted in Figure 7, you can achieve a very low stance without bending forward at the waist. However, this is an awkward and unnatural stance that greatly diminishes the potential directions and magnitude of force that can be exerted, negating any real martial value.

I know of several people who have injured their knees because of practicing form with an exaggeratedly low posture. Practicing Taiji did not cause the injury—practicing incorrectly did. There is simply no need to repeat this mistake.

The Importance of Turning the Waist

The classics tell us that "the waist and spine are the first master" and that "power is controlled by the waist." Grandmaster Feng teaches that:

> Substantial and insubstantial (*shi* 实 and *xu* 虚) change from the waist. Without turning the waist, a student cannot adjust substantial and insubstantial, cannot achieve synchronizing up and down, cannot perform unified silk-reeling, and cannot switch *jin* (劲) from inside the body. In push-hands, if a student does not use his waist, there will be no 'abandon oneself and follow others,' no 'sticking and following,' and no 'leading others to enter and fall into emptiness.' He will always be hindered and controlled by his opponent. This is why to change from the waist is important.[14]

Many form movements therefore involve turning the waist. The student must differentiate, however, between turning the waist and turning the hips. If the hips move with the waist, it is no longer "turning the waist" but rather becomes "changing the direction that the body is facing." (Of course, if the waist is turned past a certain point the hips and feet must follow.) The hips must stay solid as the waist turns to maintain a continuous, connected, spiraling silk-reeling force throughout the body. Waist turning is also exercise of one's range of motion and is essential to realize the skill of simultaneously neutralizing and releasing (*bian hua bian fa*, 边化边发).

Reverse Breathing

Moving *qigong* and Taiji form movement use a method of breathing known as "reverse breathing." This pattern of breathing has two functions: it nurtures *qi* and health, and it is an integral mechanical aspect of storing and releasing energy.

In the reverse breathing pattern, during inhalation the lower abdomen pulls inward and upward. During exhalation, the lower abdomen returns outward and downward. The Daoists observed that infants, used to pulling in nutrients from the umbilicus, breathe from the lower abdomen using this pattern. This is the opposite of a typical adult breathing pattern—hence the name "reverse" breathing. Adults tend to breathe more shallowly from the chest, with the chest and abdomen expanding on inhalation and contracting on exhalation.

Reverse breathing is important in several ways. It is a deeper, more efficient way of breathing and therefore obviously beneficial to health and respiratory function. Further, the simultaneous upward motion of the pelvic diaphragm and the downward motion of the upper diaphragm massages the internal organs, which is beneficial to circulation. It is also part of the technique of bending the spine "bow" and stretching the torso, so it is an essential aspect of storing and releasing energy. In traditional terms, reverse breathing is more conducive to sinking the *qi* and raising the spirit. Inhalation/exhalation in the reverse breathing pattern are but one of the diverse manifestations of yin and yang coordination in the form.

Reverse breathing is the method of breathing for Taijiquan practice, but paradoxically the instruction in both meditation and form practice is to forget about the breathing. The focus in *wuji* meditation is to enter quiet. Some schools do use breathing as a tool to enter quiet, but thinking about breathing is not entering true quiescence. In Taiji form movement, the focus is on *xin yi* (mind/intention), and it is definitely wrong to think about *qi* or breathing. A famous saying is, "if you practice brute strength it will break, if you practice *qi* it will be stiff, if you practice *yi* it will flow smoothly." (*Lian li ze duan; lian qi ze zhi; lian yi ze huo,* 练力则断，练气则滞，练意则活.)

The resolution of this paradox is that the breathing pattern must become so natural that you need not consider it. It is okay to practice the reverse breathing when beginning a meditation or the form, or when performing single movement *qigong* exercises. Actually, you can practice anytime—driving in your car, sitting at your desk at work—whenever you think about it. Over time, the reverse breathing pattern will internalize and become so natural that you can forget about it and move on.

Stages of Development in Form Practice

Below I have outlined five stages of development in form practice:

1. Choreography
2. *Xin yi* (mind/intention)
3. From loose and sink to soft and smooth
4. Yin and yang
5. Silk-reeling.

Understand that these stages represent general, and not absolute, areas of focus and sequences of learning. I have found that teaching form in this sequence often helps students who might be confused or overwhelmed by these stages combined. This is not to say that the stages are mutually exclusive—the achievements described in various stages can develop parallel to other achievements/stages.

Choreography

Obviously, the first step in Taijiquan is to learn a sequence of movements. Unfortunately many people, surprised by the difficulty in memorizing choreographed movement, are quickly frustrated by this beginning task and quit. Thinking that Taiji is supposed to teach them to relax (and it is), their first experience is one of tenseness caused by the self-induced pressure of keeping up with the class. Teachers from all styles of Taijiquan recognized that, to promote the art, it was necessary to develop shorter form versions that can more quickly be learned and "finished." In the Chen style, the eighty-three or so movements of the "long form" were reduced to 48-, 36-, and 24-movement forms. Similar short forms are taught in other styles. For the purpose of conducting research on novices over a relatively short period of time, I myself was forced to create 12-movement and 7-movement versions of the form.

For beginners, my advice is simply to have confidence and to tell yourself that you are the master. In so doing, you will approach the art with a more relaxed mind. Know that it does not matter in the least how quickly you can memorize a particular set of choreographed movements, how many individual movements are in the form, or how many different forms you learn. The form is only a tool to learn and internalize principles of movement. Once understood, the form is used to continue building upon the foundation of *gong* derived from *wuji* practice. No amount of quantity will make up for poor quality. If you can do the first several movements of the first routine well, you can do the whole first routine well. If you can do the first routine well, you can do other routines and weapons forms just as well. If you cannot do the first several movements of the first routine well, all other forms will be just as lacking. Ultimately when you get it, you get it, and you can do any movement as Taiji movement. At this point, the difference between forms will melt away completely. As the old Chinese martial expression goes, "I'm not afraid of someone who does a thousand forms; I'm concerned with the person that knows one form very well." (*Bu pa qian zao hui, jui pa yi zao jing,* 不怕千招会，就怕一招精.)

These simple facts are mirrored in the old, traditional way of teaching Taijiquan. When I started learning the form as a boy in China, the practice was very slow. The teacher would show one movement, and the student was expected to practice that single movement until the teacher saw that it was done correctly, or at least nearly so. Students had to arrive at class at least one hour before the teacher arrived. When the teacher did arrive, he or she would observe the practice and determine whether the quality of the movement was sufficient to move on to the next form. There was no money involved, so the instructional pace was not calculated to maximize profit. The teachers simply understood that there was little point in practicing new movements if the previous movements were not understood. It took me nearly two years to finish the Chen style first routine in this manner. Once students had finished the first form and the teacher could see that they were truly beginning to internalize the principles of movement, students were individually invited by the teacher to learn *pao cui*, the second routine in the Chen family style. When I was taught, the entire second routine was covered in a couple months. The teacher knew that once a foundation had been built, it was easy to add different movements to that foundation.

Today it is a different story. People expect to learn the form as quickly as possible, understandably equating the completion of a choreographed sequence of form movement with learning Taijiquan. I think that this is similar to the experience of other martial arts that arrived earlier in America. Many of the non-Chinese arts in America developed a belt system to reward and encourage practitioners. A high level of accomplishment is typically indicated with a black belt. Of course there are different levels of black belt, but many of my friends in these other arts tell me that, after securing a black belt (as quickly as allowed), people often feel a sense of completion and stop practicing. Earning a black belt, or completing a choreographed sequence of Taijiquan movement, is not an end point but simply one achievement along a long journey to learn and understand one's chosen martial art.

What to pay attention to. As any beginner quickly realizes, there is much to pay attention to in learning choreographed movement. Most students want to immediately start copying hand movements, even following along as the teacher is demonstrating. I always recommend that the students spend more time observing the teacher. The time you spend quietly observing is also a time you are practicing. Each form involves movement of the hands and arms, waist turning, weight shifting, and footwork or stance. You must observe all of these separately as the teacher repeatedly demonstrates.

From similar in appearance to similar in spirit. Once you have observed carefully, the quickest way to learn is to emulate the teacher's movement and pace as exactly as possible. There is no point in studying from a teacher if you have the attitude that you're going to do it your way anyway. It is very common for beginners to unintentionally add all sorts of extra movement in the forms. If you are following the teacher at the same pace and find that you are behind in the movement, find out where your extra movement is and delete it. Taiji movement is precise and efficient, and you should try to remove all unnecessary motions. Similarly, if you are moving at the same pace and find yourself ahead of the teacher, go back and determine what movement(s) you have omitted. The Taiji form strives for perfect efficiency of movement— every movement has a purpose. The *Treatise on Taijiquan* states this directly, "No excess, no deficiency."

Admittedly, everybody is unique. Everybody's body type and motions are different, and there are no two masters with identical forms. Further, all masters' forms will change over time. Everybody continues to learn with age, while at the same time everybody faces the inevitable degradation of physical ability and a changing body structure. Once you have truly learned all of the principles of movement, your form will inexorably mirror your unique character and body type. In fact, if someone does look exactly as the teacher looks, it is a likely indication that the student has not truly learned the principles of the art. No two bodies are identical, and dissimilar bodies cannot appear identical and both be truly relaxed. Nevertheless, to initially learn the principles of movement you must start with imitation. The Chinese refer to this as the natural progression from "similar in appearance to similar in spirit."

Practice. Thus far, I have not hesitated to state the obvious, so why stop now? Unless you are gifted, you cannot hope to learn the form by practicing only at class time. It is always helpful to take notes during class and to go over the day's lesson as soon as you get home while it is still fresh in your mind. During the week, practice the movements that you have learned. The sooner you can stop worrying about memorizing motions, the sooner you can concentrate on the principles of movement.

From big to small. When practicing the form, use large circles and a full range of motion. True, in application the circles are often small, and the higher the level of skill, the smaller the circles will (or can) be. But to learn the true mechanics of the intended movement and increase range of motion, strength, and circulation, it is better to practice with large, sometimes even exaggerated, motions. It is easy to adjust from big to small, but difficult to employ a large range of motion if you have always practiced with small circles. This point is conveyed in Chapter 28 of the *Yang Family Forty Chapters*:

> First practice expanding, then look to compacting.[15]

The principle of "from big to small" applies not only to arm circles, but to all body movement. Within the limit of your ability, you should approach the maximum comfortable limits of waist turning and weight shifting during form practice. In so doing, you will not only increase range of motion about the body joints, but also increase the comfortable range of motion within the base of support, effectively increasing the radius about which you are able to maintain balance.

The progression from form to push-hands is also an example of "from big to small." In the discussion of *wuji* in the previous chapter, I noted that one purpose of standing meditation is to learn to experience and maintain central equilibrium. In standing meditation, the center of mass is held constant at an optimal position for the stance practiced.[16] In going from *wuji* to Taiji, one practices moving the center of mass in all directions within the base of support. Whereas in *wuji* the goal is to find and hold the perfect balance point, in

Taiji form you learn the limits of stable movement and eventually increase the radius about which you can move and still maintain central equilibrium.

From the "big" center of mass movements of Taiji form, we then (ideally) return to "small" center of mass movements in push-hands or applications—this is the return from Taiji back to *wuji*. In push-hands you again "hold the center" and strive to maintain the center of mass at the most stable point (defined as the optimal position from which one can either defend or attack). By using the smallest center of mass movement possible, you hold in reserve larger motions *in case* they are needed. The higher the level of skill in push-hands, the less your center of mass will deviate from the optimal stance, and therefore the more stable you will be and the less likely that you can be unbalanced.

In emulating the teacher's motions as closely as possible, you have furthered the process, begun in meditation, of teaching your body to listen to your mind. Once the external pattern of the form is memorized, you can then focus on the internal aspects of the movement.

Use *Xin Yi* (Intention)

To begin to instill the mechanics of internal power in form movement, you must relax as completely as possible and use *xin yi* to generate and execute the movement. Literally translated, *xin* means heart/mind and *xin yi* together means intention—*xin yi* is commonly simplified to just *yi*. To practice *yi* means to concentrate and engage your inner nature, emphasizing the precedence of mind and spirit over physical movement.

From a traditional perspective, the Chinese say that physical movement follows the *qi*, yet the *qi* is mobilized by and follows the *yi*, the intention. Relax and emphasize mind/intention over physical ability—the body will eventually learn to listen to the mind. Over time, you will increasingly feel the power of the movement, but in a way that is quite different from the way you are generally used to experiencing strength. Most of the power will originate from the core of the body, rather than from an individual limb or muscle group.

How does one practice the form with *yi?* By consciously relaxing and emphasizing the *intention* of the movement and *awareness* of the body's structure and interaction with the environment. When practicing form, you should move with the intention to move in a specific direction, with the intention of hardness, the intention of softness, the intention to store, the intention to release, the intention of yin, the intention of yang—whatever is appropriate to the design of the form movement. Of course, all voluntary movement begins with intention, but in Taiji practice we emphasize the mental intention of the movement and do not rush to realize the result. If you can abstain from unnecessary tension, your body will ultimately follow the mind and the intended result will manifest itself, but in a way that is different from the mechanics of ordinary "external" movement. This, too, is part of the process of "accumulating hardness through softness." We practice the form with intention of hardness (where appropriate), but we keep the body relaxed. Gradually, from the softness of *yi* and conscious relaxation, a distinct hardness will be born. As stated in the classic poem, *An Explanation of Taijiquan*:

First in the mind, then in the body...[17]

When we are comfortable with and able to maintain relaxed movement, we can also imagine that we are executing the movement against a slight resistance. Here I have purposely used the modifier "slight." In keeping with the moderation principle, you should not overdo the intensity of the imagined resistance. This will likely result in tension (mental and physical), and such tension is antithetical to our practice. Through all form movements, our spirit should remain focused, calm, quiet, and reserved. Some refer to the Taiji form as "swimming in the air"—this metaphor conveys an appropriate magnitude of imagined resistance. Realize, too, that the rhythm of the form is dynamic and not static. You should not hold constant the degree of imagined resistance, but rather let it ebb and flow with the intention of the form movements. This, too, is an aspect of yin and yang in the form.

There are two fairly obvious requisites to reach the stage of practicing the form with *yi*. First, you need to have memorized the choreography—if you must think about where to move next, your mind will be occupied and therefore not focused on the intention of the movement. Second, understand that the goal of every form is to move a certain distance, in a certain direction, using certain parts of the body to express the force generated from the movement (all while maintaining central equilibrium). Added together, the Taiji form teaches how to move with power in all directions, and to potentially exert force with any part of the body without forfeiting balance. Therefore, you must clearly know the direction and intended expression of energy from every form movement. As the classic *Song of Thirteen Postures* states:

> Pay attention to every movement and *try to understand its purpose* [emphasis added], then you can comprehend the art without wasting your time and energy.[18]

Not knowing the primary purpose of every form movement is one of the most common mistakes I have observed, especially with the circular flowing motions of the Chen style. If you don't know the primary intention, you can't possibly coordinate the yin and yang of the movement. Without the coordination of yin and yang, the resulting movement will be an empty, indistinct, confused, purposeless blur (though it still might look beautiful). To better understand the intention, it is often helpful to have a rudimentary idea of a martial application of the movement. Most forms have many possible applications, some of which can be quite obvious and some of which are more hidden. Knowing one, simple application will help to focus the *yi*. Many teachers suggest that, in order to focus the *yi*, you practice the form as though the opponent is actually present. But here I will, at the risk of repeating myself, again remind the reader of the priority of the moderation principle. If you overemphasize the intention of the martial application during form practice, you may become tense and the *qi* may float into the chest. If this happens, you should simply reduce the emphasis on martial application. To help sink the *qi* to the *dantian*, you can end the session with a *qigong* exercise such as "sink *qi* and wash organs."[19]

Understandably, some believe that the more iterations of the form performed, the more they will learn and improve. This is not completely true. The rate of improvement depends as much if not more upon the quality of practice. Remember the saying in Chapter 1—*shi ban gong bei*—if you study something (anything) in the most efficient way possible, you can learn that thing in a fraction of the time. Little will be gained by practicing the form in a mindless, mechanical mode with the goal of completing as many repetitions as possible. There are two reasons why performing excessive iterations of form is an inefficient way to spend valuable practice time. First, practice without *yi* is empty practice that will not lead to the development of internal *gongfu*. After practicing correctly, you will understand that it is not at all easy to practice the form slowly with focused *yi*. If someone tells me he or she repeatedly practices many iterations of long forms during every session and over an extended period of time, my experience with the intensity and power of *yi* leads me to be skeptical of the quality of that practice. If the quality of the movement is high, you need not and should not overtrain form. Indeed, you *cannot* perform too many meaningful iterations, because, as with any activity, focus will inevitably diminish with repetition. The time to stop repetitions will become apparent when your attention shifts and/or the quality suffers. Second, know that the percentage of your practice time spent on various components of Taiji practice is a major factor in determining the *gong* you will derive. If you are like most, your practice time is limited; however, the fundamental and essential practices of sitting and standing *wuji* meditation must not be ignored in favor of form practice.

The priority of *yi*, or mind/intention, is a common principle of the internal arts. In Grandmaster Feng's words, "when practicing Taijiquan, remember to use *yi* and not to use strength. This will help a student to eliminate the stiff force or clumsy strength which he has acquired through daily activities. When he can stretch his tendons and loosen his muscles, his joints will open up and the internal *qi* can reach into the bones and marrow." Grandmaster Feng also clearly distinguishes between *yi* and *qi*, admonishing the student to *not* focus on *qi* or to try to make the *qi* move in a desired pattern; otherwise, "*qi* will become stagnant and many problems might occur."

From Loose and Sink to Soft and Smooth

After memorizing a form, the student can also begin to experience and develop *song chen* (松沉), which means "loose/relaxed" and "sink/heavy." Again, the key is to use *yi*, or mind/intention. If the mind thinks about being loose, the body will follow. In *song*, we can feel the opening of our joints, stretching of our torsos, and loosening of the tendons and muscles. When all tension is removed, the *qi* will be unobstructed and smooth. (Remember "loosen" or "relax" is not the same as "collapse.")

From *song*, we can then experience and cultivate the feeling of heaviness and sinking. By heavy and sunken, I don't mean an immobile, "double-weighted" and drooping body, but rather a relaxed, rooted, and solid posture.

We sink our *qi*, while at the same time keeping the spine and head straight and suspended, raising the spirit, and maintaining awareness and agility in the rooted posture. Because of the relaxation, the practitioner's body feels solid or heavy to someone trying to move them. A baby is a good example of the relaxed, sinking force of *song chen*. Although a baby has relatively little *li* or muscular strength, if the relaxed body of a toddler is coupled with the intention to "get down," the baby can be quite hard to hold. Another partial example is the heaviness of an unconscious adult—an unconscious person is much harder to lift than a "stiff" conscious person. The natural sinking force of *song chen* is lost in the tension accumulated with age.

Just as from the softness of standing meditation we were able to cultivate hardness, from practicing *song chen* we are eventually able to cultivate *rou shun* (柔顺), which refers to the soft and smooth motion of the body. It is said that the soft "elastic" force of Taiji is born from *rou shun*.

Yin and Yang

Yin and yang are interdependent. They are constantly alternating, giving birth to each other, everywhere in the form. Every movement has soft and hard, substantial and insubstantial, preparation and execution, store and release, open and close, light/agile and heavy/strong. Yin and yang should be *distinguished* and *very clear* in every movement, and should flow harmoniously throughout the form. The most frequent constructive criticism that my teacher would give was to note that yin and yang were not clearly distinguished in the students' movement. The constant changing of yin and yang is the rhythm of Taiji. When you catch the basic principle, when you recognize the timing of the coordination of yin and yang, all aspects of yin and yang will flow naturally in your movement.

By clearly knowing the correct intention of every movement and by relaxing and using *yi* to generate the movement, you will naturally begin to do the form using the mechanics of internal power and develop a "feel" for the yin and yang of the movement. If you expect the teacher to explain the yin and yang of each movement, you likely have not reached a level to really understand it or do it. Again, practice of *yi* and not *li* is the key to recognizing and then incorporating yin and yang into the form. If you know and practice the correct intention of a form, you will begin to feel the soft, relaxed, contracting, sinking, storing, preparatory yin phase, and the hard, solid, expanding, releasing yang phase. Have the intention of yin and the intention of yang. After a while, the intended result will manifest itself. In Grandmaster Feng's words:

> The key to mastering hardness and softness in Taiji is to learn the method of "one loose, one tight." Yin and yang are rooted in one another; so are "loose" and "tight." Before a student can apply "tight," he must first be in the "loose mode," and vice versa. The change of hardness (*gang*, 剛) and softness (*rou*, 柔) does not happen just on the physical level. It is more important for a student to apply this principle with *yi*.[20]

By "one loose, one tight," Grandmaster Feng simply means we should clearly distinguish the yin or yang aspect of the movement, and then understand how they flow into each other. This is also the meaning of the instruction from the classic *Summary of the Thirteen Postures*:

> Substantial and insubstantial must be clearly distinguished.[21]

Some of the yin/yang transitions are obvious, some are much more subtle. As brief examples of obvious or subtle yin and obvious or subtle yang, consider the following. In many motions, you must "lift" the energy to move very lightly and agilely, just as a cat moves. Even if you jump, you control the energy and land very softly. An observer can see the agile, light, yin movement—it is obvious. On the other hand, the storing yin phase can be very subtle, even imperceptible to an observer. For example, in the form "Tornado Foot" from the Chen style first routine, the intention of the movement is to turn 180 degrees to the right while sweeping or kicking the left leg. To move with agility, you must lift the energy up. However, before you can move right and the energy can go up, you must first turn the waist to the left and sink the energy. If you want to go right (with power), first you have to go left. If you want to rise, first you have to sink. The storing, preparatory yin aspect in "Tornado Foot" form happens quickly and is a very subtle movement—it is always absent in beginners' forms. It is felt by the practitioner but not seen by an observer.

Similarly, a yang aspect of movement is obviously apparent in a punching or kicking movement, especially in the Chen style if the movement is done explosively with *fajin*. A more subtle yang aspect is the strength manifested in what outwardly appears to be soft movement. It looks soft, but if you touch the advanced practitioner, you will feel the hidden strength.

Besides the cyclic flow of yin and yang between movements, yin and yang are also combined within a certain posture. For example, one side of the body may be soft, light, and yielding, while the other side may be solid, powerful, and attacking.

These are but a couple brief examples of yin/yang in the form. This is one aspect of the art you must feel and discover for yourself. If you practice correctly, with emphasis on *yi* and not *li*, you will become aware of the timing and relationship of the myriad yin and yang transitions throughout the entire form. Remembering that the yin/yang diagram *is* taiji, you will then understand why the art is called *Taijiquan*. In your practice, find how yin and yang depend on each other and seek to balance them in your movements. Push-hands practice will also greatly increase your understanding of yin and yang.

Silk-Reeling

The importance of the silk-reeling force, or *chansi jin*, was succinctly stated by Chen Xin, a 16th-generation representative of the Chen family, in his book, *Illustrated Explanations of Chen Family Taijiquan*:

> Taiji is the art of silk-reeling.

The eighth of Grandmaster Feng's 12 Principles further states:

> The silk-reeling force must be present throughout the form.

These statements are unequivocal—so what, exactly, is silk-reeling?

Silk-reeling is the spiraling, twining force generated by Taiji movement. It involves the smooth and coordinated rotation of the body's "small balls" (i.e., joints). Besides self-defense applications central to the theory of Taiji as a martial art (further discussed in the next chapter), relaxed silk-reeling movement affords the salient health benefits of gently stretching the ligaments and tendons and significantly enhancing circulation throughout the body. In traditional terms, silk-reeling is the method of circulating *zhong qi*. Silk-reeling greatly increases internal energy.

At first, beginners may become aware of the spiraling force as a disconnected or localized rotation in the arms or legs. In more advanced practitioners, the *chansi* force will be felt as originating from the middle *dantian*. The middle *dantian* is at the center of the body and therefore a critical point in the whole body connection and coordination of the spiraling force. I have listed silk-reeling last in this discussion of stages of development for a reason—it is no small achievement to realize silk-reeling force generated from the *dantian* and coordinated throughout the whole body.

Traditionally, the direction of the spiral rotation is described as either *shun* (顺) or *ni* (逆). In the following definitions of *shun* and *ni*, the reader should be aware of a distinction between the spiraling, twining motions and the force that generates these motions. The spiraling motions are a *manifestation* of Taiji movement; if the movements are performed in accordance with essential principles, then the spiraling/twining movements of the *chansi jin* will naturally be expressed and the body will be connected as one "big, rotating, Taiji ball." Conversely, disconnection of the body, inattention to posture, and tension of the muscles prevents the spiraling motions. Correct practice of *wuji* meditation, Taiji movement, and push-hands will gradually lead to the development and understanding of the coordinated *chansi* force. Simply rotating the arms or legs in clockwise or counterclockwise directions is external movement only and is not the *chansi* force.

Definitions of *shun* and *ni chan*. The following definitions are based on the original meanings of *shun* as "follow" and *ni* as "against," while *chan* is the primary character of *chansi jin*.

+ **Hand/Arm movement.** It is *shun chan* when the little finger rotates past the center of the hand toward the thumb, while at the same time the elbow closes from the outside to the inside with the sinking of the shoulder. If the arms are extended straight out, in the right arm this is clockwise rotation and in the left arm it is counterclockwise rotation.

    Ni chan is the opposite. It is *ni chan* when the thumb is rotated past the center of the palm toward the little finger, while at the same time the elbow opens outward. The shoulder should again sink during the rotation.

+ **Chest/Abdomen/Trunk.** It is *shun chan* when the chest/abdomen closes. This is called "*qi* returning to the *dantian*." When the chest/abdomen opens, it is *ni chan* and is called "*qi* emerging from the *dantian*." The trunk turns the silk-reeling of the chest/abdomen and waist/spine together. The chest and abdomen control the opening and closing of the entire body. The four limbs are open when the chest and abdomen are open and are closed when the chest and abdomen are closed.

◆ **Legs**. When the leg spirals inward, it is *shun chan*. When the leg spirals outward, it is *ni chan*.

There is some difference of opinion as to which direction is *shun* and which direction is *ni* for the leg spiral. Ultimately, there are only two possible directions of spiral, and each gives birth to the other throughout the form—another expression of yin/yang rhythm. Regardless of the name of the direction, the key point is that the spiral is present and coordinated throughout the body.

From Essential to Advanced Form Movement

The way in which I currently teach form has evolved to parallel the stages of development outlined above. The movements of the Chen style, in particular, can appear quite complicated or confusing to a beginning practitioner. Many of the circular movements of the arms are ancillary silk-reeling motions. By themselves they have practical applications and are excellent practice of Taiji movement. (Or more accurately, they are external manifestations of correct movement.) But I know from observation and teaching experience that they often confuse the beginning practitioner. The *chansi* circles make it harder for the student to learn the choreographed movement, and may also obscure the primary intention of each form movement. Without knowing the primary intention, you cannot possibly advance to the levels of exercising *yi*, understanding yin and yang, and ultimately realizing the coordinated silk-reeling force.

So that the student may quickly and easily grasp the primary intention of each form movement, I now omit some of the supplementary *chansi* circles when teaching beginners. (Incidentally, I'm not the first to do this.) After the students learn the essential movements, we then go back and refine them. The first refinement stage involves the indispensable aspects of coordinating yin and yang and realizing the silk-reeling motions of the legs, torso, chest, and arms in the essential movements themselves. When students successfully incorporate the silk-reeling, they always and invariably comment on how much more energy they feel when doing the form.

Once yin and yang and the silk-reeling of the essential movements are practiced and understood, the ancillary silk-reeling circles can then easily be reincorporated into the form. It may sound slower, but in my experience it is the most efficient way for the student to truly learn. Actually, because many of the *chansi* movements are secondary to the primary intention of a form, they can be "cut and pasted" anywhere. I know that someone doesn't understand the form if he or she becomes disconcerted when a silk-reeling circle is added, deleted, or modified. If you have learned Taiji movement, you can do any *chan-si* circle in any direction. It doesn't matter in the least. In my experience, this logical procession from essential to advanced movements is the most efficient path to understanding and actualizing the principles of Taiji movement.

Fajin

An accurate translation is the beginning point for understanding *fajin*. *Fa* means a quick or exploding "release" and *jin* means "energy." *Fajin* is the quick, explosive release of energy. Once you have accumulated a foundation of *gong*, then you can release and therefore use the energy for defensive purposes.

All Taijiquan movements are actions of storing and expressing energy in a specific direction with a specific part (or parts) of the body. The key point is to understand that relaxing and storing are the requisite skills necessary to release energy. That is one significant reason why the form is done slowly and deliberately. Once you learn how to relax and store, it is easy to release. So you are actually practicing *fajin* in every form movement. All of the necessary preparation for releasing is there in every form; one just doesn't release, as there is no reason to release (and there are several reasons not to).

Once you can feel in your practice that you are storing energy in every movement, you can then practice and experience releasing the energy. Sometimes, in the Chen style, the release of energy occurs spontaneously in the form (i.e., it just "happens" naturally). This, too, is yin and yang. Just as a classical music piece may have both soft and gentle and driving and powerful sections, explosive releasing energy naturally flows from the cache of energy stored in slow movement.

As with anything else, releasing is a skill that requires some practice. When practicing *fajin*, it is critical to pay attention to the following:

✦ **Remain relaxed**. Tension will greatly limit the energy released at the target. Stay relaxed throughout the motion until the moment of expression. At the instant of expression, it is necessary to tense up to release the energy and to avoid injuring yourself. The force generated must be transmitted through the body, but should be expressed outward and not held within the body. Immediately after expression, relax again. The longer you stay relaxed before expressing the energy, the more powerful your *fajin* will be.

✦ **Focus the energy**. The entire force of the energy released should be focused on a target. The smaller the area over which the energy is expressed, the greater the force that will be transferred to the target. This is simple physics. Ten pounds of steel and ten pounds of feathers have the same mass. But you would be much more concerned if you were being struck with the steel, because the force (mass times acceleration) is concentrated in a smaller area.

This point is emphasized in the traditional saying quoted in the introduction to this chapter—*li fa yi dian* (the released energy should focus on one point).

✦ **Do not shake the body or head**. This is closely related to the previous point. Energy is diffused throughout all moving parts. The more the body shakes or trembles during *fajin*, the less the kinetic energy that will be transferred to the target given the same starting potential energy. The highest level of skill is to transfer all energy to the target, with none being retained in the body or lost to extraneous movement. Again, Taiji movement strives for maximum efficiency. Every motion of the body should have a specific purpose.

Perhaps most importantly, do not allow your head to shake when releasing energy. It is easy to imagine the potential damage if the head or brain is shaken violently (or repeatedly). It is especially dangerous for those who have developed a foundation of *nei gong* (internal power/skill) and can generate more power.

✦ **Emphasize nurturing/gathering, not releasing**. The primary emphasis in all Taiji exercises should be in nurturing/gathering/ building energy. If you don't have the reserve, what is there to release? You do need to practice releasing, but you should limit the time spent on *fajin*. If you practice one hour, then two minutes of *fajin* is enough. Once you have "programmed" your mind and body to release in any direction (with any part of the body), there is no reason to release. If you have internalized the technique, then the power of your *fajin* is a function only of your *gong*.

When I was teaching at the Shanghai Chen Style Taiji Research Association, there was a famous local martial artist. He was very powerful, and he enjoyed the reputation that he had sought as a great fighter. It was also well known that this person emphasized *fajin* in his daily practice. When he died suddenly of unknown causes at a relatively young age, most in the martial arts community knew why. True, one can achieve a great deal of power for a short time, but if the moderation and nurturing principles are not followed, this benefit will surely be short-lived.

Taiji Form and the Nervous System

In Chapter 4, we introduced some recent studies and hypotheses for the relation between sitting and standing meditation and the nervous system. We can now build upon the ideas presented there and integrate principles of neural science specific to *voluntary movement*.

There are three principles of voluntary movement that have been extensively studied:

1. Voluntary movement is governed by motor programs,
2. Voluntary movement trades speed for accuracy, and
3. Reaction time varies with the amount of sensory input processed.[22]

The first two principles describe mechanisms of Taiji form practice, as explained below. The third principle relates specifically to push-hands, and we'll bring it up again in the next chapter.

Before we voluntarily move, the extent of the movement is represented in the brain as an abstract plan (as opposed to a series of joint movements and muscle contractions). The representation, or mental image, of the planned movement is called a *motor program.* A motor program includes movement dynamics and kinematics. In other words, a motor program includes the intended length, direction, and force of a movement.

The "eight forces" of Taiji—*peng/lu/ji/an/cai/lie/zhou/kao*—specifically characterize the direction and length (or duration) of different forces. These forces are explained in further detail in the following chapter, but the point here is that *peng/lu/ji/an/cai/lie/zhou/kao* are exactly analogous to the scientific concept of a "motor program." The Taiji form is a compilation of all combinations of *peng/lu/ji/an/cai/lie/zhou/kao.* In all form movement, correct intention *(yi)* is primary. Through repeated and correct form practice, we increase our "mental library" to include motor programs of widely variable dynamics and kinematics. This reservoir of motor programs is a rich arsenal of potential movement that can be employed in response to threatening situations. In simple traditional martial arts terms, we just say that every part of the body can be a potential weapon.

An important point to note is that the laws governing voluntary movement can be modified by learning—we *learn* motor programs by experience. Anyone, even a baby, can flail arms and punch out wildly. But the precise and complex motor programs (and the "elastic" power) of Taiji *have* to be learned. Because Taiji movement is relatively complex and is not intuitive or a function of natural ability, the form must be practiced slowly to be learned. The second principle of voluntary movement listed above states that the faster the movement, the less accurate it will be. If you practice slowly, you will ultimately learn the correct mechanics of movement. It is not possible to learn Taiji movement and power from fast movement. Once the correct motor program is instilled, however, it can be executed quickly and correctly (for example, without tensing or stiffening the body and contracting antagonistic muscles contrary to the movement). Although this principle of slow movement is an eminent feature of Taiji training, it is by no means unique to Taijiquan. For example, when I was studying violin, my teacher would insist that I begin each practice session with a slow, deliberate, and relaxed pace, emphasizing the accuracy of the fingering and bow work. By beginning slowly, it was ultimately possible to play difficult pieces at a faster tempo than if I had tried to play them quickly from the start.[23]

Voluntary Movement Requires Communication Between Different Areas of the Brain

In the introduction to the central nervous system in Chapter 4, I noted how motor programming involves communication between various brain regions. An important area of current research is the role of connections between the cerebral cortex and an area of the midbrain known as the basal ganglia.[24] The latest research suggests that the basal ganglia region is importantly involved in the formation of habits. To reach a level of effectiveness in combat (or in response to any threatening situation encountered in everyday life), all responsive movement must be internalized to the point where it is executed automatically. As the old saying goes, if you have to think about the movement, it is too late. Because Taiji combines several variables of movement, including coordination, balance, and the internalization of complex motor programs, advanced Taiji practitioners would provide excellent subjects to further investigate how the brain is involved in motor programming and to explore connections between the prefrontal cortex (responsible for initiation and programming of motor sequences), the dorsal and ventral striatum of the basal ganglia (responsible for habit formation), and the cerebellum (responsible for balance and coordination and control of voluntary movement).

The way in which movement is controlled in the brain also suggests that the basal ganglia region is "exercised" in the practice of Taijiquan. On a moment-to-moment basis, voluntary movement is regulated via communication between the motor cortex, basal ganglia, and cerebellum. The motor cortex sends information to the basal ganglia and cerebellum, and both send information back to the motor cortex via the thalamus. An interesting point is that, although different neurotransmitters are used within the basal ganglia, the overall effect of the basal ganglia on the thalamus is *inhibitory*, while the overall effect of the cerebellum is *excitatory*. In other words, an important function of the basal ganglia is to stop, or "put the brakes on," unwanted movement. As discussed above, Taiji movement strives for perfect efficiency with absolutely no extraneous or purposeless movement—as the classics say, "no excess, no deficiency." Smooth, coordinated, and efficient movement is a function of the balance between the inhibitory (yin) basal ganglia and the excitatory (yang) cerebellum systems and their communication with the motor cortex. Again, the balanced interplay of yin and yang is the very definition of Taiji.

Xie
Harmony

Chapter Six

Push-Hands

QIGONG AND FORM EXERCISES ARE PRACTICES of "knowing ourselves." In push-hands we continue learning about ourselves, and begin the practice of "knowing others." Push-hands practice is a step toward fighting, but it is not fighting. Push-hands is a training system that is done in the spirit of a game. We call it playing push-hands. The brilliance of the push-hands training system is that the theory and principles of the art can be taught safely without fighting.

The Purpose of Push-Hands Training

To begin push-hands practice, practitioners are required to give up tense or brute force and adopt the attitude that they are working with a partner to everyone's mutual benefit. The attitude with which one approaches push-hands is very important, as we will discuss in more detail later. Note that I said, "give up *tense* or brute force." A very common misconception about push-hands practice is that it should be done using no force at all. Just as using brute force is the mistake of excessive yang, a limp, powerless body is the mistake of excessive yin. You do not surrender all use of force in push-hands practice. Indeed, push-hands is a mechanism through which you (1) learn how to use the internal force that has been developed through *qigong* and form practice, and (2) continue to develop internal power.

Different people are "ready" for push-hands at different times, but it is much less efficient to start practicing without having developed a foundation of internal power from *wuji* and form practice. As the old Chinese saying goes, you can't make the wheat grow faster by pulling the sprouts up. Those who haven't developed a foundation from *wuji* and form practice have and know only brute force. If that is given up, what are they left with? How can they learn how to apply internal force if they don't possess it to begin with?

To understand the training for push-hands, we should first clearly recognize and understand the primary goal of push-hands practice. Very simply, *the ultimate goal of push-hands practice is to further develop and learn to maintain zhong ding* (central equilibrium). All of the principles and methods of practice may be considered "techniques" toward this end. You have experienced *zhong ding* in meditation practice, and learned how to maintain *zhong ding* during movement through your form practice. Now, in push-hands, you are practicing maintaining *zhong ding* while someone else is actively trying to disrupt it.

Zhong ding is an important principle in the art of Taijiquan. We briefly introduced *zhong ding* in Chapter 2 in discussing the relation between spirituality and martial arts, and then again in Chapters 4 (as a fundamental purpose of standing *wuji* meditation) and 5 (as a structural or postural principle of form movement). Before moving on to discuss the principles and techniques of push-hands, let's first summarize the essential components of *zhong ding* within the specific context of push-hands training.

Zhong Ding (Central Equilibrium)

Physically, *zhong ding* means that the body is upright, balanced, and rooted. The opposite of *zhong ding* is *pian* (偏), which refers to a leaning or oblique body position. To maintain *zhong ding*, one should keep the spine and head straight, and not bend forward or backward at the waist.[1] If you must move forward, take a step. If a force approaches from the front, *never* lean backward. Any time that you catch yourself bending the waist, stop and begin again. Find out why, and learn to neutralize the attacking force without forfeiting *zhong ding*. A goal of any repetitive practice is to instill habit and decrease reaction time. It is as easy to develop bad habits as it is to develop good habits. Bending at the waist may allow you to momentarily avoid an attacking force (provided the attacker is limited to a fixed stance), but it violates nearly every principle of Taijiquan. The moment that the waist is bent, central equilibrium is destroyed and it is extremely difficult to maintain sticking force. (Simply maintaining physical contact is *not* the sticking force of Taijiquan.)

As discussed in Chapter 2, physical balance (or the lack thereof) is first and foremost a mental function. You cannot maintain *zhong ding* in your posture if you cannot maintain a calm and balanced mind. You will not maintain *zhong ding* if your intention is fixed on attacking your opponent. Also, to maintain *zhong ding* you must relax and sink your *qi*. If your *qi* is floating, your balance will be weakened.

An experienced person could probably list a hundred things not to do in push-hands. The reason for nearly all prohibited actions is that they can cause loss of *zhong ding*. Don't let anybody take your calm or balance. Ultimately, it is your choice.

What has all this to do with self-defense? It's very simple, really. When you are unbalanced, mentally or physically, you are vulnerable to attack. Conversely, maintaining *zhong ding* affords the best options for defending yourself from attack. If you can neutralize an attack and maintain *zhong ding* while simultaneously sensing the vulnerable areas of or even unbalancing the attacker, you can counterattack at will. Any martial technique can be successful if the opponent is first unbalanced or is attacked at the weakest point. This is exactly the meaning of the words from the *Song of Comprehension and Application*:

> Neutralization generates a thousand million techniques.[2]

And so learning to neutralize a perturbation and maintain *zhong ding* (while also learning to sense or destroy the balance of your partner) is the fundamental goal of push-hands training.

Keep in mind that, though the goal of maintaining *zhong ding* is singular and straightforward, the principles and techniques of how this is accomplished are diverse. Different aspects of the art can and should be emphasized in practice at differing levels of accomplishment and in differing situations. It is easier to learn and internalize one technique or principle at a time, rather than to attempt to digest everything at once. For this reason, there is no one, single way to practice push-hands.

In this chapter, we will separately address *principles*, *techniques*, and *methods* of push-hands practice. To further explain push-hands training, I will then relate various aspects of practice to established principles of neural science. I will end the chapter with a discussion of the graduation from push-hands to fighting application.

General Principles of Push-Hands Training

Attitude

Push-hands is and should be practiced as a *qigong* exercise. As in all of Taiji practice, you should approach push-hands with the attitude of *nurturing*. This attitude is absolutely essential if you are to progress to higher levels of the art. In push-hands, we nurture both our partner and ourselves.

It is easy to check yourself and see if you are nurturing your *qi* and internal power. Just as you will feel mentally and physically "refreshed" after static or moving *qigong* drills or form, you will always feel invigorated after practicing push-hands correctly. Conversely, if you feel physically and/or mentally drained after practice, something is quite wrong. If your rate of respiration increases significantly during push-hands, you are using brute force (*li*) and not internal power (*qi*). One simple test can determine if brute force is being used. The rate of respiration will not rapidly increase in a relaxed practitioner who uses power efficiently; however, if brute force is used, the increased muscular oxygen demand will quickly precipitate heavy breathing. If you are playing with a larger, athletically inclined person, you may not easily move him or her at first. However, if such a person uses only brute force and you are able to maintain "sticking force" (discussed below), he or she will soon tire and any natural ability will promptly deteriorate. Of course, nurturing implies that you also maintain a calm mind. An excited mind will also quickly tire.

At the same time that we are nurturing ourselves, we should keep in mind that we are also nurturing our partner. In beginning push-hands patterns, we exchange attack and defense motions. We should use force in our attack, as an attack without force is absolutely without purpose or benefit to anybody, but we need to learn to control the force exerted. In doing this we learn to apply our acquired internal power, and at the same time learn to gauge and control the force exerted without losing balance. We should not use more force than the partner can handle. If your partner can handle 5 units of force, give him or her 4.9. Let your partner truly practice neutralizing, without attempting to overwhelm. If your partner can handle 1000 units of force, give 999.9. In Chinese, exerting a force in push-hands is called *wei jin* (喂劲), which literally means that the attacking force is "spoon-fed" to a partner.

Even in freestyle playing, we nurture our partner. If an attacking force upsets your balance, this is precisely the time and opportunity for learning. Ask your partner to "feed" this force to you again. Keep practicing until you find the way to neutralize it. There is no attacking force that cannot be neutralized. Consider two practitioners, **A** and **B**. If **A** continually pushes **B** backward, sooner or later **B** will understand why. **A** may improve somewhat from the exchange, but **B** will eventually progress more by learning how to neutralize a perturbation initiated by a stronger or more experienced partner.

Remember that push-hands is a game. In keeping with the moderation principle, do not approach push-hands (or any aspect of Taiji practice) as if it were a ponderous job or wearisome "workout." If you have fun with it, you will practice longer and learn more. Lastly, remember that mental training is an integral aspect of all Taiji exercises. Keep practicing with the attitude that you are improving yourself, and don't worry about what other people are doing. If some in your group just don't get it and always revert to using brute force, let them. They will learn nothing, but it is excellent practice for you.

Practice at the Limits of Your Ability

To improve in push-hands practice, you must practice at the limits of your ability. Realize, though, that there are both maximum and minimum limits to consider. While you should practice near your maximum limit of internal power exertion and range of motion, you also must learn to judge the minimum amount of force necessary and control the amount of force that you do use.

Use internal force. As emphasized in the title, Taiji is the "science of power." If no force is used, the exercise of push-hands is of minimal value to either health or martial arts. The goal, however, is to surrender external, localized, brute strength and learn to use and rely upon internal power/skill (*nei gong*).

Repeated, hands-on contact with a qualified teacher is the most direct way to understand and learn how to use internal power. In both the teacher's neutralizing and attacking motions, you will immediately perceive the difference between internal power and brute strength. Gradually, through push-hands training, you will learn to express your internal force. Just as internal power is accumulated, in part, through the use of intention or *yi* in form practice, the expression of internal force will also be realized with *yi*.

When two practitioners reach the level of understanding and expressing internal force, they can then gradually increase the magnitude of force expressed between them and thereby use the training as a means of further increasing their *gong li* (功 力), or physical strength. Again, this is a cyclical aspect of *nei gong*. The more internal power you have, the more you can use, and the more you use the more you can accumulate (if you practice correctly).

Control the force. After you understand and learn to use internal force, you should practice gauging and controlling the force necessary for neutralizing or attacking movements. The higher the level of skill, the finer the gradations of force. When you have learned to measure, finely control, and express internal force from all parts of the body that are in contact with your partner, you will begin to understand the "sticking" technique of Taijiquan.

Gauging and controlling force is an essential skill for maintaining *zhong ding* in push-hands or self-defense applications—certainly to maintain balance you cannot always respond with the maximum amount of force possible. Conversely, there is a minimum amount of force necessary for any successful neutralizing or attacking motion.

This principle of push-hands practice is also of direct benefit to everyday life. Our ability to gauge and control force deteriorates with age.[3] This decline in motor control may explain the reason for some falls in the elderly. The conscious exercise of "fine tuning" the exertion of force in Taiji practice will greatly help to ward off the inevitable decline in motor control that comes with age. At the University of Illinois, a study was recently completed that evaluated both improvements in strength and force control in Taiji practitioners.[4] Sixteen older adults received Taiji training for twenty weeks, and ten served as a control group. The study documented significant increases in both leg strength and force control in those that received the Taiji training. In other words, the Taiji practitioners both got stronger and could better control their force exertion after training. This is a significant finding, as previous studies that measured the same variables found that traditional strength training exercises did not improve the ability of older adults to control force exertion.[5] Although this study was completed on older adults, I am confident, from my experience with Taiji, that the findings are equally applicable to younger people.

Don't Overdo It

Having just noted that you must use internal force in push-hands practice to increase your skill, I will again caution that one must do so only within the limits of the nurturing and moderation principles.

First, do not rush to increase the amount of force used in push-hands. If you do, you will surely exceed your capacity to employ internal strength and will revert to brute strength. This will, of course, stall or reverse your progress and will increase your chance of injury. All injuries are debilitating, to some degree. I know of some who injured themselves quite seriously by overdoing push-hands practice. There is no reason to repeat this mistake.

Second, as you develop internal power, the force expressed in push-hands can and will grow significantly. At this point, you should listen to your body and moderate the intensity and duration of your training. The efficient way to develop a lasting foundation of internal *gongfu* is to understand push-hands as an energy nurturing/gathering exercise. If you are practicing correctly, you will feel refreshed, not drained, after push-hands.[6]

Practice with a Group

If you truly practice push-hands with *nei gong*, you will quickly understand that everybody's force is unique. Everybody "feels" different. With eyes closed, I can easily tell you which person in my class I am pushing with. It is very obvious. Because everybody is unique, it is good to gain experience from as many different partners as possible. A large group is an extremely valuable resource for this reason. Another famous martial arts saying is that "a great man needs three assistants, a great fighter needs three training partners." (*Yi ge hao han san ge bang, yi ge ba shi san ge zhuang*, 一个好汉三个帮，一个把式三个桩.) The meaning is that you must train with different people to reach a high level.

Posture

In practicing push-hands, you need to maintain all of the postural alignments that you have learned and internalized from *wuji* and form practice. Don't abandon what you have learned and revert to natural ability because of the excitement of engagement with another person. Most importantly, always maintain a natural alignment in your body posture. Never place a joint in an awkward or unnatural position. You should be constantly alert and ready to express your force in any direction at any time. If you attempt to defend yourself or express force from an awkward or unnatural position you will only hurt yourself.

Techniques of Push-Hands

The above principles allow you to continue efficiently developing *nei gong*. By understanding and practicing the *techniques* of push-hands, you gradually learn how to neutralize and counterattack while maintaining *zhong ding*.

Eight Forces of Taijiquan

Peng/lu/ji/an/cai/lie/zhou/kao are the "eight forces" (*ba fa*) of Taijiquan. The mechanics of the eight forces are first learned and internalized in form practice. In push-hands, these forces are then applied in neutralizing and attacking motions.

The eight forces are traditionally separated into two groups—*peng/lu/ji/an* are the "four cardinal directions" and *cai/lie/zhou/kao* are the "four corners," in reference to the traditional position of the respective trigrams around the Taiji symbol. Each group shares common characteristics so it makes sense to address them separately.

Peng/lu/ji/an. The classic *Song of Sparring* begins, "Be meticulous about *peng, lu, ji,* and *an.*"[7] These are the fundamental forces of beginning push-hands exercises. The meaning of *peng/lu/ji/an* is actually quite simple—it refers only to the basic directions of force. *Peng* means the force is expressed upward, *lu* means force is expressed to the side and back, *ji* means the force is expressed forward, and *an* means the force is expressed downward. The "force" means internal power/energy, which is (confusingly) sometimes also referred to as *peng.*[8]

Taiji theory stresses that you should not struggle with an opponent or meet a force "head-on." *Peng, lu,* and *an,* then, are methods by which a force is diverted without struggling and are used to "prevent the opponent from entering." If the incoming force is high, it can be quite easily diverted upward. If a force is low, the path of least resistance is to divert it downward. An off-center force acting upon the body can be led to emptiness by turning the waist and guiding the force to the side and backward. *Ji*, which is a force directed forward, is the principal attacking motion in beginning push-hands exercises.

The application of *peng/lu/ji/an* is actually nothing more than simple, basic Newtonian mechanics with a dash of common sense. Try it yourself. Stand (in central equilibrium) with a partner exerting a force straight toward your upper body, and see how little effort is required to deflect the force straight upward. (To gain an advantage in leverage, stick to the attacker's arms as far from his or her body as possible.) Similarly, have your partner push on your waist. Place your hand over the top of his or her hand, and sink your *qi* straight down. The force will fall away easily. When an attack comes at you horizontally, guide it to emptiness using a vertical force. Don't meet it head-on and struggle with it. It's all an issue of focusing and directing your energy, something that you've learned to do in form practice.

Another angle from which to view *peng/lu/ji/an* is to understand that the direction of your neutralizing force is determined by *following* the opponent. For example, when a force is low, follow it (and add to it) with *an*. It sounds simple, but it does take practice.

The theory of neutralizing is deeper than we have described thus far (we haven't discussed silk-reeling yet), and certainly there is more to the applications of *peng/lu/ji/an*. *An*, for example, is also used to quickly regain balance and root and can produce the effect of suddenly "disappearing," thus startling and unbalancing the opponent. But for now, we have enough information to understand and begin simple push-hands patterns.

Cai/lie/zhou/kao. Relative to *peng/lu/ji/an*, *cai/lie/zhou/kao* are shorter, more offensive and explosive forces. *Cai* means "pluck" and is a downward/backward, pulling/snapping force. *Lie* is a quick, explosive motion in which force is expressed in opposing directions. *Lie* is often used as a joint locking/breaking force. Because of the speed and ferocity of *lie*, it can also startle the opponent and make his or her mind "blink." *Zhou* and *kao* are similar; however, *zhou* is a short force issued through the elbow/forearm, while *kao* is an even shorter force issued from any part of the body that is touching the opponent. *Kao* means "stroke," but a more descriptive translation of the Taiji force might be "bump." *Kao* is often applied with the hips and legs to unbalance an opponent, but because it is such a short force, it can apply whenever and wherever you are touching the opponent.

There are fixed-step and moving push-hands patterns, as well as form and *fajin* drills and two person slapping/hitting (*pai da* 拍打) exercises that are designed to practice *cai/lie/zhou/kao*. However, a word of caution is in order here. Because *cai/lie/zhou/kao* are typically "shorter range" forces they are often used explosively and are more difficult to control. Only capable, sufficiently advanced practitioners who can control the power emitted should practice these forces "live" with a partner.

Overall, the combination of *peng/lu/ji/an/cai/lie/zhou/kao* describes the direction, duration, and distance of any possible expression of force. For the purpose of instruction, we can neatly define and categorize these forces, and we can drill these forces as separate exercises to learn to express force in any direction, with any part of the body, at any distance. In application, though, the boundaries can be blurred. The combination of potential directions, durations, and lengths of forces is essentially infinite. *Peng* or *an*, for example, can be performed in a quick, explosive manner. A force directed both upward and back into the opponent could be considered a combination of *peng* and *ji*. We name and define the forces in order to learn. Once your body will listen to your mind and you can express force in any direction, at any time, with any part of your body, the name of the force is irrelevant.

Adhere/connect/stick/follow (*zhan/lian/nian/shui*)

A primary focus of push-hands practice is to learn to adhere/connect/stick to and follow your partner. Taiji martial strategy fundamentally relies upon connecting with and adhering to the opponent so that you may constantly monitor the opponent's intention and balance, and therefore can more easily neutralize an attacking force and/or more efficiently time your own attack. This constant monitoring of the opponent's intention and balance is called "listening." Adhering and listening are not unique to the art of Taijiquan. The practicality of maintaining contact with an attacker is well recognized and practiced in widely diverse martial arts, from other Asian internal and external arts to European sword fighting styles.

The concept of *following* was broached in the discussion of *peng/lu/ji/an*. As the classics suggest, you should give up your own intention and follow the opponent. When you can follow and neutralize without struggling, the opponent will feel as though "in advancing there is only emptiness."

The skill of *sticking* involves much more than simply "touching." Sticking is a manifestation of one's internal force. To achieve the skill of sticking, you must exert relaxed force from every part of the body that is in contact with the opponent. No matter what the opponent does, he or she should always feel that you are right there and retreat is impossible. If you have the sticking force, wherever the opponent is insufficient your force will immediately begin to unbalance him or her. Through sticking force, you will make the (inexperienced) opponent feel very uncomfortable and he or she may quickly become nervous or stressed, and thereby unbalanced mentally as well as physically. By maintaining true sticking force, the opponent will feel as though "in retreating there is no escape."

Your skill at sticking is directly proportional to (1) the level of internal power developed through *wuji* and form practice, and (2) your ability, developed in push-hands training, to gauge and control the force exerted from all parts of the body that are touching the opponent. For example, if the leg and two arms are touching the opponent, internal power is constantly sent forward to the opponent through the leg and two arms. The trick is in judging how much force to use—in sticking training you learn to *calibrate* the force. If you use too much force, you might make the mistake of "attacking the opponent at his strength" or "meeting the opponent's force head-on," and you may unbalance yourself. If you use too little force, the opponent may be able to disconnect from you, or you might be too weak to neutralize the opponent's attack. Now, understand that different magnitudes of force are likely to be required simultaneously. In other words, the leg and two arms may all be required to exert different magnitudes of force at the same time. Further, as push-hands is a dynamic exercise, the situation is constantly changing. This requires a high degree of concentration and motor control—there is no way a beginning practitioner can be thinking about "pushing" a partner and at the same time concentrate on sticking/following. The second you think about "getting" the opponent, scoring a point, paying the bills, buying a birthday present, or any other thought besides sticking and listening, you will lose the sticking force.

Generally, the higher the skill at sticking, the less force the opponent will feel. At the highest level of ability, the opponent may not feel any force, only that you are constantly "there" and that he or she is ceaselessly uncomfortable and struggling to maintain balance. Realize, though, that this is a very high level of skill and motor control.

Again, I would emphasize that if insufficient force is used, there is no sticking—simple physical contact is not the sticking force. Sticking is unique in that, to maintain sticking in push-hands practice, you must actually start with more internal force than is necessary. If you only lightly touch, without exerting internal force, the opponent can easily disconnect from you. Gradually you can reduce the pressure applied and search for the perfect level of internal force expression—the minimum amount of force necessary to prevent the opponent from disconnecting and to afford instantaneous attack wherever the opponent is vulnerable. It is understandable that, confused by the apparent "lightness" of a master's touch, a Taiji practitioner could fall under the misconception that one should exert no force at all in push-hands. To the absolute contrary, one is *always* exerting force(s) in push-hands practice. The student may feel the lightness of the master's touch and not understand that this lightness was born from heaviness. Behind the master's light touch, a mountain is standing. If you don't see the mountain, he or she may be hiding the art from you.

Silk-Reeling

To maintain sticking while neutralizing an opponent's force, some technique is required—which is where silk-reeling comes in. The spiraling silk-reeling motions of Taijiquan described in Chapter 5 allow you to neutralize and lead an attack to emptiness *while at the same time* maintaining adhering/sticking force. This can be seen in the photographs shown here. Photo 9 illustrates a simple straight force exerted at the midsection of the body. Photo 10 shows this force being dissipated by a rotation of the trunk (two-dimensional rotation around the centerline of the body). The thing to understand is that the two-dimensional rotation about a central axis depicted in Photo 10 is *not* the silk-reeling force of Taijiquan. The attack may have been dissipated (a better word may be avoided) by the rotation, but the defender is now in an awkward position, cannot possibly maintain sticking force, and is subject to further attack (Photo 11). In Photos 12 and 13, the same initial attack is neutralized first by *engaging* the attack and then by the three-dimensional silk-reeling spiral about the *dantian*. The result is that (a) the attack is neutralized, (b) the defender is still

9

10   11

Photos 9–11. A force (push) is exerted toward the center of the body (Photo 9), and is avoided with a two-dimensional rotation of the waist (Photo 10). This is not the silk-reeling force of Taijiquan—the defender did not maintain the sticking force and has placed himself in a weakened position, subject to further attack (Photo 11).

sticking to the attacker and has maintained central equilibrium, and (c) the attack is simultaneously counterattacked.

As you can see, silk-reeling is critical for neutralization and simultaneous neutralization and attack. With silk-reeling, you can counterattack forward into the opponent's center without meeting the attack head-on and without surrendering ground. I've mentioned several times that a Taiji practitioner should be able to exert force in any direction with any part of the body. Silk-reeling is also integral to this ability—with coordinated silk-reeling every part of the body becomes a "hand." In this sense, "push-hands" is a misnomer. As all parts of the body contacting the opponent are exerting sticking force and are therefore employed in neutralization and attack, and because the relaxed force of Taiji strives to "unite the whole body as one family" in attacking, push-hands is clearly not just "hands" but is the entire body at work as hands. Perhaps a better name would be "push-body."

Photos 12 and 13. In this sequence, the same force is exerted toward the center (Photo 12), and is neutralized with a three-dimensional silk-reeling spiraling force (Photo 13). The result is that the attack is neutralized and the attacker is unbalanced. Because the defender has maintained sticking he may immediately counterattack (Photo 13). This is one simple example of an application of the silk-reeling force of Taijiquan.

Disappearing

In addition to learning how to unbalance a partner with an offensive attacking motion, practitioners should learn and practice the skill of disappearing. Actually, if he or she is in constant attack mode, disappearing is an easy way to unbalance your partner.

To unbalance with disappearing, you must sense and catch the moment when the partner is exerting force but has lost central equilibrium. In this situation, the partner will be relying on your body to hold him or her up.[9] At this instant, you can learn to "empty" the body part that is supporting the attacker. The attacker will feel as though the rug has been pulled out from beneath him. To disappear without opening yourself to a different attack or allowing the partner to fall into your center of balance, you must employ silk-reeling and maintain sticking force. With conscious practice, you will over time instinctively empty any body part that is being attacked while simultaneously attacking with another part. This is the skill of yin and yang interaction, both between you and your partner and within your own body structure. Of course, your "body must listen to your mind" before you can orchestrate such finely controlled body movement and expression of force.

"Use four ounces to neutralize one thousand pounds"

In Chapter 5, we introduced the famous classical saying that one should "use four ounces to neutralize one thousand pounds." As explained there, the "one thousand pounds" symbolizes brute strength and natural ability, while the "four ounces" symbolizes the relaxed, efficient internal power learned in Taiji practice. Above all, this saying refers to the internal power accumulated through practice, which I would primarily categorize as part of the acquired *gong* and not as technique. However there is, secondarily, also an aspect of technique sometimes necessary to realize the effect of "four ounces neutralizing one thousand pounds."

In order of degree, the ease with which one can neutralize an attacking force (and then counterattack) is a function of:

1. One's strength and power relative to the attacker,

2. The technique used for the neutralization,

3. The timing of the neutralization, and

4. The point of contact with the attacker and direction of counterattacking force.

It is easily recognizable that the relative power between attacker and defender is the most significant factor in ease of neutralization. A child cannot protect himself or herself from an attack from an adult because the difference in power is insurmountable. In push-hands, if practitioner **A**'s force is significantly greater than practitioner **B**'s, then practitioner **A** need only use "four ounces" of effort to neutralize, regardless of technique or timing. Although **A** is using little effort, **B** will feel as though he or she is attacking a brick wall! Anyone who practices Taiji correctly and begins by building *gong* will improve power considerably and will be unaffected by increasingly greater forces in push-hands.

As the difference in strength between practitioners becomes less pronounced, the combination of technique and timing determines the ease of neutralization, and the point of contact with the opponent and direction of counterattack determines the effectiveness of the counterattack. As we have discussed, *peng/lu/ji/an* and silk-reeling are the primary techniques of Taiji neutralization. The timing of the neutralization (and counterattack) is a function of one's agility (refer to the discussion of *"ling"* in Chapter 4) and adhering/connecting/listening skills. A function of listening skill is the ability to sense the balance and weaknesses of the opponent. Part of the efficiency of Taiji movement is the principle of giving up the "hard to push part" and attacking the "easy to push spot." Actually, this principle is not unique to Taijiquan—many martial arts emphasize directional attack toward the weakest part of the opponent.

If there is no significant difference in power between attacker and defender, and either (1) the direction of the neutralization force is inappropriate (i.e., the neutralization technique meets and struggles with the attacking force "head-on"), or (2) the timing is not correct, then one cannot achieve the effect of using four ounces to neutralize one thousand pounds.

Methods of Practice

Many different push-hands practices have been developed within the different styles of Taijiquan, but all may be classified as either "patterns" of movement in which the partners take turns attacking and neutralizing in predetermined motions, or "freestyle" playing in which the partners actively attempt to unbalance each other. Either may be practiced in a fixed stance or in moving. The progression should be from simple, fixed stance patterns to moving freestyle.

Fixed Stance Patterns

By eliminating the complicating variable of movement and maintaining a fixed step pattern, the beginning practitioner can focus on the principles and techniques of push-hands.

Exercise of *peng/lu/ji/an* is the starting point for all beginning fixed step patterns. In the simplest patterns, the attacker begins with a push straight forward into the defender, which is *ji*. The defender neutralizes the force using either *peng*, *lu*, or *an*, and then reattacks with *ji*, completing one cycle of the pattern. More complicated patterns can easily evolve by adding additional attacking motions.

Regardless of the pattern practiced, the way to learn the application of *peng/lu/ji/an* is to make the direction of attacking or neutralizing forces very clear. Most beginning students make the mistakes of (1) hurrying through the pattern, (2) smearing the direction of the forces, and (3) attacking at inappropriate times. The result of these mistakes is to break the pattern and thereby defeat the purpose of beginning push-hands, which is to understand the application of *peng/lu/ji/an*. For this reason, it is sometimes quite difficult to maintain a push-hands pattern with a beginning student. If an attacking force is inappropriately timed or directed, the pattern will be immediately broken. At this point the instructor has two options—to break Taiji principles and struggle against the force in hopes of maintaining a pattern (with the desire that the student will eventually learn), or to appropriately neutralize the ungraceful attack and thereby initiate "freestyle" playing (in which case the beginning student will have little chance of grasping even rudimentary aspects of push-hands).

In our training system, we begin with simple patterns of two forces—*peng/ji*, *an/ji*, or *lu/ji*, for example. Practicing simple, repetitious movements has the practical result of instilling habit and decreasing reaction time. As you repeatedly experience the situations in which *peng*, *lu*, or *an* are effective, you will eventually reach the level of automatically following and neutralizing an incoming force in the appropriate direction without thought or hesitation.

When you clearly understand the meaning and purpose of *peng/lu/ji/an*, the primary focus of fixed stance practice should be in learning to adhere/connect/stick/follow and "listen" to your partner. It is at this point that the internal force exchanged between the practitioners can be increased, and the push-hands pattern becomes an exercise to both improve neutralization skills and increase *gong li*. After you understand the meaning and purpose of *peng/lu/ji/an* and have learned to adhere/connect/stick/follow and "listen" to your partner, moving push-hands patterns may then be added to your practice.

Moving Patterns

In general, it is easier to neutralize a force with moving patterns, but at the same time it is more difficult while moving to maintain sticking and sinking, or *song chen*.

Stepping can easily be incorporated into fixed step patterns—the attacking practitioner can simply step forward when pushing, while at the same time the defending practitioner steps backward when neutralizing. Another traditional pattern that incorporates moving is *da lu* (大将). *Da* means "big," and *lu* is the backward/sideward energy of *peng/lu/ji/an*. In beginning *da lu* practice, movement is typically limited to one step forward or one step back. Other variations of *da lu* include linear and circular stepping patterns.

Once you have advanced to the level of understanding the principles and techniques of push-hands, you can create any fixed or moving pattern. By the time you reach this level, however, you will have realized that the benefit is in repetitiously practicing simple patterns with focused attention on sticking and listening. Freestyle push-hands can then be practiced to further develop sticking/listening and neutralizing skills and to continue acquiring appropriate habitual reactions.

Freestyle Push-Hands

Freestyle push-hands is a natural progression from fixed patterns. In freestyle playing, you continue primarily to practice the skills of sticking, listening, and neutralizing while also playfully attempting to disrupt the central equilibrium of your partner. In an unbalanced state, it is difficult if not impossible to defend yourself from attack. Conversely, if you can neutralize incoming forces and maintain central equilibrium while also destroying your opponent's center, you can attack at will. Note that the purpose or goal of freestyle push-hands (or any push-hands, for that matter) is *not* to push the opponent backward. It is to practice sticking/listening/neutralizing/central equilibrium, to continue nurturing your own internal force, and to "understand" the energy of the opponent. There are a myriad of ways in which balance is lost and the opportunity for attack is presented. In freestyle practice, you are learning to become aware of these possibilities. If your partner is unbalanced and you have maintained central equilibrium, and you *can* attack with a controlled force in any direction at any time with any part of your body, there is absolutely no need to perform the attack.

Some people revert to *fajin* in pushing hands and attempt to attack ferociously with *cai* or *lie* or *ji*, with the intention of joint locking or jerking the partner from his or her stance and thereby demonstrating their "superiority" in the art. Such persons are not practicing push-hands. Just the opposite— they are *avoiding* the sticking/listening/engagement/neutralizing/nurturing practice that is push-hands. I would recommend not engaging in push-hands with such people. If you do unexpectedly encounter such a person, protect yourself at all costs, and do not restrict yourself to the rules of friendly engagement in so doing. Push-hands is not fighting. Push-hands is nurturing—fighting is not. In push-hands, we strive to maintain sticking for the purpose of building *nei gong*, to everyone's mutual benefit. In fighting, one sticks only until one perceives that the attacker is vulnerable to counterattack (a skill that is developed in push-hands). When the opportunity is presented, one strikes immediately (at the attacker's most vulnerable target) in self-defense. The only motivation for practitioners to revert to *fajin* and demonstrate to an audience their "superiority" over another is to indulge the ego, an absolute indication that they do not understand the art of Taijiquan.

There is a simple way to know if you are practicing freestyle push-hands correctly—it is fun. Enjoy it, learn from it, build *gong*, nurture health, nurture your partner, and have fun.

Variables of Practice Methods

As noted in the introduction of this chapter, there is no one, correct way to practice push-hands. Different principles and techniques are emphasized and therefore specifically trained in different ways. The key is to understand the principles and techniques, and therefore understand the purpose or emphasis of any given method of practice, despite the many possible variables.

Significant variables in push-hands practice include (1) the distance between the practitioners, and (2) the amount of force used in practice. Generally, to learn sticking and develop internal power, range of motion, and neutralizing skills, you should practice as closely as possible to the partner with increasing pressures of internal force. To fine-tune sticking skills and develop listening, timing, and anticipatory skills, you can practice with a lighter touch (i.e., less force). We call these divisions "engaged" push-hands and "light" push-hands, and both should be practiced at variable distances. These are the yin and yang of push-hands methods.

Engaged Push-Hands. To use push-hands practice as a means to (1) continue growing internal power, (2) learn sticking and disappearing, and (3) improve neutralizing skills, you should practice with *constantly engaged* and increasingly greater force. Not, of course, the stiff force of globally contracted muscles, but the relaxed, supple and flexible power that we have built in meditation and form practice. This is the time that you learn to send your energy to your partner using *yi*. Actually, to remain engaged, you must use the relaxed, internal force. Regardless of aerobic conditioning, you will be unable to maintain engagement for an extended period using brute force. To see if you are using *yi* and *qi* or brute strength, do a simple test—can you exert real force in constant engagement with your partner without soon tiring?

To improve your neutralizing skills, you should also practice at closer and closer ranges. The closer to the body, the more difficult it is to neutralize an attacking force. The combination of increasing power at decreasing distance is the principle of training at the limits of your ability, both with respect to internal power and neutralizing skill. When practiced with large, exaggerated circles, it is also a training of flexibility or range of motion. When exchanging force with your partner at close range, look for and experience the most difficult situation and learn to neutralize it while maintaining *zhong ding*. If you experience and learn to handle the most difficult forces and angles of attack, initiated at close range, neutralizing from farther distances will seem much easier.

In the past, engaged push-hands training was considered secret and therefore was only practiced with known Taiji brothers. This training is based upon the mutual trust of the practitioners, as well as a mutual understanding of the principles involved. If you do not know your partner, do not show your power or engage him or her at close range. If you do, it is likely that he or she will not understand and may react unpredictably. Meeting a new partner from outside of your school is simply a time for getting acquainted. It is not the time for serious training of internal power and neutralizing skills. If you have grown your internal power and have learned to instinctively handle attacking forces at close range, it is easy to neutralize a force initiated from a greater distance. Until you are sure of the character, intention, knowledge, and ability of your partner, it is better to adhere lightly at arm's length and "listen" while politely exchanging token attacking actions.

Light Push-Hands. "Light handed" push-hands is the form of push-hands practice most known to the general public. This type of practice, in which only nominal force is exchanged between partners, is excellent training for listening and timing skills. During light push-hands, you can focus on sensing the opponent's energy and intention, with the goal of being able to "move before the opponent moves." Also, you can use this time to finely tune or "calibrate" your sticking force.

This facet of push-hands training is often emphasized in beginning practice because most students, when confronted with a real force, will immediately become tense and resort to brute force. Until a certain level of *gong* is acquired from correct *wuji* and form practices, the student simply has no internal force with which to practice engaged push-hands and any use of force is detrimental to progress. Realize, though, that if no force is used in attacking, anybody can neutralize with "four ounces" of effort. Until and unless force is used in attacking, the neutralization is pure pretense. Further, until internal power is understood, there is no true Taijiquan sticking force.

Here I will stress that "engaged" or "light" push-hands are only variables of practice methods. Different aspects of the art are emphasized or trained with each method. Once the principles of each method are understood and internalized, the yin and yang of both should be intertwined in practice. Hard and soft, empty and solid, light and heavy, all rely on each other and must be skillfully employed in Taiji push-hands training. This is the meaning of the verse from the classic *Song of Eight Words*:

> …If able to be light and agile, also strong and hard,
> then you will surely acquire adhere-connect stick-follow…[10]

Push-Hands from a Neural Science Perspective

By understanding the main purpose of push-hands as learning to maintain central equilibrium (i.e., posture control) in the face of perturbations, we can easily use principles of neural science to hypothesize the mechanisms utilized in push-hands practice.

Maintaining central equilibrium and effortless motor control is dependent upon a continuous flow of sensory information (visual, somatic sensory, and vestibular). Posture and movement are controlled by the motor system in two ways:

1. The nervous system monitors sensory signals and uses this information to act directly on a limb. This responsive action is called feedback.

2. Using sensory input and experience, the mind adopts a pro-active strategy and contracts muscles that will be necessary to maintain balance during an imminent disturbance. This anticipatory response is called feedforward.

Feedback Response in Push-Hands

To better understand feedback response, I will first give a simple example. With your eyes closed, extend your arm with palm up and elbow slightly bent and hold that position. Now, ask someone to press down on the palm. What was your response? For most of you, sensory neurons told the brain about the disturbance, and the brain told the biceps to contract with a force necessary to resist the downward force and hold the position.

The dynamic exercise and strategies of push-hands are much more complex than this simple example, but I believe that the sensory feedback response may be integral to the push-hands skill of "sticking." Sticking, as we have explained, requires the complete engagement of the opponent's force with a *responsive* force that is neither insufficient nor excessive. If your sticking force is insufficient, then the opponent will be able to disconnect from you, or you may be too weak to maintain your posture. If your sticking force is excessive, then you are wasting your energy, and likely unbalancing yourself or making the mistake of meeting the opponent's force head-on (i.e., struggling against the incoming force).

To maintain sticking force requires continuous "listening" (i.e., sensory input from all parts of the body touching the opponent) and adjustment of energy output in proportion to that of the opponent. The mechanisms of how one exerts force in push-hands are different and more complex that the simple example of the biceps contraction given above, but the sticking skill is still fundamentally the feedback response of the motor system—albeit one that has to be learned. From this angle, we can also say that a purpose of push-hands training is *to learn to change the pattern of feedback response.* Motor programs tell the nervous system how to respond to certain patterns of sensory information, and as mentioned in the previous chapter, motor programs are influenced by experience and learning. The basic strategy of push-hands is to engage and stick to the opponent, and to follow and lead his or her force to emptiness using directional force and spiraling movement (silk-reeling). These skills are not automatic; they must be learned.

Feedforward Response in Push-Hands

Feedforward is an anticipatory response—it happens before a force acts upon the body and is essential for rapid action. The feedforward response is obviously the neural mechanism of the famous Taiji classic, "The opponent moves, I move first."

The feedforward response relies on a fusion of information from the senses and experience. In push-hands training, it is equally important to learn by watching the opponent. Over time and with experience, you learn to anticipate the opponent's intention by the body language. It is not a mystery that a master can achieve the level of, "The opponent moves, I move first." It is simply experience from correct and dedicated practice of listening to many partners. It is part of the *gong* that is continually accumulated.

Even without sensory input, anticipatory actions born from experience are integral in maintaining balance. Here's a simple but interesting example. The first movement in most Taiji forms is "raise hands." Now, before you do raise your hands, you must modify the muscles that are contracted in your *legs.* If you don't, you will fall forward because of the change in the center of mass caused by the action of raising the arms. You don't consciously intend to change the contraction of muscles in the leg (or even realize that it is done)— it is an anticipatory feedforward response gained from experience. Even without any movement of the limbs, the contractions of the leg muscles are continuously being adjusted to compensate for the changes in center of mass that occur during breathing. (Thus, even during standing meditation, you are employing and exercising the anticipatory feedforward neural system.)

The key point is that both the feedforward and feedback neural mechanisms are simultaneously and continuously exercised in push-hands training. Both are essential for developing an effective strategy to handle a force (or imminent force) acting upon the body. Through these neural mechanisms, experience, and correct guidance from a qualified teacher, you can learn to anticipate and respond to perturbations and maintain posture and balance. The constant exercise of feedforward and feedback neural mechanisms also improves your reaction time.

Reaction Time and Sensory Input

Reaction time is shortest when you know which response you will have to make to neutralize an attacking force, and it is prolonged when you must choose among different responses. (The additional time required to choose among variable responses is called the "choice effect.") The more you practice push-hands, the more skilled you will become in recognizing and interpreting incoming forces, and the more you will know which response to use without having to weigh the pros and cons of different potential responses. In lay language, through push-hands practice we proceed from "thinking about" our movement to developing habitual and immediate reactions.

It is also true that reaction time varies with the amount of sensory input processed—the more data processed, the slower the reaction time. In push-hands, we are continually monitoring both visual input and somatic sensory stimuli from all parts of the body in contact with the opponent. One might initially think that the processing of all sensory input would argue for slower reaction times. However, it is also known that multiple stimuli and responses can be processed in *parallel pathways*, and that learning continuously improves the efficiency of parallel processing.[11] Because of the emphasis push-hands practice places on interpreting variable sensory input, I would contend that push-hands practice may also be described as a mechanism by which one improves the efficiency of interpreting stimuli through parallel processing.

Summary—From Push-Hands to Fighting

Push-hands is a critical training exercise to learn and understand the art of Taijiquan. We have described it as an advance from meditation and form practice, but it is also a means by which we come to better understand and therefore improve *wuji* and form practice.

Push-hands is not about defeating others. You need not, and indeed should not, be concerned with martial skills when practicing push-hands. A strong desire to develop fighting skills will only limit your ability to learn the art. Push-hands is about improving ourselves, practicing the principles of the art, and realizing how they are used to maintain mental and physical balance when confronted with a perturbation. It is learning about others, as well as continuing to learn about ourselves. As with all Taiji exercises, the lessons learned on a small scale in push-hands are ultimately applicable to the larger scale of everyday life. Push-hands can and should be practiced by anybody who truly wishes to learn the art and realize the full benefits of practice.

With correct practice, you will increase internal power and as a result will naturally gain confidence. Confidence, too, is a vital ingredient in maintaining *zhong ding*. This is another example of the circular, interrelated nature of building *gong*. The greater the internal power, the more confidence you will have. The more confidence, the more you will relax and continue to build internal *gongfu*.

If you efficiently practice the mental, physical, and spiritual aspects of the art, the hard and soft, empty and solid, with constant emphasis on nurturing, you can achieve a foundation of internal *gongfu* in three to five years. At this point, the fighting application and skills come very quickly. But understand that sparring or fighting applications are different from the core practices of the art, in that fighting is *using gong*, while meditation, form, and push-hands practice are *building gong*. It is undeniable that, in order to fine-tune fighting skills, you must practice them. But the amount of time that you need to practice sparring drills or "applications" is infinitesimal compared to the time that should be spent building *gong*. To ask whether a certain technique "works" for fighting applications reflects an immature understanding of the martial application of the art. Whether a technique "works" is a function of the *gong* supporting it. If you have the *gong*, if you have good health, agility, power, and a calm and peaceful mind, you have the necessary self-defense skills.

Actually, in several ways the achievement of building *gongfu* will decrease the likelihood that you will ever need to defend yourself from attack. Your confidence will increase in direct proportion to the *gong* developed. A calm and confident demeanor will go a long way in dissuading a potential attacker. Most people will only prey on those that they believe they can easily defeat. The weaker you are (or act), the more likely that someone will try to take advantage of you—in this way human beings are no different than any other animal. Conversely, if the manner in which you carry yourself exudes confidence, you are much less likely to be attacked. If you are attacked verbally, or even if someone is just sending "bad energy" your way, you will have the confidence, knowledge, and experience not to respond in kind. Your ego will no longer feel the necessity to "respond to a push with a push," and the likelihood of physical confrontation will be significantly reduced. If a physical attack does seem imminent and unavoidable, you will not fear the situation. Your confidence will be at a level at which you do not believe that the attacker can hurt you. For one, they are not agile enough to enter your space and strike you. Second, even if they do, their power is not sufficient to harm you. This confidence, this aloofness, will allow you to relax and therefore use the agility and power that you have developed. A famous saying emphasizes the importance of confidence:

艺高人胆大，胆大艺更高。

Yi gao ren dan da; dan da yi geng gao.

Higher skill will yield greater confidence;
Greater confidence can further enhance the skill.

In sensing your willingness to accept a challenge, the potential attacker may very well reconsider. More than once, someone has approached a master with the intention of attacking, only to turn back after looking him or her in the eye.

If you are in the unavoidable position of physically defending yourself, the attack will likely be fast, furious, and unpredictable. It is not possible to train defensive techniques for all potential modes of attack, and there will be no time for thinking. In real fighting, there are no techniques *per se*; there is only agility, power, confidence, and experience developed over the course of training. If "your mind is not the least bit detained," you will respond effortlessly and correctly.[12] If you haven't reached the level of martial skill to where you could always negate an attack without hurting the attacker, remember that being kind to an attacker may be an act of unkindness to yourself. Do not hesitate, and do not stop defending yourself until you know that the attacker cannot hurt you.

Yang
Nurturing

Chapter Seven

Why Practice Taijiquan?

IN DECIDING TO READ THIS BOOK, you presumably already had some interest and motivation to practice Taijiquan. Perhaps you already had an answer to "Why practice Taijiquan?" Whether you wished primarily to acquire martial arts skills or to improve your health, you will have realized by now, these are inextricably intertwined. The benefits of practicing Taijiquan correctly are many and varied, and may come as surprise additions to your original goal. Chapters 4, 5, and 6 on the core practices of meditation, Taiji form, and push-hands emphasized the reasons for practicing each of these exercises and gave some suggestions for possible neural mechanisms at work. We have yet, however, to discuss what benefits could result from practicing a complete curriculum based on these essential practices, and to summarize the neural mechanisms that may make these benefits possible.

Taijiquan is a deep and profound art, but depending upon the sincerity and adeptness of the student it is possible to realize the benefits of practice relatively quickly. Not too long ago, the door to the complete art was closed to the general public, and only the most superficial aspects were popularly known. Today, however, extensive literature and diverse instruction have paralleled the meteoric rise in the popularity of Taijiquan (as well as other internal martial arts). Many of the leading teachers in China have published books, articles, and videos and now travel worldwide sharing the art. The problem today lies not in finding direction but rather in avoiding the diluted instruction that is an inevitable result of the mass commercialization of the art. What will never change is that the art of Taijiquan cannot be fully learned from a book or videotape or weekend seminar, but must be handed to the student by a capable teacher. A good teacher is essential in communicating and demonstrating the essential principles of Taiji. The more time you spend with such a teacher, the more you will learn.

Assuming you have found quality instruction, *how you practice* determines how much you will benefit from the art. A well-known saying from the internal martial arts tradition pointedly advises:

拳贵得法。

Quan gui de fa.

To learn martial arts, the most important thing
is to practice in the proper way.

In order to "walk a straight path" and quickly realize the benefits of Taiji, you need to practice correctly and efficiently, and this book was written with these goals in mind. To practice correctly, you need to understand the fundamental principles and theories of the art without being overwhelmed or confused by sometimes intentionally obscure literature. It's best to stay grounded in reality and practical experience and not rely on your own interpretations of esoteric writings. Such conjecture, however well intended, can easily yield misguided or even preposterous conclusions. To practice efficiently, you should concentrate on the core exercises outlined in this book—*wuji* meditation, Taiji form movement, and push-hands, and limit time spent on extraneous subjects. In any endeavor, people are sometimes captivated by the elaborate and complicated. However, the core exercises of Taijiquan, the important and essential practices, are not complicated. They are simple, though not necessarily easy. The more complicated your practice, the less efficient it will be. Because Taiji is a wide art, with many different styles and options for practice, there is no shortage of potential detours. If you are lucky enough to have ample time, it is fine to follow tangents of the art that interest you. But most people today do not have a lot of time and must practice efficiently if they hope to progress. When you realize the foundation of internal *gongfu* through practicing these core exercises, all aspects of the art are within your grasp. If you do not focus on the essential foundation, however, you will never enter the door.

To understand the symbiotic relationships between different exercises and to design and practice an efficient curriculum, you should also understand the purposes of the core practices. Again, quality instruction and guidance are necessary. Do you know exactly why you practice the way you do? If you don't know where you are going, you can't possibly design an efficient way to get there. It is always fair and reasonable to ask your teacher, "Why?" Many seemingly different exercises, once understood, actually serve identical purposes. There is no need to waste time duplicating exercises to the detriment or even exclusion of other fundamental practices. You also need to be able to recognize when you have arrived at an intermediate destination, so that you can adjust your practice accordingly and continue improving without wasting time.

In order to reap the full benefits of Taijiquan practice and avoid false turns, it is important to remember in all of your practice the essential principles of nurturing and naturalness. *The straight path to realize internal gongfu is to always practice in a manner that nurtures your internal energy.* Whatever the exercise, you should focus on nurturing and developing your energy. Eventually, the habits and lessons you learn in practice will carry over into everyday life. Rather than trying to force a particular result (using physical or mental force), let things happen naturally. Taijiquan must be learned step by step; it cannot be rushed. Notwithstanding the claims of snake oil salesmen, there is no secret shortcut, no magical pill, and no mystery. The accumulation of internal *gongfu* is realized only with sincere and dedicated effort.

Once you have learned the fundamental principles and core practices of Taijiquan, the benefits of practicing a complete curriculum are real and abundant. In the following sections, I will first summarize the various benefits of an integrated approach, and then describe the neural mechanisms that may, at least in part, explain why it works the way it does.

Benefits of Taiji Practice

The table below lists some of the potential benefits claimed for Taijiquan practice. Many of these benefits of practice are well established, either from centuries of practical experience or from scientific research. Even if a benefit has been satisfactorily "proven" by Western scientific standards, it is still appropriate to refer to it as "potential," because the extent of the benefit depends upon the quality of both instruction and practice. Although the benefits listed below reflect research thus far, future research will certainly add to this list as our understanding of the benefits of practicing Taijiquan increases.

Because this book is not a complete study of the health benefits of Taiji practice, but rather a guide to the fundamental exercises of Taiji, I have divided the benefits of Taiji into primary, secondary, and holistic categories. Although these categories are certainly not mutually exclusive, Taiji was created as a martial art, and so specific benefits that yield improvements in martial skill are listed as primary, while other specific therapeutic benefits are listed as secondary and broader benefits as holistic. By no means is this categorization intended to lessen the importance of any potential benefit—it is only to emphasize why the core exercises of *wuji* meditation, form movement, and push-hands described in this book were initially created. Certainly if you begin Taiji practice hoping to improve or cure a specific medical condition, then that benefit is primary, not secondary, to you. Indeed, throughout Chinese martial arts history, many of the most famous practitioners were initially motivated to practice because of poor health. The holistic category lists benefits that are perhaps the least expected and most difficult to quantify, but sometimes recognized as the most significant in people's lives.

Potential Benefits of Taiji Practice

Primary (Skill-Related)	Secondary (Therapeutic)	Holistic
Postural control/balance	Digestion/bowel function	Avoidance or repair of stress-related injuries/illness
Flexibility	Cardio-respiratory function	
Coordination	Immune system function	
Agility	Prevention or treatment of arthritis	Social interaction/sense of community
Strength/power	Cognitive function (e.g., attention, concentration, learning, memory)	Spiritual development (calmness/peace/tranquility)
Sensitivity/awareness		
Reaction time	Prevention of osteoporosis	
Quality of sleep	Physical improvements in multiple sclerosis patients	

Primary Benefits

The primary benefits of Taiji training are the skill variables that the Taiji training system was designed to enhance. Postural control and balance, flexibility, coordination, agility, strength and power, sensitivity and awareness, reaction time, quality of sleep, and confidence—these are the *gong*, or essential foundational skills, developed through Taiji practice. They are indispensable for martial skill and are the support and foundation for technique. To be sure, strategy and technique are part of the martial training system. But without the fundamental skills, there can be no high level of *gongfu*—hence the many famous sayings in the internal martial arts tradition emphasizing the priority of accumulating *gong*.

Postural control and balance: Taiji training certainly emphasizes postural control and balance, which, along with cardio-respiratory function, are among the most commonly measured variables to date in Western scientific studies of the art. Postural control and balance are practiced in standing meditation, Taiji form, and push-hands practices.

In the relaxation of standing meditation, we nurture our awareness of body structure and the sensation of maintaining perfect balance—where the body's center of mass is held at an optimum point above the base of support. A straight, centered, and balanced body is a primary requisite of the Taiji principle of *zhong ding* (central equilibrium). The postural principles of gently straightening the spine, relaxing and "sinking and rooting" the body, and slightly bending the knees (i.e., slightly lowering the center of mass) are physical strategies for maintaining balance, and are first learned and internalized in standing meditation practice.

In contrast to standing meditation, where the center of mass is held stationary, in Taiji form practice the weight constantly flows from right to left, forward to back, and therefore the center of mass is constantly shifting within the limits of the base of support. In form movements, we thus practice maintaining *zhong ding* while moving (and therefore exerting a force) in all directions. The form movements eventually increase the range within the base of support in which we can comfortably maintain balance. As in any martial art, many of the movements are striking or kicking motions, and so in form practice we also internalize the ability to execute attacking motions without forfeiting balance. The kicking motions in Taiji provide a simple illustration. In contrast to other martial arts, which require the practitioner to lean over to a large extent to execute some of the kicks, kicking motions in Taiji are always done with a relatively straight and centered body. In the self-defense strategies of Taiji, maintaining *zhong ding* is the first priority, more so than "getting" the opponent.

Finally, the goal of push-hands training is to maintain postural control and balance while your partner is actively trying to disrupt it. Although in form movements the center of mass is purposely shifted to the limits of the base of support, in push-hands we strive to maintain the center of mass at an optimal position above the base of support. Larger movements (weight shifting or stepping) are held in reserve in case they are needed. In push-hands, the higher the skill, the less a practitioner has to move to maintain perfect balance, regardless of the force and direction of the perturbation. At the highest level of skill, the neutralizing and counterattacking motion may not even be apparent to an observer, a fact that may have contributed to the proliferation of myths about the "mysterious powers" of Taiji.

Although physical balance and postural control are among the most studied of the benefits of Taiji training, I will again emphasize that in Taiji practice, mental balance training is equally, if not more, important than physical balance training. If the mind is unbalanced, the body will soon follow. "Centering" means balance of mind *and* body—there is no *zhong ding* without a calm and centered mind.

Flexibility: Flexibility refers primarily to the range of motion around the body's joints. Taiji form movements are purposely executed in large "circles" to increase the range of motion and thus improve flexibility. In Taiji practice, we open and rotate the joints, stretch the torso, and loosen the tendons and muscles. In so doing, circulation also immediately improves—in traditional terms, the *qi* flows smoothly and unobstructed. The improvement in flexibility and circulation is immediately obvious to the practitioner.

In particular, the "silk-reeling force" that is a culmination of movement performed in accordance with Taiji principles involves the coordinated rotation and motion of all body joints. It is said that when the "eighteen balls" (i.e., the joints) are coordinated, the body becomes one "big, rotating, Taiji ball." This silk-reeling force of Taiji can only happen with a relaxed body and fluid, synchronized movement about the joints.

Coordination: It is not easy to list the myriad ways in which coordination is exercised in Taiji. All of the skills of Taiji rely upon the harmonious interaction of different systems. For example, besides simple physical strategies (i.e., postural principles) employed for maintaining balance, balance is also a function of the coordination between sensory and motor systems. Also, strength and power rely in part upon the coordinated and efficient engagement of muscles. To make the body move as one family and realize the combined force of Taiji, the practitioner must coordinate weight shifting, waist turning, and "opening and closing" of the chest, as well as learn the optimal pattern of agonist and antagonist muscle contractions. Taiji practice works to improve these interactions of the body's various systems.

A sense of rhythm is yet another aspect of coordination. The dynamic interaction of yin and yang forms the rhythm of Taiji movement. In all movement, there is the continual dance of hard/soft, high/low, store/release, light/heavy, left/right, front/back, open/close, neutralize/attack, and movement/stillness. The coordination of these "complementary opposites" must be realized to understand Taiji movement. All of these individual aspects of coordination combine to yield the fluid, controlled, and graceful movements of Taiji. I doubt that anyone can watch a skilled Taiji practitioner and not be impressed with the harmony of body movement.

Agility: Agility is a broad term that presupposes the three benefits we've already discussed—balance, flexibility, and coordination. It is also suppleness and lightness, the ability to move instantly with ease and grace. In Taiji terminology, light and instantaneous movement is referred to as *ling*. *Ling* also and importantly includes a mental aspect—it is a calm awareness that yields the ability to perceive a situation and intuit or anticipate an opponent's movement. Although it may at first seem paradoxical, it is traditionally taught that meditation practice is essential for developing the light, instantaneous reaction or movement characteristic of agility.

Taiji practice improves not only the degree of agility, but also its duration. The ability to move with agility decreases in proportion to the degree of fatigue. Taiji practice prizes the constant gathering and nurturing of energy and strives to avoid inefficient energy consumption. In this way, the Taiji practitioner learns to maintain agility in engagement, while that of a perhaps more naturally endowed opponent decreases rapidly with use of "stiff" or "brute" force.

Strength and power: In the classic poem *Treatise on Taijiquan,* Taiji is called "the science of power." But as it also emphasizes, this power is different from brute force or natural ability—it is a strength that has to be learned. According to the principles of Taiji practice, hardness comes from softness. We first have to relax and seek "softness," both to nurture and build our energy and to "de-program" our habitual tendency to stiffen the body and globally contract the muscles when threatened or needing to exert force. From this softness, we gradually develop a hardness, or tangible strength, of a distinctly different quality. In traditional terms, the power of Taiji is described as a strong and solid but also smooth, elastic, and economical force. This strength is referred to as "internal power," to distinguish it from the "external" rigid and inefficient strength of brute force or globally contracted muscles.

Again, meditation, form, and push-hands practices are all integral to the development of internal power. Standing meditation exercises are the foundation of the form movements, and internal power is first developed in standing meditation. The strength of the energy gathered from standing meditation is eventually quite obvious to the practitioner—it is an expanding, solid feeling, analogous to the elastic strength of an inflated ball. This fundamental strength is called *peng* energy. In standing meditation we are also directly exercising and strengthening the muscles that support our posture—especially, I believe, the core stabilizing muscles of the trunk, spine, and pelvis that are essential to both balance and overall power. Further, because the knees are constantly slightly bent (in both standing meditation and form practice), the leg muscles are continuously exercised and strengthened. When asked the simple question of how best to improve overall power, every master that I have studied with responded the same—do more standing meditation.

Form practice then teaches the practitioner the mechanics of efficient movement and force generation. By purposely relaxing and emphasizing intention in our motions, the body gradually and naturally adopts the ideal pattern of agonist and antagonist muscle action for the desired movement. The practitioner will then begin to feel an increased strength originating from the legs and torso. Exactly which muscles are used in Taiji movement (and standing meditation) is an interesting question and a possible subject for future research.

In addition to improving the efficiency of muscle action, Taiji practice teaches controlling the direction and magnitude of force. All form movements are intended in a specific direction, and the body must move in a coordinated manner in that direction for the individual movement to be correct. As the traditional saying states, "The released energy focuses on one point." In order to maintain your balance, force exertion must also be controlled. Force control was the subject of a study at the University of Illinois.[1] In that study, mentioned in Chapter 6, it was found that older Taiji practitioners increased both knee extensor strength and force control. This was a significant finding, as studies of traditional knee extensor strength training exercises had not found a concurrent increase in the ability to control force.

In push-hands we then (playfully) practice both issuing and controlling power with a partner. If practiced correctly in a mutually cooperative manner and with understanding of the principles and purposes of practice, push-hands is also a form of resistance training that further increases strength. The economical use of energy is also an eminent feature of internal power, which is why the classical literature of Taijiquan states, "Four ounces can deflect one thousand pounds." Push-hands provides a self-test for determining whether you are using internal power or brute force. If you are using internal force, you will tire much less quickly than a partner using brute force. This could easily be evaluated in the laboratory with simple physiologic measurements, such as heart rate and oxygen uptake, before, during, and after freestyle push-hands playing.

Sensitivity/awareness: I am not aware of any Western studies that have addressed sensitivity or awareness, likely because of difficulties in precisely defining and measuring these variables. But from my personal practice and experience, I do not hesitate to include them as important benefits and goals of the Taiji training system. The two are different, but somewhat overlapping, so I have grouped them together for the purpose of this summary.

Awareness is purely a mental function. A heightened awareness of your own body structure and physical state is developed through standing meditation, form movement, and push-hands practice. A heightened awareness of your environment, and of your reactions and interaction with the environment, naturally grows from the quietness and tranquility of meditation practice. Indeed, we can characterize meditation as a state of "quiet awareness." As Grandmaster Feng teaches, the *gongfu* of quietness and tranquility is the most important benefit of our practice.

In addition to awareness of others, sensitivity also means the capacity to respond to stimulation. Push-hands, especially, is sensitivity training. In push-hands, you are in constant contact with your partner, always trying to "listen" and sense his or her intention. The more sensitive your listening skills, the more quickly you can identify your partner's intention and the more easily you can neutralize the attack.

Reaction time: The ability to move quickly is a product of increased agility, sensitivity, and awareness. However, to decrease reaction time effectively, you must be *aware* of what responsive movement is appropriate and be *able* to execute that movement. (It does no good if you can react quickly to a car coming at you, when your reaction is to jump into the middle of the road.) The capability to move in any direction is developed in form practice. In the choreographed form movements, we practice repetitive motion in myriad directions and thereby instill a wide variety of motor programs that are eventually internalized and therefore can happen quickly without thought. One reason the Taiji form movements are practiced slowly (besides the principle of nurturing energy) is because they are different from "ordinary" movement and cannot (initially) be executed quickly and precisely, any more than a beginning violin player can pick up an instrument and immediately jump into a fast and difficult piece of music. After the movement is internalized, however, it can be done quickly with precision.

Awareness of appropriate responses comes from the experience of practicing push-hands with multiple partners. In push-hands, through good old trial and error, you learn which neutralizing movements are effective in a given situation and which are not. This experience eliminates the need to "choose" among various options, thereby decreasing reaction time.

Quality of sleep: Initially, quality of sleep might seem outside this group of skill-related benefits of Taiji practice. But in my experience good quality sleep is an important benefit of Taiji training, essential for health and accumulation of martial skills. Sleep is commonly known to consist of five cyclical stages: four distinctly different stages of non-rapid eye movement sleep and one stage of rapid eye movement sleep. Stage four is a deep level of sleep that is important for many body functions, including tissue repair, antibody production, and the regulation of various hormones and neurotransmitters.

The *qigong* meditation exercises, especially, improve the quality of sleep. The finding, mentioned in Chapter 4, that meditators had significantly higher blood melatonin levels might explain one reason why. Good sleep is not only a benefit of *qigong* meditation exercises but is also essential for doing these exercises efficiently. The traditional teaching is that physically tired persons should get rest and should not attempt to practice the meditation exercises. A physically tired person attempting meditation will tend to enter a dull, unaware stupor (or may even fall asleep), which is absolutely contrary to the state of quiet awareness and inward reflection that is the goal of meditation. If practicing repeatedly in an incorrect manner, the tired practitioner could mistakenly come to believe that a drifting or comatose daze is the correct meditative state. These persons will habitually wander down the wrong path and will neither understand meditation nor reap its benefits. (However, I should note here that traditional teachings also assert that the meditation exercises are beneficial to and should be practiced by "mentally" tired persons—they will restore the practitioner's spirit and energy.)

This is another example of the interrelated nature of the Taiji training system. The meditation practices improve the quality of sleep, and good sleep is important to practice the meditation exercises correctly. Good sleep is essential for acquiring and maintaining skill over an extended period—it is a requisite for the continual process of acquiring internal *gongfu*.

Confidence: If you are practicing correctly, you will feel the improvements in all of the above listed skill variables. Improved confidence will inevitably follow. Also, if practiced correctly, the experience at handling perturbations in push-hands will add to your confidence.

Confidence is of course a crucial aspect of martial ability, which is why I have grouped it with the primary benefits instead of the broader holistic category. Confidence grows from the accumulation of *gong*, and as noted in the famous saying quoted in Chapter 2, "First *gong*, second confidence, third technique," is ultimately is more important than technique. Given any two persons with approximately equal skills and physical abilities, confidence is the determining factor in deciding the victor. Rarely, if ever, has anyone walked away from a confrontation saying, "I didn't think I would win."

The observant reader may have recognized that, though Taijiquan is a martial art, all of these skill-related benefits are, fundamentally, also health benefits. That is why there is no possible way to separate the health and martial aspects of the art. If you don't have good health, you can't possibly develop your martial skill. In fact, the principles of practice assert that you should not be overly concerned with acquiring fighting skill—such an attitude will, in many ways, prevent you from acquiring all of the fundamental *gong*. If you shortsightedly practice in a manner that does not nurture your health and energy, any martial ability that is gained will be short-lived. Ultimately, we should look to the examples of the true masters of the art. Those who have practiced correctly are strong and vibrant well into their senior years.

Other Therapeutic Benefits

Over the years, Taijiquan has become well known as an exercise to maintain and restore health. The reported therapeutic benefits of Taiji include, among other things, improvements in digestion and bowel function, cardio-respiratory function, immune system, and cognitive function (e.g., attention, concentration, learning, memory). Physical and psychosocial improvements in multiple sclerosis patients have also been documented, and Taiji is often cited as beneficial in the prevention or treatment of arthritis and osteoporosis. The reported therapeutic benefits have received sporadic attention within the Western scientific community. Some benefits, like bowel function, have not been studied at all and are only known anecdotally, whereas others have been evaluated in several excellent studies. Considering the primary benefits of the art and the potential neural mechanisms of practice discussed below, many other illnesses could easily be added to this list of potential therapeutic benefits. For example, the better quality sleep realized from practice could help fibromyalgia patients (who frequently suffer from poor quality sleep), and the multiple neural mechanisms involved suggest potential application in the treatment of neural dysfunctions such as Parkinson's disease.

The purpose of this book is to explain Taiji practice, and so a thorough evaluation of all documented, reported, or potential health benefits is beyond the scope of this work. For those interested, I have included as Appendix II a summary of select Taiji studies completed since 1987. This appendix includes the author, year, study design, subject groups, and a summary of the findings. Full references for the studies are found in Research References.

Holistic Benefits

Still other benefits of Taiji practice include avoidance or repair of stress-related injuries or illnesses, opportunity for social interaction and a sense of community, and spiritual development. These are somewhat broader benefits, and so I have separated them from the skill-related or other therapeutic groupings.

Stress is widely regarded as the underlying cause of many illnesses. The American Institute of Stress, quoting a 1983 *Time* magazine article, refers to stress as America's number one health problem.[2] Stress can be measured by testing for physiological responses characteristic of sympathetic dominance, such as increases in blood sugar, heart rate, and blood pressure. Taiji, of course, is designed to teach practitioners to relax and thereby reduce or avoid stress. A traditional saying emphasizes the role of stress reduction through practice of Taiji (or any *qigong*) in healing:

气功能祛病，缘由在松静。

Qigong neng qu bing, yuan you zai song jing.

Song (relaxation) and *jing* (tranquility/quietness)
are the reasons why *qigong* can heal.

Unfortunately, as mentioned in Chapter 5, a frequent problem with beginning students is that their stress often increases because of the tensions and difficulties of learning choreographed movement and "keeping up with the rest of the class." It is the responsibility of the instructors to emphasize and remind the students to relax in practice—it does not matter in the least how quickly they learn the choreography. Nor does it matter how many different sequences of movements are learned because, once you understand the principles and mechanics of Taiji motion, any movement can be done as Taiji movement. Because the level of exertion is easily adjustable, everyone, regardless of age or natural ability, can learn the form movements. Just relax, and understand Taiji practice as a continual process of acquiring *gong*. There is no hurry.

In the Chinese martial arts traditions of both internal and external styles, the school is considered a second family. The instructor is called teacher/father or teacher/mother, and fellow students are referred to as brothers or sisters. In Chapter 3, I mentioned the traditional saying, "Different spirits won't enter the same temple"; that is, kindred spirits will tend to select the same teachers and schools. Over time, strong friendships are forged between fellow students, and these friendships are certainly a valuable benefit.

Chapter 2 discussed the spiritual aspects of Taiji practice at length, and throughout the book, I have emphasized the importance of developing a spiritual calmness, peace, and tranquility. Every human activity, if done in awareness, can be a spiritual exercise. Taiji is no exception. As Chen Xin wrote, Taiji is a little dao from which the big Dao can be glimpsed.

The skill-related, therapeutic, and holistic benefits described above are some of the main reasons for practicing Taiji. In addition to this rather dry table of benefits, I would add one other important reason why you would practice Taiji—because it is fun, and to summarize all the potential benefits, it just makes you feel good. Taiji practice is serious, but it is also fun and joyous and should make you feel happy. This too, of course, is an important holistic health benefit. There is a Chinese saying:

笑一笑，十年少；愁一愁，白了头。

Xiao yi xiao, shi nian shao; chou yi chou, bai le tou.

Smile one smile and you are ten years younger.
Add more worries and you gain more white hair.

Possible Neural Mechanisms of Practice

Why does Taiji produce so many varied and significant benefits? The nurturing principles of *qigong* in general, and the Taiji training system in particular, are quite different from the "no pain, no gain" mentality of many exercise regimens, and that is likely a reason why they are so broadly effective. But I believe we can now start to look deeper and identify the mechanisms at work. In concluding Chapters 4, 5, and 6, I described several neural mechanisms that may help to explain why Taiji works the way it does. It is possible that standing and sitting meditation, form practice, and push-hands all directly exercise and develop specific aspects of the nervous system. Taken together, practicing the complete Taiji curriculum may be a holistic approach to heighten the function and efficiency of the entire central and peripheral nervous system.

Sitting and standing meditation exercises are a common foundation of all internal martial arts. Scientific studies have measured physiologic responses in both novice and advanced sitting meditators. The physiologic patterns observed in beginning meditators are characteristic of a decrease in sympathetic activity and marked increase in parasympathetic dominance. The physiologic pattern in beginning meditation stages is so familiar it is now referred to by the scientific community as the "relaxation response." But the switch to parasympathetic dominance is only the gateway to deeper meditation and ultimate modification and control of both sympathetic and parasympathetic activity. The practical benefit of the *"gong"* of calmness and autonomic control accumulated in sitting meditation practice is that the adept practitioner, when confronted with a threatening or stressful situation, can remain relaxed and alert and is not controlled by the "fight or flight" extreme of sympathetic activity that is the ordinary response to danger or stress. (Of course, other variables such as confidence and experience also affect the ability of a person to remain calm.)

Another possible mechanism to explain improvements in agility traditionally attributed to sitting meditation is that sitting meditation may encourage the synthesis of neurotransmitters and/or specific or optimal neurotransmitter profiles that are essential for coordinated movement. For example, in the study referred to in Chapter 4, significant increases in dopamine were documented in meditators.[3]

Relaxation in standing meditation is a conscious and fundamental exercise of sensory and motor systems and the integration of these systems. In standing meditation, we exercise posture control by processing the continual flow of sensory information (visual, somatosensory, and vestibular) and learning to adopt the ideal patterns of contraction and relaxation of agonist and antagonist muscle groups. It is exercise of both the efficient use and strength of muscles. The efficient employment of muscle groups is a key aspect of the soft, elastic, "internal" power of Taiji, in direct contrast to the rigid and stiff force of globally contracted muscles. How directly or deeply (and therefore how efficiently) you exercise these various aspects of the nervous system is a function of how deeply you can enter a state of "quiet awareness" during practice.

After realizing the fundamental improvements afforded by standing and sitting meditation, we then further develop the somatic sensory system in form and push-hands practice. In practicing moving *qigong* or form, we are consciously improving our agility/coordination and ability to execute a desired motion, which is to say that we are practicing our motor skills. Every form is movement toward a goal, and the knowledge of that goal (i.e., intention) is a critical aspect of practice. Ultimately we want to develop our ability to the level at which we can move in any direction, at any time, with any part of our body, with desired speed and magnitude, and do so as efficiently as possible with no wasted or extraneous motion. The motor programs of Taijiquan are relatively complex and must be learned—they are gradually realized only through slow practice. The repetitious practice of the coordinated and efficient choreographed movements of Taiji could possibly provide researchers with a means to further investigate how the brain is involved in motor programming and to explore connections between the prefrontal cortex (responsible for initiation and programming of motor sequences), the dorsal and ventral striatum of the basal ganglia (responsible for habit formation), and the cerebellum (responsible for balance and coordination and control of voluntary movement). The balance between the inhibitory basal ganglia and excitatory cerebellum systems is perhaps significantly "optimized" in the controlled and coordinated movements of Taiji.

To round off this complete exercise program of neural function, we then practice push-hands as a direct exercise of our sensory "feedback" and predictive "feedforward" neural systems. In push-hands, we experience, sense, and learn to predict physical perturbations and subsequently train the body to adjust to or neutralize the perturbation with the ultimate goal of always maintaining our physical and mental central equilibrium. A Taiji strategy for accomplishing this is to "stick" and "listen" to the partner. To learn the skill of sticking, we must learn to maintain constant contact with the partner and to exert a responsive force that is neither insufficient nor excessive. If the force is insufficient, the partner can easily disconnect from us. If it is excessive, we are making the mistake of matching force against force, and we may also unbalance ourselves. This calibrated, responsive force of sticking is a continual and focused exercise of the feedback neural system.

Through experience, we learn to recognize and interpret incoming forces and determine effective neutralizing motions, which is the feedforward neural mechanism. The response time to a disturbance is ultimately decreased by a combination of experience (which decreases the choices necessary) and, possibly, by increased efficiency of parallel sensory input processing.

Closing

Understanding the Complete Art

In writing this book, I have tried to go beyond merely illustrating form movements or applications. My hope is that I have at least introduced the complete art, including mental, physical, and spiritual aspects, and explained the principles and methods of practice that will allow you to realize the full potential benefits of Taijiquan as quickly as possible. If nothing else, you should now understand that the core practices of *wuji* meditation, form movement, and push-hands are essential and interrelated, and that Taijiquan is much more than repetitious practice of a choreographed, slow movement form.

I have also attempted to detail the fundamental principles and criteria for Taiji form movement beyond the superficial differences of common "styles." Any choreographed form, if it is correct and performed in accordance with those principles, will teach the practitioner the mechanics of powerful movement and expression of force. The myriad combinations of *peng/lu/ji/an/cai/lie/zhou/kao* contain all possibilities of direction, duration, and length of force, and all Taiji movement, if done correctly, will yield the twining/spiraling movements of the silk-reeling force. Taiji movement is practice of hard and soft, opening and closing, storing and releasing, neutralizing and attacking—*yin* and *yang* continually flowing in rhythm. Once the movement is understood and internalized, any movement can be done as Taiji movement, and in fact this level must be achieved before a practitioner can apply the art in a freestyle fighting situation. The manner in which an advanced practitioner will express movement in his or her form practice is ultimately a function of personality, knowledge, physical body structure and capability, and spirit. To be sure, there are differences in *theories* of practice (e.g., speed of movement, height of stance, amount of explosive force expressed, etc.), and these differences can be *very* important. But at some point in your practice the difference between the form movements themselves should melt away completely.

Traditional Teachings and Modern Research

I have observed with interest how many Westerners view Taiji (and other Asian arts) as a mysterious Oriental practice. While this perception will always yield a certain baseline of interest, in the long run it is not at all helpful in bringing the many potential benefits of Taiji practice to the largest possible audience. To broadly communicate the methods, principles, and benefits of practice, I have interwoven contemporary explanations with traditional sayings and language. In so doing, I hope that the ideas have been made clear, or that I have at least introduced a different angle from which you can ponder the art. We should look to Western science to further understand the art, but at the same time we should not discard the traditional language and theory as antiquated or useless. Traditional sayings and teachings have helped people to learn the art for centuries; why cast them aside now? The traditional teachings also serve to indicate potential directions for future scientific research. For example, knowing the (formerly quite secret) traditional teaching that sitting meditation can improve agility allows us to formulate otherwise unforeseen hypotheses on the relationship between *wuji* meditation practice and the nervous system. I view traditional Eastern theory and the Western scientific approach as complementary opposites—yin and yang. Both can help us to further our understanding and continue to improve our practice.

Although the contemporary terminology and ideas presented herein may at times appear over-simplified to the scientist, another purpose of this book was to situate Taiji in the realm of scientific concepts and to forward hypotheses that may, in part, explain the mechanisms of practice. With the burgeoning interest in Taiji by the Western scientific community, I also hope that this book will serve as a resource for those planning research studies. I did not hesitate to include benefits that have not yet been thoroughly evaluated through scientific methods in the listing of benefits above, fully hoping that the potential for the benefit may spark interest in concerned researchers.

However, it is imperative that the Western scientific community understands the art of Taiji if they are to validly evaluate its mechanisms and benefits. Of immediate concern, none of the Western studies to date has included, or even mentioned, *wuji* meditation training, which is a fundamental component of the Taiji curriculum that can and should be practiced in the earliest stages of learning. (Push-hands, too, is a pillar of Taiji practice, but it cannot be practiced in any real degree until a foundation of skill is dveloped through *wuji* meditation and form training.) It would be a disservice to our understanding of Taijiquan and humanity if future scientific research were founded on an incomplete understanding of the art. It is absolutely the responsibility of those conducting research to search out competent advisors.

Lastly, I hope I've not been too successful in explaining theory, to the point where intellectual understanding is confused with true experiential knowing. No number of my words will make the art fully clear—it is a path you must walk to understand. I hope this book will help you to walk a straight path. One final word of advice:

Duo zhuyi yang sheng

Pay attention to nurturing!

A Brief History of Taijiquan and the Modern Chen Style

BEFORE TACKLING THE SUBJECT OF THE HISTORY OF TAIJIQUAN, I wish to alert the novice Taiji student that the origin of the art has long been controversial. Sound historical documentation on the origins and early transmission of the art is scarce, and what documentation is available is patchy and sometimes contradictory. For example, consider the writings of Li Yiyu (1832–1892), author of several seminal Taiji texts and student of Wu Yuxiang (1812–1880), the founder of the Wu/Hao style of Taijiquan. The 1867 *Ma Tongwen* manuscript of Li Yiyu's *Short Preface to Taijiquan* names the Daoist Zhang Sanfeng as the creator of Taiji. By 1881, however, in the *Three Old Manuscripts* version of this same verse, Li Yiyu had apparently changed his mind when he wrote, "The creator of Taijiquan is unknown."[1]

Partisan camps are loath to admit that the founder of their style may have studied from a master of a "competing" family style. It is not surprising, then, that many of the origin theories espoused by Taijiquan practitioners attempt both to validate their form as the true progeny of their proposed creator of Taijiquan, and to downplay or even exclude the possible influence of other styles. The scarcity of historical documentation and the abundance of loopholes within that documentation certainly provide opportunities for creative minds to advance self-serving theories. Even unbiased scholars—if there is such a thing—disagree on such matters as authorship of classical texts and the historicity of certain key figures. To the scholars, I would say, "research on"—the information at least provides interesting reading. To the bickering partisan camps, I would invite you to look inward and evaluate your motives. To those interested in realizing the benefits of the art (those for whom this book is written), I would say that it doesn't matter who history credits for creating

Taijiquan. The writer, E.L. Doctorow, I think had it right: "History is the present. That's why every generation writes it anew. But what most people think of as history is its end product, myth."[2] What does matter is the knowledge and quality of your teacher, and the effort that you put forth to understand and learn the art.

I will further preface this "brief history" with the disclaimer that I am not a trained historian and have done no significant research of my own. Here I am only summarizing what others have already reported. My purpose is simply to provide an outline for interested readers who may not yet be familiar with the history of the art. Other, much more complete, works on the history of Taiji are available, and the reader should refer to those for a more thorough exposition. Douglas Wile's *Lost T'ai-chi Classics from the Late Ch'ing Dynasty* (1996), in particular, is an excellent and well-balanced scholarly work.

Theories of Origin

The two principal creators of Taijiquan championed by different camps are **Chen Wangting** (1600–1680) of the Chen Village in Henan province, and **Zhang Sanfeng**, an "immortal" Daoist.[3] Most accounts of Zhang place him in the Ming dynasty (1368–1644) but mention no association with martial arts, while others that do mention martial arts place him in the Song dynasty (960–1279).[4] Those trying to discredit the originality of the Chen family style have offered various suppositions as to how the art was later transmitted to the Chen Village. The scholar Xu Zhen (1898–1967) argued that the mysterious **Wang Zongyue** brought the art to the village,[5] while his contemporary, Tang Hao (1897–1959), concluded from the same evidence that Wang Zongyue was a student and recorder of the Chen masters.[6] Others variously posit that **Jiang Fa**, another mysterious figure of unaccounted origin, taught either Chen Wangting or **Chen Changxing** (1771–1853) in the Chen Village or brought the art to the nearby Zhaobao Village.[7]

The various theories on the origins of Taijiquan are perhaps best summarized by Douglas Wile in his excellent work *Lost T'ai-chi Classics from the Late Ch'ing Dynasty*. Wile distills the competing camps into two groups — the "idealists" or "fundamentalists" who emphasize the priority of Daoist philosophy in the development of the internal arts, and the "materialists" or "evolutionists" who argue the origins based on transmission of form. Wile writes, "It is this radical bifurcation of perspectives that causes idealists to dismiss Ch'en Village as a hick town and Wang-t'ing as a lowly militia battalion commander, and materialists to minimize the perennial influence of Taoist ideas and the possibility of multiple advents of old wine in new bottles." While relatively few argue the "materialist" view that all modern orthodox forms of Taijiquan evolved from teachings in the Chen Village, it is also true that a tradition of "internal martial arts" is mentioned in texts predating, or are parallel to the early years of, Taijiquan. For example, the writings of Chang Naizhou (1724?–1783?), a native of Sishui (the modern Xingyang) in Henan, are similar in tone and content, and sometimes parallel, the Wu/Li classical texts and Chen Xin's (1849–1929) writings from the Chen Village.[8] Also, advocates of Zhang Sanfeng frequently quote Huang Zongxi's (1610–1685) *Epitaph for Wang Zhengnan*:

> The Shaolin Temple is famous for its fighting monks. However, their art stresses only offense, which allows an opponent to take advantage of this for a counter-attack. Then there is the so-called internal school that uses stillness to control movement and can easily throw an opponent. Therefore we call Shaolin the External School. The Internal School originated with Chang San-feng of the Sung dynasty.[9]

As Wile points out, however, there is no way to draw a line connecting the fragments of "internal school" references with the art developed in the Chen Village. An obvious resolution to the debate is to accept that, although the Chen villagers obviously did not invent the characteristically Daoist theories common to the broader category of "internal martial arts," they did assimilate these pre-existing ideas, and other martial arts styles, in forging their own unique art.

Wile resolves the discrepancy between the idealist and materialist camps in the following manner:

> When tracing the origins on the level of theory, one is free to go all the way back to the Lao Tzu and *I Ching*, add any number of legendary Taoists and martial arts heroes and pick up the Internal School on the way to Ch'en Village or Chao-pao. However, if one is tracing the evolution of a specific movement form, then, starting with Yang and Wu, one works backward to the Chen family, Ch'i Chi-kuang, and his antecedents.[10]

Either way, the evolution of modern Taiji goes through the Chen family village, and so it is there that I will focus.

History of the Chen Family Style
and Evolution of Modern Styles of Taijiquan

The history of Chen style Taiji begins with Chen Wangting, a 9th-generation descendent of the Chen family. *The Genealogy of the Chen Families* attests that it was he who originated the Chen family martial art:

> Wangting, alias Zouting, was a knight at the end of the Ming dynasty and a scholar in the early years of the Qing Dynasty. Known in Shandong Province as a master of martial arts, defeating once more than 1000 "bandits," he was the originator of the bare-handed and armed combat boxing of the Chen school.[11]

In Chen Wangting's own words:

> Recalling past years, how bravely I fought to wipe out the enemy troops, and what risks I went through! All the favors bestowed upon me are now in vain! Now old and feeble, I am accompanied only by the book of 'Huang Ting.' Life consists in creating actions of boxing when feeling depressed, doing fieldwork when the season comes, and spending leisure time teaching disciples and children so that they can become worthy members of the society.[12]

Tang Hao concluded from his research that the original Chen family art compiled by Chen Wangting contained seven routines—a 108-posture "Long Range Boxing" form, five sets of forms collectively referred to as the "13 Postures," and Cannon Boxing, or *Pao Cui*. There are several existing texts from the Chen Village that document the old form practices, including: *Book of Wenxiu Hall, Sanxing Version, Boxing and Weapons Collection — Chen's Notes from Liangyi Hall*, and *Boxing and Weapon Collection of Chen Family Passed Through Generations*.[13] These texts, however, give contradictory explanations for the classification of "Cannon Boxing" and the names of the five sets of forms of the "13 Postures." For example, the Liangyi Hall version includes "Cannon Boxing" as the second of the five sets of 13 Postures, but the (likely older) Wenxiu version states that the second and third sets of the 13 Postures were lost, and mentions "Cannon Boxing" apart from the remaining first, fourth, and fifth sets of the 13 Postures.[14]

Although the extent to which is not known, Chen Wangting did borrow from pre-existing martial arts when compiling the movements of his forms. Tang Hao noted that (1) 29 of 32 forms recorded in late Ming Dynasty general and national hero Qi Jiguang's (1528–1587) *Cannon of Boxing* are contained in the seven sets of routines created by Chen Wangting, and (2) Chen Wangting copied lines of text for his *Song of the Cannon of Boxing* from Qi Jiguang's *Cannon of Boxing*.[15] The Chen family texts suggest the possible influence of pre-existing arts such as *Taizu* Long Range Boxing (*Taizu Chang Quan*), and *Duan Da*. For example, the last two verses of the *Sanxing Version's* boxing formula for the fourth set of the 13 Postures suggest, "If you want to know where this martial art comes from, the answer is *Taizu Xia Nan Tang*."[16] (*Taizu* Long Range Boxing is one of sixteen martial arts compiled in Qi Jiguang's *Cannon of Boxing*.) Further, the Chen family texts separate the old Chen family art into either "long-range" or "short-range" boxing techniques. *Duan Da*, a well-known short-range boxing style, is listed by name among the several short-range forms or techniques identified. Weapons forms mentioned in the Chen family texts also implicate pre-existing sources. For example, Tang Hao found that some stick postures were identical to Shaolin postures (the stick was reportedly a favorite weapon of Shaolin monks), and the "24 Spears" mentioned in spear registers are identical with those described in Qi Jiguang's *New Book of Effective Techniques* (*Ji Xiao Xin Shu*).[17] Gu Liuxin (1908–1991), a martial arts scholar and one of the 18th-generation representatives of the Chen style, concludes in his introduction to *Chen Style Taijiquan*, "Though it is impossible to verify what he assimilated specifically from boxing of other schools, it can be presumed from the great number of forms in his seven sets of shadow boxing routines that Chen also absorbed many strong points of boxing of many schools existing at the time."[18]

While Chen Wangting borrowed external form movements from existing arts, he also forged new boxing theories, presumably influenced by Daoist philosophical principles and practices such as those detailed in the Daoist text *Huangting Jing*.[19] Chen Wangting's *Song of the Canon Boxing* begins with the verse, "Changes of actions such as extending and bending are so unexpected as to be totally unpredictable, I rely on all kinds of subtle body movements such as twisting and swirling." Tang Hao noted that these words express principles of body movement that are totally absent in books on martial arts by late Ming Dynasty authors.[20] The 17th-century description of movements as "twisting and swirling" immediately brings to mind the *chansi jin* or "silk-reeling force," a principal characteristic of the Chen family art today.

Following the cultural norm, Chen Wangting's art was passed to successive generations of the Chen family. After five generations, the art was received by the 14th-generation practitioners **Chen Changxing** (1771–1853) and **Chen Youben** (1780–1858). This was a seminal period in the history of Taiji, as it (1) marked both the genesis of divisions within the Chen family style and the birth of other modern styles of Taiji, and (2) was the period in which the first and second routines of the Chen family style, still practiced today, were created.

Chen Youben was reportedly a top master of the Chen family art. The *Genealogy of the Chen Family* states,

> Chen Youben and his brother Chen Youheng were both Xiang Sheng (students of the ancient local school) and learnt Taijiquan, especially (Chen) Youben, who received "the dragon's pearl" (i.e., true transmission of Taijiquan), and trained his sons and brother's sons in the art (of Taijiquan), had a modest carriage, always as if (his skill) was inferior (to others), at that time most of [the] people who excelled in Taijiquan were his disciples…(Chen) Youben's disciples—Chen Qingping, Chen Youlun, Chen Fengzhang, Chen Sande, Chen Tingdong had certain achievements, Chen Gengyun also called him [Chen Youben] a teacher.[21]

Although there are diverse explanations for how and why, Chen Youben's art became variously labeled as both a "new style" and a "small style," differentiated from other forms which were labeled "old style" or "big style." These labels were added by significantly later generations of practitioners or researchers, and I am aware of no textual evidence that anyone in Chen Youben's time, or even up to two generations later, considered his art as a variant style. We will discuss this further in the sections below on old versus new and big versus small styles.

It was also at this time that Chen Changxing is credited with condensing the movements from Chen Wangting's seven sets into the first routine (*yilu*) and second routine (*erlu*, or *paocui*), which are still practiced today. By most accounts, Chen Wangting's original forms included rigorous movements designed for battlefield training prior to the introduction of firearms. This makes sense, as much of his life was spent in such combat. After the introduction of firearms, some of the movements were outdated and no longer practical and were dispensed by Chen Changxing when he arranged the first and second routines.

Besides composing the first and second routines, Chen Changxing is also famously known as the teacher of **Yang Luchan**. Reliable, specific details of Yang's life are sparse and stories of how he came to practice in the Chen Village vary, but his assimilation and interpretation of the art were most certainly crucial in the history of Taiji. Yang Luchan then traveled to Beijing, where he quickly became a renowned martial artist and earned the title, "Yang the Invincible." Yang Luchan's descendents openly taught a modified version of the Chen form in Beijing, and therefore first opened the potential benefits of the art to the public. The Chen family did not openly teach their art until the 1920s to 1930s, when **Chen Ziming** (?–1951, 17th-generation), **Chen Fake** (1887–1957, 17th-generation), and **Chen Zhaopei** (1883–1972, 18th-generation) all taught outside of the Chen Village.

With this background, we can now outline the widely accepted evolution of the five most popular modern styles of Taijiquan: Chen, Yang, Wu, Wu/Hao, and Sun. Yang style originated from Yang Luchan, who learned from Chen Changxing of the Chen Village. Wu style originated from **Wu Quanyou** (1834–1902), who had studied with Yang Luchan. **Wu Yuxiang** also studied from Yang Luchan, and learned the small frame of the Chen style from **Chen Qingping** (1795–1868), eventually creating the Wu/Hao style. **Sun Lutang** (1861–1932) created the Sun style after studying in a direct line of descendents from Wu Yuxiang. (Sun learned from **Hao Weizheng** (1849–1920), who had learned from **Li Yiyu** (1832–1892), who had learned from Wu Yuxiang.)

The most recently recognized "style" of Taiji to emerge is that of my teacher, **Feng Zhiqiang** (b. 1928) of Beijing. Since the late 1990s, his training curriculum has been referred to as *Chen Style Xinyi Hunyuan Taiji* (sometimes simplified to *Hunyuan* Taiji). For many years he was pressured to call his art "Feng Style," but out of humility he refused to do so. "Chen Style" and "Xinyi" refer to the fact that he was a top student of, and deeply respects, both Chen Fake (a 17th-generation master of the Chen family style) and Xinyi master **Hu Yaozhen** (1879–1973). The term *"hunyuan"* (unified, primordial) is generally revered within the Chinese internal martial arts community for its depth of meaning, and is commonly referenced by different internal martial art styles.

This is, of course, a much abbreviated description of the evolution of only a few of the modern styles of Taiji. Each deserves its own book on the topic, but here I will focus specifically on developments of the modern Chen style.

Chen Style—Old versus New, Big versus Small

Within the Chen style today, there are divisions of old and new, big and small styles. The differentiation between old and new styles, especially, is a source of considerable confusion and dispute. There is no definitive, non-partisan conclusion, but I will summarize common opinions of what constitutes old and new styles, and show why these differing views are quite natural and to be expected. We'll then revisit the issue of big and small styles, practiced in both Zhaobao and the Chen Village.

Before beginning, one point should be made clear. All of these distinctions of old, new, big, or small are relatively recent. Chen Xin's *Illustrated Explanations of Chen Family Taijiquan* makes no mention of these styles, but he does write, "I am afraid of the passing of time and impatient to wait anymore; I'm also afraid that (the martial art) will divide into schools and branches and true knowledge will be lost. For this reason in my leisure time I do my outmost [*sic*] to explain and clarify deep secrets [of the art], and describe it in great detail."[22] This passage hints that divisions may have been starting to brew within the Chen Village even during Chen Xin's time.

Old Style (*Laojia*) versus New Style (*Xinjia*)

The first assessment of old and new styles occurs in the research of Tang Hao in the 1930s. Tang stated that Chen Youben created a "new style" by dispensing with some of the more rigorous movements of the traditional form.[23] Chen's new style, passed on through his nephew Chen Qingping, soon became known as the "small style." Small style practitioners, however, while acknowledging a difference between big and small styles, strongly deny that Chen Youben created a new style or, as claimed by Tang, that he intentionally dispensed with difficult movements. (Refer to the following section for further discussion of small style.)

My teacher, Feng Zhiqiang, offers a different view of old and new styles. In an interview conducted for *T'ai Chi Magazine*, Master Feng explained that "old style" referred to Chen Wangting's original forms, and that the significant modifications by Chen Changxing were a "new style."[24] This is an eminently logical explanation, as this surely marked the most significant form change between generations. According to this view, the old style no longer exists, since no one practices the extensive forms initially created by Chen Wangting.

A more recent explanation of old and new styles refers to the unique form movements developed by Chen Fake in his later years in Beijing, and inherited by his youngest son, **Chen Zhaokui** (1928–1981). Chen Fake left the Chen Village to teach in Beijing in 1928, and he lived there until his death in 1957. Chen Fake's youngest son, Chen Zhaokui, first returned to visit the Chen Village in 1965.[25] The villagers immediately perceived external differences between Chen Zhaokui's form movements and the traditional form being taught by **Chen Zhaopei** (1893–1972), the top 18th-generation teacher in the village at that time. **Wu Xiubao** (b. 1931), a student of both Chen Zhaopei and Chen Zhaokui, explains that Chen Zhaokui's form was different in that: (1) it contained relatively more *fajin* that was executed over shorter distances (i.e., more "inch force"), (2) it contained relatively more "tight and refined" silk-reeling circles, and (3) it was performed in a lower stance than the form taught by Chen Zhaopei. These differences eventually led some to characterize Chen Zhaokui's form as a "new style," versus the "old style" form taught by Chen Zhaopei. This modern understanding of the new style has gained momentum and is advanced by 19th-generation practitioners today. One wonders, however, if Chen Fake had not left the Chen Village, whether his form movements would have been labeled "new," or if, as the leading master of the 17th generation, his teachings would have simply been assimilated into the village art.

Old and new designations are, of course, entirely relative, and it is to be expected that different generations would have different opinions. To me, the various incarnations of "new styles" simply reflect the fact that Taiji is a living art, necessarily and constantly molded by the unique understandings and insights from each successive generation—it is not and cannot possibly be rigidly locked to the understandings of previous generations. For example, no one knows exactly what Chen Wangting, or even Chen Changxing, thought, practiced, and taught. Further, the *art* of Taiji is ultimately a manifestation of one's entire being—physical, mental, and spiritual. No two artists can produce the same work, and no two masters look alike. In this light, the greatest practitioners from every generation represent and pass on a "new style" to succeeding generations.

Big Style (*Da Jia*) versus Small Style (*Xiao Jia*)

Today, there is an accepted differentiation of "big" and "small" frame versions of the Chen style, but as you might have guessed, there is disagreement on the origins of these forms. When discussing big and small frame form versions, inevitably the question arises as to which came first, followed just as inevitably by a divergence of opinion. The reader is forewarned—the discussion of big and small frame versions, in combination with the various old and new characterizations, can get quite confusing. Don't try to reconcile the ensuing discussion of big and small with the above discussion of old and new—I will summarize all for you after introducing the big and small frame versions.

As their names imply, the big and small forms differ in the size, or range of motion, of external form movement. The small frame form is not as well known as the big frame, simply because the exponents of small style did not, historically, engage in teaching outsiders to the extent that big style practitioners have. Chen Fake, who was among the first and possibly most well known to teach the Chen family style outside of the village, was a big style practitioner, as are many of the current generation of well-known Chen style masters. This is beginning to change, however, as small style teachers are now reportedly also beginning to teach outside of the Chen Village.

A small frame form is practiced both in the Chen Village and nearby Zhaobao Village. As noted above, Tang Hao claimed that Chen Youben created a new style, which, passed on through his nephew and student Chen Qingping, soon became known as the "small style." After marriage, Chen Qingping lived in the nearby Zhaobao Village, and many claim this to be the origin of the art, known as Zhaobao style, still practiced in that village. (Many Zhaobao advocates, however, assert that Jiang Fa originated the art of Taiji in the Zhaobao Village. Refer to Endnote 7 for further discussion of Jiang Fa.) Contemporary small style practitioners within the Chen Village are led by the 18th-generation representatives **Chen Kezhong** and **Chen Boxiang**.

According to Tang Hao's characterization, the form version practiced by Chen Changxing would be the corresponding "big style." And, since Tang Hao claimed that the small style was new, by elimination Chen Changxing's big frame version must be the older form. (Confusing, isn't it?) Small style practitioners, however, object to the classification of their style as "new," claiming that the big style was developed after the small style, and therefore the small style is the older of the two. Small style advocates anecdotally assert that Chen Youben created the *big* style specifically for the purpose of teaching Chen Changxing's son, **Chen Gengyun**. The story related by small style advocates is that Chen Gengyun was anxious to learn Taiji quickly, in order to join his father who was often traveling as a caravan security escort. So that he might learn more quickly, Chen Youben made the circles larger (therefore easier to understand and perform), and increased emphasis on *fajin* expression. (One cannot but wonder, if this story is true, what Chen Changxing thought the first time he saw his son demonstrate a "modified" form.) This "bigger" form version was retained by subsequent generations and was reportedly passed to Chen Gengyun's grandson, Chen Fake.[26]

There is a paradoxical saying that I think is very important in understanding the (seeming) difference of small and big form versions, and it is this: "Big style is not big, and small style is not small."[27] As explained in Chapter 5, if form movement is done correctly, the size of the movement is irrelevant. But generally speaking, the more advanced a practitioner is, the smaller he or she *can* perform the movements (with the spiraling silk-reeling force that is a product of correct movement). The epitome of martial application is to neutralize and counterattack with the minimum necessary motion—"no excess, no deficiency," to again quote the classics. This fact, I think, may well be the source of legends of how Taiji masters have thrown opponents away with just their *qi*. There is no mysterious force involved in such incidents, it is simply that the movements of a true master may be so small and refined as to be indiscernible, and therefore incomprehensible, to an unknowing observer. A perfect recipe for legend—a highly skilled person and an uninformed observer.

Although smaller and smaller circles are possible in advanced stages of form practice, in order to initially learn the movement, and to increase your range of motion, it is helpful to first practice with larger circles. (Please do not jump promptly to a microscopic form, believing that you have quickly mastered Taiji movement.) Once you understand and can do the movement, you can perform any given circular movements in any radius—there is absolutely no difference in the mechanics of *how* the movement is generated. Practitioners of both big and small frame versions hold this principle of "from big to small," and that is the explanation of the saying, "Big is not big and small is not small."

Some believe that a smaller frame form version is better suited for older or less physically fit persons, while a big frame form is more fitting for the younger, stronger, and more martially minded persons. While it is certainly true that the range of motion must be adjusted according to the physical capability of beginners, it is also true that, as just explained, smaller movements can represent a higher level of achievement. Actually, the range of motion, height of stance, and speed of *any* Taiji form sequence can be varied to suit the practitioner's physical capabilities, and that is one reason why Taiji is such a remarkable exercise. Whether the practitioner's interest is in health or martial arts, it is advisable for beginners to gradually *increase* the range of motion of form movements to improve physical capabilities. As I said in Chapter 5, if you only practice in small movements, it is difficult to apply big movements if they are needed. If you practice with big movements, in due course you will be able to do either small or big movements. You should, eventually, have both—big and small, yin *and* yang.

Summary of Old and New and Big and Small

I promised I would summarize the various old, new, big, and small characterizations, so here it is. Don't blame me if it is confusing—I had nothing to do with any of it.

✦ **Chen Changxing** created a new style by distilling the older forms initially created by Chen Wangting. But the new style is a meaningless characterization because the old style no longer exists; or

✦ **Chen Youben** created a new style, which became the small style of his nephew Chen Qingping. The small style is therefore new, compared to the old (big) style represented by Chen Changxing; or

✦ **Chen Youben** created the big style to teach Chen Gengyun; therefore, the small style is old and the big style is new; or

✦ **Chen Fake**, who practiced the big style, created a new style (in comparison to the old big style represented by Chen Zhaopei).

Does that clear it up? Facetious comments aside, to make some sense of all of this, remember the following two sayings:

1. The small style is not small and the big style is not big; and
2. Old is relative and there is nothing new under the sun.
   (That one, I made up.)

About History and Styles—Concluding Remarks

So what, in the end, are we to make of the surfeit of historical accounts and styles of Taiji that have evolved to date? That the history of an art that arose hundreds of years ago should be uncertain is not surprising given the nature of human memory and history itself. Today many researchers at the forefronts of psychology do not believe human memory preserves completely faithful and full records of events. That earlier widespread belief has been replaced by the hypothesis that memories are constructed. They are based in part on the traces of past events retained in the brain, but these traces are believed to be incomplete. Our memories are also a function of ideas and events in the *present*. People reconstruct their memories to fit their changing ideas, especially those that concern their sense of themselves. The collective memories of groups and cultures, whether carried forward in written histories or as oral traditions also have a constructed character. They too contain a variety of distortions and are adjusted to fit as best they can the incomplete sources and ever shifting ideas held by the historians, their patrons, and their readers. Thus the accounts in our history books may differ dramatically in different political regimes. In the same way, versions of the history of Taiji have been rewritten to fit the interests of particular camps.[28]

The proliferation of "styles," I think, is inevitable, given the number of influential characters over the course of Taiji history: Chen Wangting, Chen Changxing, Yang Luchan, Chen Youben, Wu Yuxian, Chen Qingping, Wu Quanyou, Sun Lutang, Chen Fake, Chen Zhaokui, Feng Zhiqiang, to name a few. All of these important figures have been ascribed as originators of a "new style" at some point, either during or after their lifetime. Why? Because of the reasons mentioned above: (1) Taiji is a *living* art, constantly molded by the unique insights from each successive generation, and (2) the *art* of Taiji is, ultimately, a personal expression of one's entire being. No two masters look exactly alike. Many people follow the lead of and copy the works, or styles, of great artists, but few reach the level of mastery whereby their own unique artistic expression leaves a lasting imprint on the psyche of followers.

For these reasons, I respectfully disagree with those who reminisce about the unachievable greatness and absolute authority of past masters (pick your generation). It is true that some professional martial artists of the past had much more time to practice than most of us living in modern society, but it is equally true that what one learns is a function of the efficiency of one's practice and mental and physical capabilities. Overtraining does not yield desired results. With valid research and modern technological capabilities, I believe that we will soon understand more about the art than was imaginable by past generations. Here's to the next generation that will benefit from our understanding—may they improve upon it and share their knowledge and experience with the following generation!

Role of Wu Xiubao in the Recent Transmission of Chen Style Taiji

Wu Xiubao, my first teacher, is currently living in Jiaozuo near the Chen Village. Because of his love of Taiji and his enabling position in the Communist Party, Wu Xiubao has done much to improve the living condition of the people of Chen Village, where he is greatly admired and respected. He also played a significant, but largely unheralded, role in the recent transmission of the Chen family art. In January 2003, I returned to Jiaozuo and, upon visiting him, learned more about his experience and knowledge of the Chen style. Following is a portion of the history that he told me.

Wu Xiubao began his studies of the small frame Chen style Taiji with Yan Lixiang, under whom he studied from 1944 to 1960. In 1960, he began studies with Chen Qingzhou (b. 1933), and in 1966 began studying directly under the 18th-generation master Chen Zhaopei. Wu Xiubao spoke highly of Chen Zhaopei's martial ability and his personal character. He relayed one story that, when Chen Zhaopei was already an old man, a martial artist from nearby Shandong Province came to the Chen Village with an open challenge to any takers. Saying that he was already an old man and didn't care if he "lost face," Chen Zhaopei accepted the challenge and won convincingly. As another testament to Chen Zhaopei's character, Wu Xiubao noted that he frequently offered to pay Chen Zhaopei for teaching him, but that Chen Zhaopei always refused money, accepting only a gift of coal and supply of sweet potatoes.

After several years, Chen Zhaopei told Wu Xiubao that there was no one else in the Chen Village who could further elevate his skills, and that if he wanted to further his study he must go to Beijing to study with Chen Zhaokui. (As noted above, Chen Zhaokui is the youngest son of Chen Fake. Since Chen Fake had left the Chen Village in 1928, Chen Zhaokui grew up in Beijing.) So in 1969, Wu Xiubao traveled to Beijing carrying a note from Chen Zhaopei asking Chen Zhaokui to accept him as a student. When Chen Zhaokui read the note, he proclaimed, "You have studied with my number five brother (meaning that Chen Zhaopei was Chen Zhaokui's second cousin), let me see what you have learned." After Wu Xiubao demonstrated his form, Chen Zhaokui commented, "You have worked hard, but there is still much to learn. We will have to study gradually, piece by piece."

Wu Xiubao continued studying with Chen Zhaokui from that meeting in 1969 until Chen Zhaokui's death in 1981. Throughout the 1970s, Wu Xiubao would frequently travel to Beijing (about five times a year, each time for 8 to 10 days) and study with Chen Zhaokui in the evenings. From 1971 to 1981, Chen Zhaokui would travel to Jiazuo during the month of October, and stay at Wu Xiubao's house as his guest.

Wu Xiubao quickly developed a deep respect for Chen Zhaokui's martial ability, frequently commenting in our interview that Chen Zhaokui's skill was so high that when he threw an opponent his movement was so small and refined that it was often not possible to see what technique or movement he had performed. It was during this period in the 1970s that Wu Xiubao began to play a role in the transmission of the Chen style. This was a time of political unrest in China, and the younger generation in the Chen Village was segregated from and unable to study with Chen Zhaokui, who by then was considered by many to be one of the greatest living practitioners of the 18th-generation of the Chen family. Upon returning from his frequent trips to Beijing, Wu Xiubao openly shared what he learned from Chen Zhaokui with an eager younger generation still living in and around the Chen Village.

Ultimately, at the request of younger generation practitioners, Wu Xiubao was instrumental in persuading Chen Zhaokui to return to the Chen Village and teach, obviously a pivotal occurrence in the transmission of the

Chen style Taijiquan. Chen Zhaokui taught in the Chen Village for a period of one week in 1973, one month in 1974, and two months in 1976. In subsequent years, he spent a few months in nearby Zhengzhou, the capital city of Henan Province, and in my hometown of Jiazuo, and taught others then.[29] Many Chen style practitioners owe their current knowledge and understanding of the art in part to the efforts of Wu Xiubao in convincing Chen Zhaokui to teach.

Missing Taiji Link Discovered

To lighten this rather studious discourse on Taiji history, and with tongue now firmly planted in cheek, I here take the opportunity to announce that I have found a missing link in the Taiji puzzle—a heretofore unknown, but very ancient, Taiji art called "Crawfish Taiji." As luck would have it, I happened to meet a self-proclaimed 333rd-generation practitioner of this art—we'll call him Bob—at a seminar I was giving. Bob explained that he was actually attending the seminar to evaluate whether any of the students were worthy to receive his art. Unfortunately, none were, but I was able to convince Bob to give a brief talk and demonstration. A native of New Orleans, Bob began his talk by introducing the history of the art. The originator of this very ancient Taiji training system, reverently referred to as the "Grand Crawdaddy" by proponents of the style, hailed from Atlantis. Records of the origin and early lineage were lost when Atlantis was submerged, but Bob explained that the Grand Crawdaddy had moved to China, and it was actually he who, in Bob's own words, "Started the Wudang mountain thing." Stories abound about the Grand Crawdaddy. One famous poem relates the story of the time he dreamt he was a crawfish, but upon awakening, couldn't decide if he was a man dreaming that he was a crawfish, or a crawfish dreaming that he was a man. Tradition also asserts that the Grand Crawdaddy was an immortal who, after living three thousand years, flew to heaven on the back of a winged crawfish.

Bob did yield a hint of skepticism about the history of Crawfish Taiji, ultimately confessing that the origin stories weren't well documented but, since he was a practitioner of the style, he had to "buy into it." Derivations from the original Crawfish Taiji include the newer "Five Crustaceans" style, but apparently some groups of Five Crustaceans practitioners now argue that their art evolved independently. Anyway, Bob was then kind enough to give a brief demonstration of *qigong*, forms, and applications of the art. Crawfish Taiji practices include a hard style *qigong*, called "red fist" and "red body," reminiscent of the much later "iron hand" and "golden body" *qigong* of some external styles. For the beginning red fist exercise, Crawfish practitioners place their hands in a barrel of pinching crabs. Later, when they are immune to localized pain, they immerse the entire body and realize the invincible red body. The similarity of this Crawfish *qigong* to other hard style arts has apparently led some to conclude that all martial arts in China can be traced to the influence of the Grand Crawdaddy.

The Crawfish Taiji form looked similar to many modern Taiji forms. Beginning with the slow and graceful "Raise Hands and Retrieve Crawfish," Bob then amazed the group with a powerful "Break the Shell" splitting *fa jin* movement. The next form movements were called "Eating the Crawfish" and "Drinking from the Fermented Grain Cup," which Bob explained as being hidden elbow-striking techniques. To demonstrate applications, Bob took a volunteer from the audience who avowed no previous acquaintance with him. Stating that this was the highest level of the art—that he could reveal publicly—Bob then astounded the group with a demonstration of "empty force." Separated by a distance of approximately ten feet, Bob inflicted the pain of the "Crawfish Pinch" on the helpless volunteer. To finish the demonstration, and to show that the hand that can kill can also heal, Bob then revived the volunteer with an empty force healing *qigong*.

After his demonstration, Bob passed around a sign-up sheet for his seminars. For those unable to travel to study with Bob in person, he has promised that a series of books and videos are "in the works" and will soon be available for purchase.

The ability to laugh at ourselves is a valuable gift, indeed.

Yang Yang with participants of a Taiji intervention study at the University of Illinois, Urbana-Champaign, 2004.

Taiji Research: Selected Studies

Full reference information for the studies listed here can be found in Research References beginning on page 203. Abbreviations are summarized on page 185.

Study	Category/Design *Participants*	Results
Van Deusen (1987)	Rheumatoid arthritis / RCT *Rheumatoid arthritis patients,* *Taiji: 7, Control: 16*	Taiji has positive effects on the range of motion of the upper extremities.
Jin (1989)	Physiological and psychological / RCT *Healthy adults, Beginners: 33,* *Practitioners: 33*	Taiji practice has positive effects as moderate exercise in selected psychological and physiological measures.
Kirsteins (1991)	Rheumatoid arthritis / CS *Rheumatoid arthritis patients,* *Taiji: 40, Control: 20*	"Taiji appears safe to rheumatoid arthritis patients and may serve as an alternative for their exercise therapy and part of their rehabilitation program."
Tse (1992)	Postural control / CSS *Healthy community-dwelling older* *adults, Taiji: 9, Non-Taiji: 9*	Taiji has positive effects on postural control.
Lai (1995)	Cardiorespiratory / COH *Healthy community-dwelling older* *adults, Taiji: 45, Control: 39*	Taiji practice may delay the decline of cardiorespiratory function of older adults.

Lan (1996)	Cardiorespiratory/CCS *Healthy community-dwelling older adults, Taiji: 41, Control: 35*	"Taiji practitioners have higher peak oxygen uptake and higher oxygen uptake at the ventilatory threshold. Taiji can be prescribed as a conditioning exercise for older adults."
Schaller (1996)	Cardiorespiratory and balance/ NRCT *Community-dwelling older adults, Taiji: 24, Control: 22*	Taiji practice improved balance but not systolic and diastolic blood pressure. Taiji might help community-dwelling elders improve their balance.
Wolf (1996)	Cardiorespiratory function and fall prevention/RCT *Community-dwelling older adults, Taiji: 72, Balance: 64, Education: 64*	Taiji training reduced the rate of falls and fear of falling, and lowered blood pressure.
Wolfson (1996)	Fall prevention/RCT *Healthy community-dwelling older adults, Balance: 28, Strength: 28, Balance + Strength: 27, Control: 27*	Taiji training has the effect of maintaining the significant balance and strength gains obtained in strength and balance training.
Jacobson (1997)	Balance training/RCT *Healthy middle-aged adults, Taiji: 12, Control: 12*	Taiji training improved lateral body stability and the strength of the dominant knee extensor significantly. Taiji may be a low stress method for lateral stability and the strength of knee extensor.
Kutner (1997)	Psychological/RCT *Community-dwelling older adults, Taiji: 72, Balance: 64, Education: 64*	Both Taiji and balance training increased participants' confidence in balance and movement, but only Taiji affected participants' daily activities and their overall life.
Lan (1998)	Fitness/NRCT *Community-dwelling older adults, Taiji: 20, Control: 18*	Taiji group significantly improved VO₂ max, flexibility and strength of knee extensor and flexor. A 12-month Taiji program appears effective to improve older adults' fitness.

Yan (1998)	Postural and motor control/NRCT *Older adults at nursing home, Taiji: 28, Walking: 10*	Taiji practice may improve older adults' dynamic balance and smoothness of arm movement.
Hain (1999)	Postural control/NCT *22 persons with mild balance disorders*	Taiji training significantly improved balance.
Husted (1999)	Psychosocial and physical/NCT *19 patients with multiple sclerosis*	An 8-week Taiji training increased participants' walking speed by 21% and hamstring flexibility by 28%. Patients also improved in vitality, social funtioning, mental health, and ability to carry out physical and emotional roles.
Lan (1999)	Cardiorespiratory/NRCT *Low-risk patients with coronary artery bypass surgery, Taiji: 9, Control: 11*	Taiji training increased VO_2 peak and peak work rate. Taiji also increased ventilatory threshold VO_2 and work rate. Taiji practice can favorably enhance cardio-respiratory function for low risk patients with coronary artery bypass surgery.
Yan (1999)	Motor control/NRCT *Older adults, Taiji: 12, Walking/jogging: 8*	Taiji practice reduced the force variability in arm movement.
Hong (2000)	Balance, flexibility, and cardio-respiratory/CSS *Healthy older male adults, Taiji: 28, Control: 30*	Taiji practice may have favorable effects on older adults' balance, flexibility, and cardiorespiratory fitness.
Lan (2000)	Strength and endurance/NCT *41 healthy community-dwelling older adults*	A 6-month Taiji program increased participants' concentric and eccentric knee extensor peak torque and knee extensor endurance ratio. Taiji training may improve muscular strength and endurance of knee extensors in elderly individuals.

Lin (2000)	Postural control/CSS _Healthy community-dwelling older adults, Taiji: 14, Control: 14_	Regular Taiji practice might lead to better postural control, especially in the more complicated conditions with disturbed visual and somatosensory information.
Li (2001)	Self-efficacy and self-perceived physical function/RCT _Healthy elderly participants, Taiji: 49, Control: 45_	Taiji training has positive effects on self-efficacy and self-perceived physical function.
Wang (2001)	Cardiorespiratory/CCS _Healthy community-dwelling elderly males, Taiji: 10, Control: 10_	Compared to their sedentary counterparts, Taiji practitioners had higher cutaneous microcirculatory function during exercise.
Christou (2003)	Strength and force control/NRCT _Healthy community-dwelling older adults, Taiji: 16, Control: 10_	A 20-week Taiji program is effective in improving knee extensor strength and force control in older adults.
Irwin (2003)	Immunity/RCT _Older adults with impairments of health status and at risk for shingles, Taiji: 18, Wait: 18_	A 15-week Taiji training boosts shingles immunity significantly.
Rosengren (2003)	Taiji skill acquisition/NCT _16 healthy community-dwelling older adults_	Intervention programs that use Taiji should be at least 4 months long for individuals to achieve a moderate level of Taiji skill.
Song (2003)	Osteoarthritis/RCT _Older women with osteoarthritis, Taiji: 22, Control: 21_	A 12-week Taiji program is effective in improving osteoarthritis patients' arthritic symptoms, balance, and physical functioning.
Taggart (2003)	Fibromyalgia/NCT _21 patients with fibromyalgia completed a 6-week Taiji program._	Taiji is potentially beneficial to patients with fibromyalgia.

Chan (2004)	Bone density/RCT	A 12-month Taiji program is beneficial for slowing bone loss in weight-bearing bones in early postmenopausal women.
	Healthy postmenopausal women, Taiji: 67, Control: 65	
Han (2004)	Rheumatoid arthritis/R	Taiji does not aggravate symptoms of rheumatoid arthritis. Taiji is effective in improving lower extremity range of motion, in particular ankle range of motion, for rheumatoid arthritis patients.
	Rheumatoid arthritis patients	
Lan (2004)	Aerobic assessment/ES	"Taiji is exercise with moderate intensity. It is an aerobic exercise and suitable for participants of different ages and gender to improve their functional capacity."
	100 community-dwelling Taiji practitioners were divided into three groups: young: 25-44 yrs.; middle-aged: 45-64 yrs.; elderly: 65-80 yrs.	
Li (2004)	Sleep/RCT	A 6-month Taiji program has positive effect on self-rated sleep quality of aerobic assessment. Taiji is an aerobic exercise with moderate intensity.
	Community-dwelling older adults with moderate sleep complaints, Taiji: 62, Low-impact exercise: 56	

ABBREVIATIONS

CCS case control studies
COH cohort study
CS comparative study
CSS cross-sectional study
ES evaluation study
NCT non-controlled trial
NRCT non-randomized controlled trial
R review
RCT randomized clinical trial

Notes

Chapter 1: Introduction

1. Refer to Appendix I for a discussion of the history of Taiji.

2. For a detailed analysis of the origin and symbolism of the Taiji Diagram, see Gu, M.D. (2003). The Taiji Diagram: A meta-sign in Chinese thought. *Journal of Chinese Philosophy*, *30(2)*, 195–218.

3. In spoken language, "Taijiquan" is commonly abridged to "Taiji."

4. Wile, D. (1996). *Lost T'ai Ch'i Classics from the Late Ch'ing Dynasty*. Albany, NY: SUNY Press, 75.

5. Yang, J. M. (1987). *Advanced Yang Style Tai Chi Chuan—Volume I, Tai Chi Theory and Tai Chi Jing*. Jamaica Plain, MA: YMAA Publication Center, 238.

Chapter 2: The Foundation

1. In attempting to explain human *qi*, some modern theories have focused on the similarities between *qi* and bioelectric fields, but this academic approach narrows the broader definition of *qi* as the universal, energetic intermediary between physical essence (*jing*) and spirit (*shen*). In the broader sense, the energy and movement of *qi* is what produces all things. As a "vital life force," the Chinese concept of *qi* is essentially identical to the Indian *prana*, Greek *pneuma*, Latin *spiritus*, and Japanese *ki*. The Indian *Upanishads*, written between 800–400 BCE, beautifully summarize *prana*: "Prana is the soul of the universe, assuming all forms, it is the light that animates and illuminates all" (*Prasna Upanishad*).

    Qi is intangible—it is therefore an abstract concept or theory and not a distinct, observable, physical "thing." In this, however, it is not too different from scientific theories now universally accepted, such as gravity or energy.

    The scientific approach is to accept theory where that theory is in 100% agreement with observation, even if known physical processes do not currently explain the theory itself. Gravity is an example. The force of gravity has not been explained by any proven distinct physical phenomena, but we accept the "theory" that gravitational force exists because it does accurately and precisely explain other physical phenomena. (With 100% certainty, no one on earth has ever fallen up.) Since gravity is not explainable as a proven separate, fundamental entity, we only have theories of gravity (e.g., the proposed "graviton" particle, or Einstein's theory that gravity is the shortest path through curved space/time). "Energy" is another example of an accepted, yet unexplained, theory. No one can say what energy is. We can classify it as chemical, electrical, kinetic, etc., or we can state a function of energy (the capacity to do work), but we don't know what energy is. We only know that energy is that which is always "conserved" (i.e., that which can neither be created nor destroyed). In the words of the celebrated physicist Richard Feynman, "It is important to realize that in physics today, we have no knowledge of what energy *is*. We do not have a picture that energy comes in little blobs of a definite amount. It is an abstract thing in that it does not tell us the mechanism or the *reasons* for various formulas." (Feynman, R.P. (1995). *Six Easy Pieces.* Reading, MA: Perseus Books, 71–72).

From this perspective, then, gravity and energy are no different than *qi*. No one can describe *qi* as a distinct, physical entity, but we do have theories of *qi*. We have *classifications* of *qi*, and Chinese medical theory can describe the *function* of *qi*, all based upon centuries of observation.

Beyond theory, *qi* and energy or gravity have another, perhaps much more important, aspect in common—you can feel them (or, maybe more accurately, feel the effects of them). The reader can easily find elsewhere intellectual hypotheses of what *qi* "is." I will only point the way for you to experience it yourself in your practice.

2. Yang, Y., and Grubisich, S. (2000). Feng Zhiqiang Tells About the Importance of Internal Work. *T'ai Chi*, 24(3), 13.

3. Duke University has established a *Center for the Study of Religion/Spirituality and Health*, accessible at www.dukespiritualityandhealth.org.

4. Wile, 89.

5. Chen Xin. (1996). *The Illustration of Chen Style Taijiquan.* Taibei: Wuzhou Publishing House, 145.

6. Wile, 70–71. Slight modification in translation from Chinese by Yang Yang.

7. Grandmaster Feng's twelve principles were first published in his book, *Entering the Door to Chen Style Taijiquan* (Beijing: People's Physical Culture Press, 1993). The twelve principles are summarized on page 21.

8. Yusufali (Trans.). *Qur'an* (13:003). Accessed August 2004 from www.usc.edu/dept/MSA/quran. Sponsored by University of Southern California.

9. Yusufali (Trans.). *Qur'an* (53:043).

10. Müller, F. M. (Trans.). (1879–1884). *Brihadaranayka Upanishad*, Part 1, First Adhyaya, Fourth Brahmana. In *The Sacred Books of the East*. Accessed August 2004 from www.intratext.com/IXT/ENG0070/_P84.HTM#8Y. Intra-text digital library website sponsored by Èulogos.

11. Nukariya, K. (1913). *The Religion of the Samurai: A Study of Zen Philosophy and Discipline in China and Japan*. Accessed August 2004 from www.intratext.com/IXT/ENG0082/_P2Y.HTM#WIT. Intra-text digital library website sponsored by Èulogos.

12. Suzuki, D. T. (1914). *A Brief History of Early Chinese Philosophy*. London: Probsthain & Co., 17–18.

13. From Burnet, J. (1920). *Early Greek Philosophy*. (3rd ed.). London: Adam and Charles Black. Accessed October 2004 from www.wku.edu/~jan.garrett/302/302herac.htm. Sponsored by Western Kentucky University.

14. Das, B. (1932). *Essential Unity of All Religions*. Wheaton, IL: Theosophical Publishing House, 43.

15. Gotshalk, R. (1985). *Bhagavad Gita, Translation and Commentary*. Delhi: Motilal Barnarsidass, 25–26.

16. Yusufali (Trans.). *Qur'an* (5:087).

17. Nitobe, I. (1931). *Japan*. New York: Scribner & Sons, 322.

18. "Nothing in Excess" and "Know Thyself" are the two famous inscriptions on Apollo's temple at Delphi. Inazo Nitobe writes in *Japan* that these are complimentary—moderation is a requisite for knowing oneself. In Nitobe's words, "If you have too much of anything, you cannot know yourself . . . The moral equipoise—the Golden Mean—is the attainment of the godhead" (322).

19. Miller, R. J. (Ed.). (1985). *The Complete Gospels, Annotated Scholars Version*. Santa Rosa, CA: Polebridge Press. Accessed August 2004 from www.westarinstitute.org/Polebridge/Title/Complete/Thomas/thomas.html. Sponsored by Westar Institute.

20. Prabhavananda and Manchester, F. (1947). *The Upanishads, Breath of the Eternal*. Hollywood, CA: Vedanta Press, 65.

21. Das, 137–138.

22. Kwok, M. H., Palmer, M., and Ramsay, J. (Trans.). (1993). *Tao Te Ching*. Rockport, MA: Element, 38, 102, 145.

23. Abridged from Suzuki, *A Brief History*, 51–56, by Bhagavan Das, *Essential Unity*, 336.

24. *Dantian* is usually translated as "elixir field," and is an area in the body where *qi* is collected and stored. There are three *dantians* in the body—upper, middle, and lower—but *qigong* masters have different opinions as to their specific localities. According to *Chinese Qigong in a Practical English-Chinese Library of TCM* (Shanghai: Publishing House of Shanghai University of Traditional Chinese Medicine, 1990,

Chief Editor Zhang Enqin), the upper *dantian* is either inside the *Baihu* acupoint (Hundred Convergences, *Du* 20) on top of the head (and called *niwan*, or "mud ball"), or inside the acupoint *Yintang* (Glabella, Extra 1) between the two eyebrows (called *Zuqiao*, or "Progenitor Orifice"). The middle *dantian*, called *Jianggong* (Scarlet Palace), is believed by some to be inside the acupoint *Shanzhong* (Middle Chest, *Ren* 17) between the two nipples, and by others to be located in the naval. The lower *dantian* is variously ascribed three different locations. The first is the area of the lower abdomen, below the naval (specifically, the area in the upper two-thirds of the line joining the umbilicus and symphesis pubis). The second opinion is that the lower *dantian* is located at the acupoint *Hiuyin* (Converging Yin, *Ren* 1), between the anus and genitals. The third opinion is that the lower *dantian* is *Yongquan* (Pouring Spring, K1), on the soles of the feet. Generally, the phrase "sink the *qi* to the *dantian*" refers to the "lower *dantian*" in the lower abdomen (about $1\frac{1}{2}$ to 2 inches below the naval and 1 to 2 inches deep).

25. Here I am not advocating the elimination of all desire, rather only an awareness of how egoistic desire controls and unbalances all human beings, and that it must be surrendered to enter a state of quiescence. The ego is a tricky thing, however. Do not deceive yourself by thinking, "OK, I will surrender the ego for a short time now, and *then* I will get what I want." The only attitude that will work is a sincere effort to improve yourself and an openness or willingness to accept what you discover, regardless of how uncomfortable that may initially make you.

26. Abridged from Takuan Soho. (1986). *The Unfettered Mind, Writings of the Zen Master to the Sword Master*. (William Scott Wilson, Trans.). New York: Kodansha International, Ltd., 1–32.

27. *Fa jin* is discussed further in Chapter 5.

28. To which the *Oxyrhynchus Papyrus 654, Logion 2* adds, "and whoever *knows himself* shall find it" (emphasis added). Mark and Luke's version of this saying of Jesus (and that in the Gospel of Thomas) are similar: "If anyone says to you, 'Look, here is the Christ,' or 'Look, there he is,' do not believe it." The meaning is the same—the Kingdom of Heaven is not to be seen in external "things," but internally. (Information about papyrus writings was taken from Throckmorton, B. (Ed.). (1979). *Gospel Parallels, A Synopsis of the First Three Gospels*. (4th ed.). Nashville, TN: Thomas Nelson Publishers, 125.)

29. Miller, R. J. (Ed.). (1985). *The Complete Gospels, Annotated Scholars Version*. Santa Rosa, CA: Polebridge Press. Accessed August 2004 from www.westarinstitute.org/Polebridge/Title/Complete/Thomas/thomas.html. Sponsored by Westar Institute.

30. Prabhavananda and Manchester, 189.

31. Prabhavananda and Manchester, 132.

32. Prabhavananda and Manchester, 30–31.

33. Das, 329.

34. Das, 98. (The song is in reference to 50:016 of the *Qur'an*: "For we are nearer to him than his jugular vein.")

35. Saint Theresa of Avila. (1997). *The Way of Perfection*. (The Benedictines of Stanbrook, Trans.). Rockford, IL: Tan Books and Publishers Inc., 159.

36. Merton, T. (1998). *Contemplation in a World of Action*. Notre Dame, IN: University of Notre Dame Press, 160–161.

37. Rumi, Maulana Jalalu-'d-din Muhammad. (1898). *The Mathnawi*. (E.H. Whinfield, Trans.). Accessed August 2004 from www.intratext.com/IXT/ENG0134/_P2F.HTM#$CV. Intra-text digital library website sponsored by Èulogos.

38. Legge, J. (Trans.). (1930). *The Four Books: Analects*. Shanghai: The Chinese Book Company, 228.

39. We should not overlook the fact that esoteric language, metaphors and allegories, can serve several purposes. First, they keep one occupied and continuously searching, *through personal effort*, for understanding and enlightenment. There is a real danger in things being explained too clearly—one could easily confuse intellectual understanding with real knowing and therefore unwittingly stall or even reverse progress. We can read the ingredients of root beer, but we will only know the taste if we drink it ourselves. Second, for the purpose of instructing each soul according to its aptitude, all spiritual traditions assert that the deeper truths are veiled in scriptural writings. As Paul said, "I could not talk to you as spiritual men but only as men of flesh, as infants in Christ. I fed you milk, and did not give you solid food because you were not ready for it" (I Corinthians 3:1–2). Origen wrote, "But that there should be certain doctrines, not known to the multitude, which are divulged after the exoteric ones have been taught, is not a peculiarity of Christianity alone, but also of philosophic systems in which certain truths are exoteric and others esoteric." The saying attributed to Jesus is more emphatic, "Do not give what is holy to dogs or toss your pearls before swine. They will trample them underfoot at best, and perhaps even tear you to shreds" (Matthew 7:6). And "Therefore I speak to them in parables and allegories because they, seeing, see not, and hearing, they hear not, neither do they understand" (Matthew 11:13), an echo of the ancient Hindu *Rig Veda*, "There may be someone who sees the words and yet indeed does not see them; may be another one who hears these words but indeed does not hear them" [*Rigveda* R.V. 10:71:4] (Swami Satyaprakash Saraswati and Satyakam Vidhyalank, *Rigveda Samhiti* Volume XII, 4309).

40. Muller, M. (1893). *Introduction to the Science of Religion*. London: Longmans, Green and Co., 92.

41. There is a passage with similar meaning in Luke: "But it is easier for heaven and earth to pass away than for one dot of the law to become void" (Luke 16:17).

42. From the *Second Apology of Justin Martyr*, Ch. XIII, and *First Apology of Justin Martyr*, Ch. XLVI, respectively. Accessed August 2004 from faculty.fullerton.edu/bstarr/ JUSTIN.htm. Sponsored by Professor Brad Starr, California State University, Fullerton.

43. Yusufali (Trans.). *Qur'an* (041:043).

44. Yusufali (Trans.). *Qur'an* (041:043, 005:044–048).

45. Das, 67.

46. Saint Augustine, *Confessions*, 12.25.34. (E.B. Pusey, Trans.). Accessed August 2004 from www.georgetown.edu/faculty/jod. Sponsored by James J. O'Donnell of Georgetown University.

47. Takuan, 22.

48. Rumi, Maulana Jalalu-'d-din Muhammad. (1990). *The Mathnawi*, Book I, Vs. 3086. (Camile Helminski and Kabir Helminski, Trans.) In *Rumi: Daylight*. Putney, VT: Threshold Books, 72.

49. Eckhart, M. (1941). *Talks of Instruction*. (Raymond Blakney, Trans.). In *Meister Eckhart, A Modern Translation*. New York: Harper & Brothers Publishers, 23–24.

50. *Selected Sayings of Sri Ramakrishna*. Accessed August 2004 from www.geocities.com/ neovedanta/srks.html. Sponsored by Neovedanta Group.

51. As cited in Das, 38.

Chapter 3: Finding a Teacher

1. As with most sayings, don't interpret this literally. If you find a teacher you are comfortable with, don't say to yourself, "Well, it hasn't been three years yet so I can't start studying." The meaning is simply that one is responsible for selecting a teacher (and the teacher is responsible for accepting a student).

2. The word *shifu* has two basic meanings. The more common usage of the word is as a respectful title for artists (martial or otherwise) or craftsmen. The less common meaning is "teacher/father," which is reserved for close relationships such as that between teacher and disciple in the martial arts. The two meanings are differentiated in written Chinese by the character for "*fu*."

3. There is another saying with a similar meaning: 人不知我，我独知人。Ren bu zhi wo, wo du zhi ren—Other people do not know me, but I know other people.

4. This was true within a certain style of an art, but admittedly there was, and remains today, a degree of competition and mistrust between different arts. Especially in the West, it is now much more common for people to seek knowledge from other internal arts. I believe that this open attitude will serve to continually raise the overall level of Taiji in the West.

Chapter 4: *Wuji* Meditation

1. It should be noted that other internal martial arts besides Taiji also refer to form movement as "moving pole," further accentuating the importance of standing meditation in all internal martial arts practice.

2. Wile, 67.

3. Wang, Fengming. (n.d.). *Special Taoist Taiji Stick and Ruler Qigong*. Helsinki, Finland: European Chen Style Hun Yuan Taiji Association.

4. *Baihui* is an acupuncture point on the rear center of the top of the head (where a beanie might be worn).

5. Balance is controlled by a combination of (1) the vestibular system of the inner ear, (2) vision, and (3) the somatic sensory system. At any time, two of these three systems are typically dominant. Until improvement is realized from the standing meditation practice, persons with degraded capacity of either the vestibular or somatic sensory systems will encounter some difficulty in maintaining balance with eyes closed.

6. All physiological functions, including sexual activity, will deteriorate with age. However, with correct *qigong* practice, one can improve the quality and lengthen the life span of active sexuality. As with any natural function, there is a healthy and a diseased state of sexual desire. In the diseased state, sexual desire awakens either too frequently or too infrequently. Over time and with correct practice one's physical and mental heath will improve, and sexual desire will awaken with a natural and healthy frequency (unique to the individual and his or her age).

7. *Peng jin* has two basic meanings. The *peng jin* referred to here is the expanding aspect of one's internal energy/power, or *nei gong*. This meaning is exemplified in the description of *peng jin* as *"yi qi gudang,"* which literally means that *yi* (mind/intention) and *qi* are expanding/vibrating. This energy feels strong and is obvious both to the practitioner and anyone touching him or her.

    The second meaning of *peng jin* refers to the first of the "eight forces" of Taijiquan: *peng/lu/ji/an/cai/lie/zhou/kao*. These eight forces refer to the direction and duration of an expression of force. *Peng* is simply a force directed upward. (The eight forces are explained in detail in the discussion of push-hands in Chapter 6.) Some have combined these two definitions of *peng jin* by saying that *peng* is "a force directed upward and outward." This is accurate, but fails to communicate the full meaning of the term *peng jin*.

8. This fluttering sensation can vary in intensity from subtle to quite strong. I remember once lying in bed in my dormitory room in China, when I felt this quite strongly. I jumped down and, not recognizing the cause of the sensation, mistakenly told my roommate that we were having an earthquake.

9. Lau, D.C. (Trans.). (1994). *Tao Te Ching*, Mawangdui Manuscripts. New York: Alfred A. Knopf, Inc., 20.

10. Bynner, W. (Trans.). (1944). *The Way of Life According to Lao Tzu*. New York: Putnam, 75.

11. Saint Theresa of Avila wrote the following about the feeling of meditation (what she calls "recollection"): "If this recollection is genuine it is easily discerned, for it produces a certain effect that I cannot describe, but which will be recognized by those who know it from personal experience." (From *The Way of Perfection*. Rockford, IL: Tan Books and Publishers Inc., 1997, 161.)

12. This summary of the central nervous system was contributed by Wendy Heller, professor of Psychology at the University of Illinois, Urbana-Champaign.

13. It is sometimes necessary to have co-contraction where both agonist and antagonist muscles are active simultaneously. For example, when descending stairs the hamstrings undergo concentric contraction while the quadriceps experience eccentric contraction to stabilize the knee and prevent collapse. My purpose in introducing the fundamental biomechanical concept of agonist and antagonist muscle contraction is simply to illustrate that, from both traditional Taiji and Western scientific perspectives, relaxation (of specific muscle groups) is necessary for efficient movement and force exertion, and that unnecessary muscle tension is inefficient and counterproductive. More to the point, the Taiji training process will improve the coordination between antagonist and agonist muscle groups, a continuous process in both static and dynamic postures.

14. For current scientific studies on the health benefits of meditation, see the relevant section in Further Reading listed at the end of the book.

15. Young, J. D., & Taylor, E. (1998). Meditation as a voluntary hypometabolic state of biological estivation. *News in Physiological Science 13*, 149–153.

16. Young & Taylor. (1998).

17. Kjaer, T. W., Bertelsen, C., Piccini, P., Brooks, D., Alving, J., & Lou, H. C. (2002). Increased dopamine tone during meditation-induced change of consciousness. *Cognitive Brain Research, 13*(2), 255–259.

18. Tooley, G. A., Armstrong, S. M., Norman, T. R., & Sali, A. (2000). Acute increases in night-time plasma melatonin levels following a period of meditation. *Biological Psychology, 53*(1), 69–78.

19. Yue, G., & Cole, K. J. (1992). Strength increases from the motor program: Comparison of training with maximal voluntary and imagined muscle contractions. *Journal of Neurophysiology, 67*(5), 1114–1123.

20. Core Strength Training. (2002). Sports Science Exchange Roundtable 47, *13*(1). Accessed August 2004 from www.gssiweb.com/reflib/refs/311/CORE_STRENGTH_RT.cfm?btid=1. Sponsored by Gatorade Sports Science Institute.

21. Core Strength Training. (2002).

22. The importance of core musculature is implied in the classical literature of Taiji. The poem *Thirteen Postures: Comprehending External and Internal Training* famously states, "Power is issued from the spine." It is exactly the core musculature that flexes the spine. I suspect that the concept of "core strength training," though a relatively new area of focus for Western exercise regimens, has been around for centuries in the internal martial arts.

23. Of course, for the purpose of instruction, this is an idealized summary. Nowadays almost everyone begins Taiji by memorizing choreographed form movement. But the most efficient way to progress is to start *wuji* practice as soon as possible.

Chapter 5: Taiji Form Movement

1. Shen Shou. (1991). *Taijiquan Classics*. Beijing: People's Physical Culture Press, 25. Trans. Yang Yang.

2. Mair, V. (Trans.). (1990). *Tao Te Ching*, Mawangdui Manuscripts. New York: Bantam, 60.

3. Lau, D.C. (Trans.). (1994). *Tao Te Ching*, Mawangdui Manuscripts. New York: Alfred A. Knopf, Inc., 84.

4. Chen Changxing. (1999). *Important Words on Martial Applications*. (Jarek Szymanski, Trans.). Accessed August 2004 from www.chinafrominside.com/ma/taiji/chenchangxingIWMA.html. Sponsored by Jarek Szymanski. Refer to Appendix I for a discussion of Chen Changxing's historical role in the development of Taijiquan.

5. Certain silk-reeling exercises are intended to emphasize flexibility and range of motion and to promote circulation, and are therefore purposely executed in large exaggerated motions that extend beyond the "normal" range of movement.

6. Greer, J. M. (2000). Swordsmanship and Esoteric Spirituality; An Introduction to Gerard Thibault's Academie de l'Espee. *Journal of Asian Martial Arts*, 9(2), 23.

7. There are a number of other important factors that affect the total force output of a muscle, including velocity at which it is changing length, level of activation of the fiber, and passive tension of the non-contractile tissue.

8. Abridged from McArdle, W., Katch, F., and Katch, V. (1996). *Exercise Physiology: Energy, Nutrition, and Human Performance*. (4th ed.). Philadelphia, PA: Williams and Watkins, 325–326.

9. The ankles, knees, and hips are the joints in the lower body used to maintain balance.

10. That is why some bridges have an arch design. The force or "load" of the vehicles passing over the bridge is transferred to the abutments (the base supports that are securely connected to the ground) at the ends of the bridge. The same is true for

arched dams—the dams are arched in the upstream direction to transfer the force of the water to the abutments anchoring the sides of the dams.

11. According to *Chinese Acupuncture and Moxibustion* (Chief Editor Cheng Xinnong, Beijing: Foreign Languages Press, 1987, 51–52), *zhong qi* is post-birth (i.e., acquired) *qi* formed from the combination of *qing qi* (clean *qi*), which is inhaled by the lungs, and *qi* of food essence produced by the spleen and stomach. *Zhong qi* is stored in the chest and has two main functions: (1) to promote function of the lungs in controlling respiration, and (2) to promote the heart's function of controlling the blood and blood vessels. The strength or weakness of speech and respiration, and the circulation of *qi* and blood, coldness and warmth, and the motor ability of the four limbs and trunk are all associated with the quality of *zhong qi*.

12. More technically, the center of mass is the weighted average of the center of mass of each body segment in 3-D space. As the position of the arms, legs, and body changes, so too does the distribution of body mass. As a result, the location of the center of mass changes continually during movement. For ease of illustration, the arms are omitted from Figures 1–7, and the center of mass is shown in the torso, where it is in a standing position with the arms at the sides.

13. There are two benefits of temporarily achieving a low posture. First, a low posture strengthens leg muscles at different parts of the range of motion than high postures. A general rule is that static exercises such as postures and stances are effective in strength gain for approximately ± 15 degrees around the joint angle. Second, a significantly lower center of mass may be temporarily necessary or advantageous in push-hands. However, an experienced practitioner should not have to revert to excessive mechanical movement to neutralize a force.

14. Quote taken from a seminar lesson given in Champaign, Illinois, July, 2001.

15. Wile, Chinese text on page 146. Trans. Yang Yang.

16. The precise location of the center of mass varies with different standing postures. In a staggered stance, the center of mass (i.e., "weight") will be more toward the back leg. The optimal position of any stance is where the center of mass is at a spot most advantageous for either neutralizing or attacking. The key point is that the optimal posture is first instilled during quiet standing, and then refined through form and practical experience in push-hands.

17. Shen Shou. (1991). *Taijiquan Classics*. Beijing: People's Physical Culture Press, 44. Trans. Yang Yang.

18. Shen Shou, 34. Trans. Yang Yang.

19. "Sink *Qi* and Wash Organs" is one of Grandmaster Feng's *hunyuan qigong* exercises. In this exercise, the practitioner raises his or her hands above the head, gently stretching the body, and then slowly lowers the hands down the front center of the body. The practitioner imagines that the *qi* enters the top of the head and flows downwards through the body, "washing the organs." A common description of the

sensation experienced during this exercise is one of a bucket or shower of water flowing through the inside of the body.

20. Quote taken from Seminar in Champaign, Illinois, July, 2001.

21. Shen Shou, 50. Trans. Yang Yang.

22. Kandel, E., Schwartz, J., and Jessel, T. (2000). *Principles of Neural Science*. New York: McGraw-Hill, 658–662.

23. I recently had a conversation that underscores this example with the manager of the internationally renowned guitarist, Manuel Barreuco. The manager commented that Master Barreuco tells his guitar students to begin practicing slowly, using Taiji as an example.

24. Personal communication with Wendy Heller, professor of Psychology at the University of Illinois, Urbana-Champaign.

Chapter 6: Push-Hands

1. Of course, you should not "lock" the body in a fixed position. Flexibility about all of the joints, within the limits of complete stability, is desirable.

2. Yang, J. M., *Advanced Yang Style Tai Chi Chuan*, 255.

3. Enoka, R. M., Christou, E. A., Hunter, S. K., et al. (2003). Mechanisms that contribute to differences in motor performance between young and old adults. *Journal of Electromyography and Kinesiology, 13*, 1–12; and Tracy, B. L. and Enoka, R. M. (2002). Older adults are less steady during submaximal isometric contractions with the knee extensor muscles. *Journal of Applied Physiology, 92*, 1004–1012.

4. Christou, E. A., Rosengren, K. S., and Yang, Y. (2003). Taiji training improves knee extensor strength and force control in older adults. *The Journal of Gerontology. Series A, Biological Sciences and Medical Sciences, 58(8)*, 763–766.

5. Tracy, B. L., Kern, D. S., Mehoudar, O. D., Sehnert, S. M., Byrnes, W. C., & Enoka, R. M. (2001). Strength training does not improve the steadiness of muscle contractions in the knee extensors of older adults. *Medicine and Science in Sports and Exercise, 33*, s254; and Bellew, J. W. (2002). The effect of strength training on control of force in older men and women. *Aging Clinical and Experimental Research, 14*, 35–41.

6. As the internal force exchanged between two practitioners increases, it is important to wear good quality shoes. The force will bear upon the feet, and good shoes will help protect them from injury. In plain and simple English, get rid of those cheap slippers that are popular among some Taiji practitioners and get yourself a good pair of sneakers.

7. I believe that the common English translations of *peng, lu, ji,* and *an* as "ward-off," "rollback," "press," and "push" are incomplete and have led to very creative, but

completely inaccurate, interpretations, so I have intentionally retained the Chinese terms without translation.

8. The dual use of the term *peng* was addressed in Chapter 4. In the remainder of this chapter, *peng* is used to describe the upward direction of the "four cardinal directions."

9. Disappearing is also a skill that can be done with agile movement before contact is made.

10. Shen Shou, 229. Trans. Yang Yang.

11. Kandel, Schwartz, and Jessel, 662.

12. This is in reference to the Takuan quote in Chapter 2.

Chapter 7: Why Practice Taiji?

1. Christou, Rosengren, & Yang. (2003).

2. Why is there more stress today? Accessed August 2004 from www.stress.org/problem.htm. Sponsored by American Institute of Stress.

3. Kjaer, et al. (2002).

Appendix I: A Brief History of Taijiquan and the Modern Chen Style

1. Wile, 115.

2. Doctorow, E. L. (1988). *Writers at Work: The Paris Review Interviews,* Eighth Series, Ed. George Plimpton. New York: Viking. Accessed August 2004 from *Columbia World of Quotations* at www.bartleby.com/66/60/16860.html. Sponsored by Bartleby.

3. To make reading a little easier, from this section forward the first occurrence of each name of historical Taiji personages is represented in boldface type.

4. Wile, 109.

5. It cannot go without notice that Xu Zhen, the scholar who argued that Wang Zongyue brought the art to the Chen Village, was a student of Wu/Hao Taiji, and therefore his research conclusions serve to endorse the authenticity of his own lineage while at the same time diminishing the role of Chen Wangting and his descendents. His contemporary, Tang Hao, who concluded that the Chen Village was the origin of Taiji, eventually became a student of the 17th-generation Chen family master Chen Fake. In personal communication in August 2003, Jarek Szymanski stated that Xu Zhen began his Wu/Hao style under Hao Yueru in 1931, before he wrote his research. Tang Hao studied under Chen Fake much later, probably beginning in the early 1950s. Both men were in touch with Chen Ziming since the early 1930s. Jarek provides a brief biography of these two scholars at www.chinafrominside.com/ma/taiji/chenboxingmanuals.html.

6. Wile, 111. We do not know whether Wang Zongyue was a real historical figure or was conjured by Wu Yuxiang as a fictitious author of Taiji classical texts. Wile notes on page 112, "Whatever truth may exist in any account of Wang Zongyue is purely accidental, as we do not have a single, bona fide historical document. Nevertheless, this inconvenience has not prevented generations of authors from assigning specific dates and native places to Wang." Wile further notices, "None of these authors felt obliged to cite their sources," and the proposed dates for Wang span 600 years (from the Song to the Qing Dynasties).

7. To my knowledge, there are no primary sources that document the life of Jiang Fa; however, Chen family tradition does assert his existence. Chen Xin's writings mention that Jiang Fa was a servant of Chen Wangting (Wile, 114). Anecdotal stories in the Chen Village explain that Jiang Fa traveled to the Chen Village to hide after a peasant uprising that he supported was put down. Many speculate that Jiang Fa is the mysterious figure standing behind a seated Chen Wangting in the famous portrait of Chen Wangting in the Chen family shrine. Other, unsubstantiated, accounts of Jiang Fa place him variously in the 17th and 18th centuries, and as the teacher of either Chen Changxing or Chen Qingping.

8. At www.chinafrominside.com/ma/otherstyles/CNZbook.html, Jarek Szymanski, using the fragments of *Dictionary of Chinese Martial Arts Personages* and *Si Shui County Gazetteer* published in the December 1, 1988, edition of *Wuhun* magazine, lists Chang Naizhou's birth and death as 1724–1783. Wile, however, states on page 118 of *Lost T'ai-chi Classics* that Zhang Naizhou's precise birth and death dates are not known.

9. Wile, 25–26.

10. Wile, 116. Note that Wile uses the Wade-Giles system for transliterating Chinese words and, in keeping with conventional writing styles, I have retained the Wade-Giles when quoting his work. In *pinyin*, "Lao Tzu" is written as "Laozi," "Chao-pao" is written as "Zhaobao," and "Ch'i Chi-kuang" is written as "Qi Jiguang."

11. Feng Zhiqiang, Feng Dabiao, and Chen Xiaowang. (1984). *Chen Style Taijiquan*. Hong Kong: Hai Feng Publishing Co., 2.

12. Feng, Feng, and Chen, 3.

13. Szymanski, J. (2000). *Brief Analysis of Chen Family Boxing Manuals*. Accessed August 2004 fromwww.chinafrominside.com/ma/taiji/chenboxingmanuals.html. Sponsored by Jarek Szymanski.

14. Szymanski. (2000).

15. Feng, Feng, and Chen, 2.

16. Szymanski. (2000).

17. Szymanski. (2000).

18. Feng, Feng, and Chen, 3.

19. The *Huangting Jing,* or "Yellow Court Classic," is a long poem dating from second century A.D. It describes *qigong* and meditation practices, what some term *neidan* or "internal alchemy," from the *Shangqing* Daoist tradition. It is one of the most popular Daoist texts and is part of the Daoist Canon.

20. Feng, Feng, and Chen, 2.

21. Excerpt from Jian Ge. (2002). Small Frame of Chen Style Taijiquan. *Shaolin Yu Taiji,* 9/2002. (Jarek Szymanski, Trans.) Accessed August 2004 from www.chinafrominside.com/ma/taiji/xiaojia.html#6. Sponsored by Jarek Szymanski.

22. Jian Ge. (2002).

23. Feng, Feng, and Chen, 7.

24. Yang, Y. and Grubisich, S. (2000). Feng Zhiqiang discusses the importance of internal work. *T'ai Chi Magazine,* 24(3), 13.

25. Personal communication with Wu Xiubao, August, 2003.

26. Jian Ge. (2002).

27. Jian Ge. (2002).

28. This description of history and memory was contributed by Lillian Hoddeson, professor of History at the University of Illinois, Urbana-Champaign. Hoddeson presently teaches a course on Memory and the Construction of Identity and Culture. For a popular account of the current view of memory, see Schacter, Daniel L., *Searching for Memory: The Brain, the Mind and the Past* (New York: Basic Books, 1996).

29. Specific details of Chen Zhaokui's later years are provided by Cheng Jincai. (2002). *Chen Style Taijiquan—A Classical Explanation* (in Chinese). Houston: International Chen Style Tai Chi Development Center, 286–288.

Research References

Part I: Selected Research on the Health Benefits of Taijiquan

Bellew, J. W. (2002). The effect of strength training on control of force in older men and women. *Aging Clinical and Experimental Research, 14,* 35–41.

Chan, K., Qin, L., Lau, M., Woo, J., Au, S., Choy, W., Lee, K., & Lee, S. (2004). A randomized, prospective study of the effects of Tai Chi Chun exercise on bone mineral density in postmenopausal women. *Archives of Physical Medicine & Rehabilitation, 85*(5), 717–722.

Channer, K. S., Barrow, D., Barrow, R., Osborne, M., & Ives, G. (1996). Changes in haemodynamic parameters following Tai Chi Chuan and aerobic exercise in patients recovering from acute myocardial infarction. *Postgraduate Medical Journal, 72*(848), 349–351.

Christou, E. A., Rosengren, K. S., & Yang, Y. (2003). Taiji training improves knee extensor strength and force control in older adults. *The Journals of Gerontology. Series A, Biological Sciences and Medical Sciences, 58*(8), 763–766.

Hain, T. C. (1999). Effects of T'ai Chi on balance. *Archives of Otolaryngology—Head and Neck Surgery, 125*(11), 1191–1195.

Han, A., Robinson, V., Judd, M., Taixiang, W., Wells, G., & Tugwell, P. (2004). Tai chi for treating rheumatoid arthritis. *Cochrane Database of Systematic Reviews, 2004:(3):* CD 004849.

Hong, Y., Li, J. X., & Robinson, P. D. (2000). Balance control, flexibility, and cardiorespiratory fitness among older Tai Chi practitioners. *British Journal of Sports Medicine, 34*(1), 29–34.

Husted, C., Pham, L., Hekking, A., & Niederman, R. (1999). Improving quality of life for people with chronic conditions: The example of t'ai chi and multiple sclerosis. *Alternative Therapies In Health and Medicine, 5*(5), 70–74.

Irwin, M. R., Pike, J. L., Cole, J. C., & Oxman, M. N. (2003). Effects of a behavioral intervention, Tai Chi Chih, on varicella-zoster virus specific immunity and health functioning in older adults. *Psychosomatic Medicine, 65*(5), 824–830.

Jacobson, B. H., Chen, H. C., Cashel, C., & Guerrero, L. (1997). The effect of T'ai Chi Chuan training on balance, kinesthetic sense, and strength. *Perceptual and Motor Skills, 84*(1), 27–33.

Jin, P. (1989). Changes in heart rate, noradrenaline, cortisol and mood during Tai Chi. *Journal of Psychosomatic Research, 33*(2), 197–206.

Jin, P. (1992). Efficacy of Tai Chi, brisk walking, meditation, and reading in reducing mental and emotional stress. *Journal of Psychosomatic Research, 36*(4), 361–370.

Kirsteins, A. E., Dietz, F., & Hwang, S. M. (1991). Evaluating the safety and potential use of a weight-bearing exercise, Tai-Chi Chuan, for rheumatoid arthritis patients. *American Journal of Physical Medicine and Rehabilitation, 70*(3), 136–141.

Kutner, N. G., Barnhart, H., Wolf, S. L., McNeely, E., & Xu, T. (1997). Self-report benefits of Tai Chi practice by older adults. *The Journals of Gerontology. Series B, Psychological Sciences and Social Sciences, 52*(5), 242–246.

Lai, J. S., Lan, C., Wong, M. K., & Teng, S. H. (1995). Two-year trends in cardiorespiratory function among older Tai Chi Chuan practitioners and sedentary subjects. *Journal of the American Geriatrics Society, 43*(11), 1222–1227.

Lan, C., Chen, S. Y., & Lai, J. S. (2004). Relative exercise intensity of Tai Chi Chuan is similar in different ages and gender. *American Journal of Chinese Medicine, 32*(1), 151–160.

Lan, C., Chen, S. Y., Lai, J. S., & Wong, M. K. (1999). The effect of Tai Chi on cardiorespiratory function in patients with coronary artery bypass surgery. *Medicine and Science in Sports and Exercise, 31*(5), 634–638.

Lan, C., Lai, J. S., & Chen, S. Y. (2002). Tai chi chuan: an ancient wisdom on exercise and health promotion. *Sports Medicine, 32*(4), 217–224.

Lan, C., Lai, J. S., Chen, S. Y., & Wong, M. K. (1998). 12-month Tai Chi training in the elderly: its effect on health fitness. *Medicine and Science in Sports and Exercise, 30*(3), 345–351.

Lan, C., Lai, J. S., Chen, S. Y., & Wong, M. K. (2000). Tai Chi Chuan to improve muscular strength and endurance in elderly individuals: A pilot study. *Archives of Physical Medicine and Rehabilitation, 81*(5), 604–607.

Lan, C., Lai, J. S., Wong, M. K., & Yu, M. L. (1996). Cardiorespiratory function, flexibility, and body composition among geriatric Tai Chi Chuan practitioners. *Archives of Physical Medicine and Rehabilitation, 77*(6), 612–616.

Li, F., Fisher, K. J., Harmer, P., Irbe, D., Tearse, R. G., & Weimer, C. (2004). Tai chi and self-rated quality of sleep and daytime sleepiness in older adults: a randomized controlled trial. *Journal of American Geriatrics Society, 52*(6): 892–900.

Li, F., McAuley E, et al. (2001). Tai Chi enhances self-efficacy and exercise behavior in older adults. *Journal of Aging and Physical Activity. 9*, 161–171.

Lin, Y. C., Wong, A. M., Chou, S. W., Tang, F. T., & Wong, P. Y. (2000). The effects of Tai Chi Chuan on postural stability in the elderly: Preliminary report. *Changgeng Yi Xue Za Zhi, 23*(4), 197–204.

Rosengren, K. (2003). Quantification of Taiji learning in older adults. *Journal of American Geriatrics Society, 51*, 1–2.

Schaller, K. J. (1996). Tai Chi Chih: An exercise option for older adults. *Journal of Gerontological Nursing, 22*(10), 12–17.

Song, R., Lee, E. O., Lam, P., & Bae, S. C. (2003). Effects of tai chi exercise on pain, balance, muscle strength, and perceived difficulties in physical functioning in older women with osteoarthritis: A randomized clinical trial. *Journal of Rheumatology, 30*(9), 2039–2044.

Taggart, H. M., Arslanian, C. L., Bae, S., & Singh, K. (2003). Effects of T'ai Chi exercise on fibromyalgia symptoms and health-related quality of life. *Orthopaedic Nursing, 22*(5), 353–360.

Tracy, B. L., Kern, D. S., Mehoudar, O. D., Sehnert, S. M., Byrnes, W. C., & Enoka, R. M. (2001). Strength training does not improve the steadiness of muscle contractions in the knee extensors of older adults. *Medicine and Science In Sports and Exercise, 33*, S254.

Tse, S. K., & Bailey, D. M. (1992). T'ai chi and postural control in the well elderly. *American Journal of Occupational Therapy, 46*(4), 295–300.

Van Deusen, J., & Harlowe, D. (1987). The efficacy of the ROM Dance Program for adults with rheumatoid arthritis. *American Journal of Occupational Therapy, 41*(2), 90–95.

Wang, J. S., Lan, C., & Wong, M. K. (2001). Tai Chi Chuan training to enhance microcirculatory function in healthy elderly men. *Archives of Physical Medicine and Rehabilitation, 82*(9), 1176–1180.

Wolf, S. L., Barnhart, H. X., Kutner, N. G., McNeely, E., Coogler, C., & Xu, T. (1996). Reducing frailty and falls in older persons: An investigation of Tai Chi and computerized balance training. Atlanta FICSIT Group. Frailty and Injuries: Cooperative Studies of Intervention Techniques. *Journal of the American Geriatrics Society, 44*(5), 489–497.

Wolf, S. L., Coogler, C., & Xu, T. (1997). Exploring the basis for Tai Chi Chuan as a therapeutic exercise approach. *Archives of Physical Medicine and Rehabilitation, 78*(8), 886–892.

Wolfson, L., Whipple, R., Derby, C., Judge, J., King, M., Amerman, P., Schmidt, J., & Smyers, D. (1996). Balance and strength training in older adults: Intervention gains and Tai Chi maintenance. *Journal of the American Geriatrics Society, 44*(5), 498–506.

Wu, G., Liu, W., Hitt, J., & Millon, D. (2004). Spatial, temporal and muscle action patterns of Tai Chi gait. *Journal of Electromyography Kinesiology, 14*(3): 343–354.

Yan, J. H. (1998). Tai Chi practice improves senior citizens' balance and arm movement control. *Journal of Aging and Physical Activity, 6*, 271–284.

Yan, J. H. (1999). Tai chi practice reduces movement force variability for seniors. *Journal of Gerontology. Series A, Biological Sciences and Medical Sciences, 54*(12), M629–634.

Part II: Selected Research on the Health Benefits of Meditation

Barnes, V. A., Treiber, F. A., Turner, J. R., Davis, H., & Strong, W. B. (1999). Acute effects of transcendental meditation on hemodynamic functioning in middle-aged adults. *Psychosomatic Medicine, 61*(4), 525–531.

Barnes, V. A., Treiber, F. A., & Davis, H. (2001). Impact of Transcendental Meditation on cardiovascular function at rest and during acute stress in adolescents with high normal blood pressure. *Journal of Psychosomatic Research, 51*(4), 597–605.

Bujatti, M., & Riederer, P. (1976). Serotonin, noradrenaline, dopamine metabolites in transcendental meditation-technique. *Journal of Neural Transmission, 39*(3), 257–267.

Elias, A. N., Guich, S., & Wilson, A. F. (2000). Ketosis with enhanced GABAergic tone promotes physiological changes in transcendental meditation. *Medical Hypotheses, 54*(4), 660–662.

Infante, J. R., Peran, F., Martinez, M., Roldan, A., Poyatos, R., Ruiz, C., Samaniego, F., & Garrido, F. (1998). ACTH and beta-endorphin in transcendental meditation. *Physiology & Behavior, 64*(3), 311–315.

Infante, J. R., Torres-Avisbal, M., Pinel, P., Vallejo, J. A., Peran, F., Gonzalez, F., Contreras, P., Pacheco, C., Roldan, A., & Latre, J. M. (2001). Catecholamine levels in practitioners of the transcendental meditation technique. *Physiology & Behavior, 72*(1–2), 141–146.

Kjaer, T. W., Bertelsen, C., Piccini, P., Brooks, D., Alving, J., & Lou, H. C. (2002). Increased dopamine tone during meditation-induced change of consciousness. *Cognitive Brain Research, 13*(2), 255–259.

Kubota, Y., Sato, W., Toichi, M., Murai, T., Okada, T., Hayashi, A., & Sengoku, A. (2001). Frontal midline theta rhythm is correlated with cardiac autonomic activities during the performance of an attention demanding meditation procedure. *Cognitive Brain Research, 11*(2), 281–287.

Lazar, S. W., Bush, G., Gollub, R. L., Fricchione, G. L., Khalsa, G., & Benson, H. (2000). Functional brain mapping of the relaxation response and meditation. *Neuroreport, 11*(7), 1581–1585.

Lou, H. C., Kjaer, T. W., Friberg, L., Wildschiodtz, G., Holm, S., & Nowak, M. (1999). A ^{15}O-H2O PET study of meditation and the resting state of normal consciousness. *Human Brain Mapping, 7*(2), 98–105.

Peng, C. K., Mietus, J. E., Liu, Y., Khalsa, G., Douglas, P. S., & Benson, H., & Goldberger, A. L. (1999). Exaggerated heart rate oscillations during two meditation techniques. *International Journal of Cardiology, 70*(2), 101–107.

Sakakibara, M., Takeuchi, S., & Hayano, J. (1994). Effect of relaxation training on cardiac parasympathetic tone. *Psychophysiology, 31*(3), 223–228.

Tooley, G. A., Armstrong, S. M., Norman, T. R., & Sali, A. (2000). Acute increases in night-time plasma melatonin levels following a period of meditation. *Biological Psychology, 53*(1), 69–78.

Travis, F. (2001). Autonomic and EEG patterns distinguish transcending from other experiences during Transcendental Meditation practice. *International Journal of Psychophysiology, 42*(1), 1–9.

Travis, F., & Wallace, R. K. (1999). Autonomic and EEG patterns during eyes-closed rest and transcendental meditation (TM) practice: The basis for a neural model of TM practice. *Consciousness and Cognition, 8*(3), 302–318.

Young, J. D., & Taylor, E. (1998). Meditation as a voluntary hypometabolic state of biological estivation. *News in Physiological Sciences, 13*, 149–153.

Index of Chinese Sayings

Chapter 1: Introduction

事半功倍。 *Shì bàn gōng bèi.* Half the work, double the result (i.e., if you practice and study efficiently, you can learn in a fraction of the time).

Chapter 2: The Foundation

练拳不练功, 到老一场空。 *Liàn quán bù liàn gōng, dào lǎo yī chǎng kōng.* If you practice form (external movement), but do not practice *gong*, even if you practice your whole life, your art will be empty.

力不敌法, 法不敌功。 *Lì bù dí fǎ, fǎ bù dí gōng.* Brute strength cannot defeat technique, technique cannot defeat *gong*.

一功、二胆、三技巧。 *Yī gōng, èr dǎn, sān jì qiǎo.* First *gong*, second confidence, third technique.

教拳不教功。 *Jiāo quán bù jiāo gōng.* I will teach you form (external movement) but not *gong*.

功夫特别深。 *Gōng fu tè bié shēn.* (A person's) skill is very deep.

空架子, 没有功夫。 *Kōng jià zi, méi yǒu gōng fu.* Empty form, no *gongfu*.

药补不如食补, 食补不如气补, 气补不如神补。 *Yào bǔ bù rú shí bǔ, shí bǔ bù rú qì bǔ, qì bǔ bù rú shén bǔ.* To improve your health, medicine is not as good as food/nutrition; food/nutrition is not as good as *qi(gong)*; *qi(gong)* is not as good as spiritual nourishment.

拳以德立, 无德无拳。 *Quán yǐ dé lì, wú dé wú quán.* Virtue is the foundation of boxing skill; without virtue there is no (high level of) boxing skill.

拳无拳，意无意，无拳无意求真意。*Quán wú quán, yì wú yì, wú quán wú yì qiú zhēn yì.* Form without form. Intention without intention. Go beyond form and intention to search for the true meaning.

吾日三省吾身。*Wǔ rì sān xing wǔ shēn.* One should look inward three times a day.

Chapter 3: Finding a Teacher

徒访师三年，师访徒三年。*Tú fǎng shī sān nián, shī fǎng tú sān nián.* It takes three years for a student to find a teacher, and three years for the teacher to decide whether he or she will accept a student.

不是一家和尚不进一家庙。*Bù shì yī jiā hé shàng, bù jìn yī jiā miào.* Different spirits won't enter the same temple.

今天你叫我爷，明天你叫我孙子。*Jīn tiān ni jiào wǒ yé, míng tiān ni jiào wǒ sūn zi.* Today you call me grandfather, tomorrow you will call me grandson.

诀窍奥秘，须经明师口传心授。*Jué qiào ào mì, xū jīng míng shī kǒu chuān xīn shòu.* Tricks of the trade and secrets of practice must be passed on by sincere instruction from a teacher who understands the art.

藏而不露。*Cáng ér bù lòu.* Show your power to no one.

人不知我，我独知人。*Rén bù zhī wǒ, wǒ dú zhī rén.* Other people don't know me, but I know other people.

师父领进门，修行在个人。*Shī fu lǐng jìn mén, xiū xíng zài gè rén.* The teacher will lead you to the door, but it is up to the student to improve.

一点就透。*Yī diǎn jiù tòu.* One touch will penetrate (i.e., when a student has reached a certain level of understanding and ability, brief instruction from the teacher is all that is necessary).

山外有山，天外有天，能人背后有能人。*Shān wài yǒu shān, tiān wài yǒu tiān, néng rén bèi hòu yǒu néng ren.* Beyond this mountain, there is another (bigger) mountain; beyond this world, there is another (bigger) world; beyond a master, there is another (better) master.

远路的和尚会念经。*Yuǎn lù de hé shàng huì niàn jīng.* The faraway monk is the smartest.

苦练十年，不如名师一点。*Kǔ liàn shí nián, bù rú míng shī yī diǎn.* One word from a knowledgeable teacher will save ten years of hard practice.

Chapter 4: *Wuji* Meditation

无极为太极之母。*Wú jí wèi tài jí zhī mǔ.* Wuji is the mother of Taiji.

无极生太极。*Wú jí shēng Tài jí.* Wuji gives birth to Taiji.

不静不见动之奇。*Bù jìng bù jiàn dòng zhī qí.* If you don't have quiet or tranquility, you will never see the miracle of moving.

太极太和。*Tài jí tài hé.* Taiji requires peacefulness/harmony (also, Taiji leads to harmony).

练拳不站桩，吃饭没粮仓。*Liàn quán bù zhàn zhuāng, chī fàn méi liáng cāng.* Practicing form (external movement) without practicing "standing pole" is like eating food with no grain in the storage bin.

百动不如一静，百练不如一站。*Bǎi dòng bù rú yī jìng, bǎi liàn bù rú yī zhàn.* One hundred movements are not as good as one stillness; one hundred practices are not as good as one standing (pole).

练后满身汗，避风如避箭。*Liàn hòu mǎn shēn hàn, bì fēng rú bì jiàn.* When you sweat after practice, you should avoid wind as you avoid arrows.

Chapter 5: Taiji Form

周身一家，力发一点，点点透骨。*Zhōu shēn yī jiā, lì fā yī diǎn, diǎn diǎn tòu gū?* The whole body is one family, the released energy should focus on one point, [as a result] every touch can penetrate the bone.

练力则断，练气则滞，练意则活。*Liàn lì zé duàn; liàn qì zé zhì; liàn yì zé huó.* If you practice brute strength, it will break; if you practice *qi*, it will be stiff; if you practice *yi*, it will flow smoothly.

由形似到神似。*Yóu xíng sì dào shén sì.* From similar in appearance to similar in spirit.

不怕千招会，就怕一招精。*Bù pà qiān zāo huì, jiù pà yī zhāo jīng.* I am not afraid of someone who knows a thousand forms (techniques); I am concerned with the person that does one form (technique) very well.

Chapter 6: Push-Hands

一个好汉三个帮，一个把式三个桩。*Yī gè hǎo hàn sān gè bāng, yī gè bǎ shì sān gè zhuāng.* A great man needs three assistants; a great fighter needs three training partners.

舍己从人。 *Shě jǐ cóng rén.* Give up yourself and follow your partner/opponent.

艺高人胆大，胆大艺更高。 *Yì gāo rén dǎn dà; dǎn dà yì gèng gāo.* Higher skill can inspire greater confidence. Greater confidence can further enhance the skill.

Chapter 7: Why Practice Taijiquan?

拳贵得法。 *Quán guì dé fǎ.* To learn martial arts, the most important thing is to practice in the proper way.

气功能祛病，缘由在松静。 *Qì gōng néng qū bìng, yuán yóu zài sōng jìng.* Song (relaxation) and jing (tranquility/quietness) are the reasons why qigong can heal you.

笑一笑，十年少；愁一愁，白了头。 *Xiào yī xiào, shí nián shào; chóu yī chóu, bái le tóu.* Smile one smile and you are ten years younger. Add more worries and you gain more white hair.

多注意养生。 *Duō zhù yì yǎng shēn.* Pay attention to nurturing.

Index

agility. See also *ling*
  fundamental aspect of *gong*, 5, 15,
    139, 146
  improved by meditation, 69
an (downward force), 78, 85, 111,
    122–123, 130–132
Aquinas, St. Thomas, quote from
    introduction to *Summa Theologica*, 7
autonomic nervous system, 67, 69
awareness, increased by practice,
    5, 21, 53, 63, 74, 83, 84, 99,
    146–147, 149, 151–152

ba fa (eight forces), 78, 122–124
basal ganglia, role in motor skills, 112,
    158
base of support, 87–91, 98, 147–148
benefits (of Taiji practice), 5, 8, 146–156
Big Style (vs. Small Style), 172–175
breathing
  and meditation, 59
  reverse, 50, 93–94

cai (pluck), 78, 111, 122–124,
cannon fist. See *pao cui*

center of mass, 50, 53, 71, 87–91,
    98–99, 137–138, 147, 196
central equilibrium. See *zhong ding*
Chang Naizhou, 165, 199
chansi jin (silk-reeling force), 82, 87, 93,
    105–108, 126–130, 137, 148
Chen Changxing, 83, 164, 168–175,
    195, 199
Chen Fake, 169, 171–175, 177, 198
Chen Gengyun, 168, 173–174
Chen Qingping, 168–170, 172,
    174–175, 199
Chen Qingzhou, 176
Chen Village, 1, 10, 19, 164–166,
    169–172, 176–178, 198–199
Chen Wangting, 164, 166–168, 170–171,
    174–175, 198–199
Chen Xin, 10, 19, 33, 105, 155, 165, 170,
    188, 199
Chen Youben, 168, 170, 172–175
Chen Youheng, 168
Chen Zhaokui, 1, 41, 171, 175,
    177–178, 200
Chen Zhaopei, 1, 169, 171, 174,
    176–177
Chen Ziming, 169

classical writings (of Taijiquan)
  esoteric nature of, 10–11
  quotations from, 4, 19–20, 26,
    47, 77, 79, 98, 100–101, 104, 117,
    135, 137
confidence, 153
  developed in practice, 5, 57, 75, 139
  importance of, 16, 95, 139–140, 157
core musculature, strengthened in Taiji
    practice, 72–73, 150, 195

da lu (big rollback), 132
da zuo. See meditation, sitting
daily life (relation to practice), 18, 24,
    33, 53, 84, 120, 139, 145
Dao De Jing, quotations from, 7, 25,
    61, 81
de Mello, Anthony, quotation from
    Sadhana: A Way to God, 60

efficiency of movement, learned from
    form practice, 77, 79, 97, 148,
    150, 157
ego (overcoming), 24–29, 59, 140
eight forces. See ba fa
er lu (second routine). See pao cui
external martial arts, 3, 8

fajin (quick release energy), 28, 84, 104,
    108–110, 124, 133
feedback response, 136–137
feedforward response, 137
Feng Zhiqiang, 36, 41
  originator of Chen Shi Xin Yi Hunyuan
    Taiji, 169
  teachings of, 20, 47, 64, 93, 102,
    104–105, 151
  twelve principles of, 21
fight or flight response, 67

fighting. See martial applications
five bows, 50, 82, 84–86
form (choreographed movement)
  as "moving standing pole," 47
  different versions of, 4, 37, 95–96,
    175–176
  neural mechanisms of, 110–113
  principles of, 3, 77–94
  purpose of, 116, 122–123, 146–153,
    157–158
  reflection of inner spirit, 4, 19
  stages of development, 94–107
  vs. fighting, 36

gong
  defined, 5, 15–17
  development of, 8, 18, 26–27, 36,
    40, 45–46, 52, 102, 137, 139, 153
  foundation of martial skill,
    3, 28, 37, 40, 52, 110, 129, 135,
    139, 146
  of sitting meditation, 63–64, 156–157
gong li (strength), 120, 131–132
gongfu, defined, 16. See also gong
Gu Liuxin, 167

Hao Weizheng, 169
health
  benefits of practice, 8, 18, 94, 105,
    145–156
  vs. martial skill, 5–6, 37–38, 69–70,
    139. See also gong
Heller, Wendy, contributions to text,
    194, 197
history
  effect of memory upon, 175
  of Taijiquan, 163–176
Hu Yaozhen, 169
Huang Zongxi, 165
Huangting Jing (Yello Court Classic), 200
hunyuan (unified, primordial), 169

intention. *See also* *xin yi*
  importance in practice, 72, 92,
    102–104
  University of Iowa study document-
    ing strength increases from, 72
internal power. *See also* *peng jin*
  controlling magnitude of, 118, 120
  description of, 78–80
  fundamental aspect of *gong*, 16, 18,
    36, 129
  mechanical aspects of, 73
  methods of development, 92, 99,
    103, 115, 120, 133–134, 149–151
  reliance of skill of "sticking" upon,
    125, 135
  self-test for using, 118
  understanding, 39, 75, 119

ji (forward force), 78, 111, 122–123,
    130–131, 133
Jiang Fa, 164, 172, 199
Jiazuo (hometown of Yang Yang), 1
joint movement, 66. *See also* range
    of motion
  principles for Taiji practice, 83, 85,
    122

kao (bump), 78, 111, 122–124, 159

Laozi. *See* *Dao De Jing*, quotations from
li (ordinary strength), 103, 105, 118
Li Yiyu, 163, 169
lie (split), 78, 111, 122–124, 159
ling (lightness/agility), 39, 63, 69, 149.
    See also agility
listening, 124–125, 130, 132–135, 137, 151
low posture, arguments against, 86–93,
lu (rollback), 78, 111, 122–123, 131–132,
    159

martial
  applications, 17, 26, 52, 75, 84,
    86, 101, 117, 124, 130, 133,
    140–141, 147
  arts of China, 3, 5
  danger of over-emphasizing, 9,
    27–29, 38, 110, 139, 153
  dual cultivation with spiritual, 4,
    19–20, 33
  foundation of self-defense skill.
    See *gong*
  root of Taijiquan, 8, 77–78, 146
  vs. health. *See* health vs. martial skill
meditation. *See also* *wuji*
  fundamental component of
    practice, 6–7, 17, 45, 80, 139, 144,
    147, 149–150
  improvements in quality of sleep,
    69, 152
  neural mechanisms, 68–73, 156–157
  omission in research studies, 12, 160
  physiologic changes during, 68–70,
    157
  sitting, 57–64, 160
  standing, 45–57, 79, 81, 103, 138,
    147, 151
moderation principle, 17–18, 21–24,
    32, 38, 54–55, 63, 100–101, 119, 121
morality, relation to martial skill, 19,
    46, 74. *See also* *xui lian*
motor programs, 110–112, 137, 152, 157
multiple training partners
    (necessity of), 121

nei gong (internal power/skill), 109,
    119–120
nervous system
  and form movement, 110–113
  and push-hands, 136–138
  and sitting meditation, 68–70
  and standing meditation, 70–73
  overview, 64–67

About the Author

YANG YANG WAS BORN in 1961 in Henan Province near the Chen Village in China, from where all modern styles of Taiji can trace their heritage. Diagnosed with a congenital heart condition as a child, he began studying Taiji at the age of twelve, and credits his practice of Taiji for curing his heart condition and enabling him to pass the physical exam necessary for acceptance to universities in China.

For six years Master Yang studied Taiji with local teachers before leaving in 1979 to attend the China Textile University in Shanghai, where he earned an engineering degree. During the next few years, he met and studied with Gu Liuxin, Chen Zhaokui, and Feng Zhiqiang, all famous 18th-generation masters of the Chen Style of Taijiquan.

Winning first place in the Shanghai University Martial Arts Championships for three straight years (1981–1983) and being voted Best Overall Martial Artist (1983) earned Master Yang a job as an instructor with the Shanghai Chen Style Research Association. In order to continue his studies of Taiji with Grandmaster Feng Zhiqiang, however, he moved to Beijing in 1985. He enrolled at the China University of Political Science and Law, where he earned a law degree in 1987. The following year (1988), he was granted the formal title of disciple of Grandmaster Feng.

Master Yang practiced business law in China for several years before coming to the United States to study for a master's degree in Economics at Illinois State University.

Currently the Director of the Center for Taiji Studies™ in Champaign, Illinois, Master Yang is also pursuing a doctorate degree in Kinesiology at the University of Illinois, Urbana-Champaign, where his research focuses directly on the benefits and mechanisms of Taiji practice. Master Yang's Taiji studies now span more than 30 years.